The C ORIGINAL NIGHT STALKER

EAST AREA RAPIST

GOLDEN STATE KILLER

BY ANNE PENN

MY NAME IS LAURIE

MURDER ON HIS MIND

EDITION II

THIS BOOK IS DEDICATED

TO ALL OF THE VICTIMS AND TO

LYMAN JONES & VEONIA SMITH

WHO WERE MY GRANDPARENTS

Printed in the United States of America

Final Cover Graphics Adjustments created by Tim

Because of the dynamic nature of the Internet any Web addresses or links contained in this book may have changed since publication and may no longer be valid.

We now know the name of the suspect responsible for all of the crimes that many have written and speculated about for 42 years. I will not change this publication because this story needed to be told the way it was. This story was my journey through the reality of having a family member or members be victims of murder. In these cases, this happened to be the work of a serial killer. There are so many countless people living with the murder of someone they loved everywhere. Many women are killed by a domestic partner. This is a sad fact. Their families have experienced the loss of a loved one by the hands of a murderer as well.

After I wrote this book I heard many stories from people on various Facebook pages, messages on boards and blogs. Those of us who have experienced the loss of a loved one to murder many times find out who took them away from us. Sometimes it takes the wheels of justice a very long time to put the perp in jail. Sometimes there are never any answers for the victims of violent crime. These cases, these murders, and this murderer almost passed into history without being identified, and without giving us answers. Because of DNA, even if we had not found the criminal soon he still would have been identified even after we collectively had passed into history. It was inevitable that this man's name would be found.

Hopefully in the future waiting 42 years to find the creep will never happen again.

Hopefully men and women will also not be wrongly convicted or at least less often than in previous times in history. DNA will be the tool now and in the future that helps us know as in this case with a 100% DNA match that we have the right suspect in a cage.

I believe when you read through this story you will hear, and know how the world once was when this criminal started to terrorize. You will also be able to hear and read about his crimes, his MO and what it was like to struggle with the fact that the perpetrator lived free for so, so long. You will also hear, and maybe feel the frustration and the struggle with what it was like to have so many unanswered questions from everywhere for so long. Joseph James DeAngelo began his crimes as the Visalia Ransacker in 1973, morphed into the East Area Rapist from 1976-1979, and then was called the Original Night Stalker as he murdered until 1986.

The cases went cold in almost every jurisdiction over time. For long periods of time there was no cold case unit anywhere. The criminal thought he had been missed, he was free to come out of hiding as it were, to live without discovery or punishment. He thought he was home free. In approximately 1980 until about 1990 this man was not on anyone's radar.

He laid low. He became a family man who hid behind his family. Otherwise this creep was in plain sight all along. You will see one woman's investigation into who this man is and where he was. I was right in my assessment of him and was right about where he would be found. We wait to hear all of the details that law enforcement will put together.

Thank you for reading this story.

Anne/Laurie

Praise for this book: Kevin M. Sullivan is the author of twelve books, a former investigative journalist for both print and online media, and is a recognized authority on serial sex killer, Ted Bundy.

Kevin says: I first heard about the East Area Rapist of Sacramento, CA in 2012 when I was doing research for a book about Richard Chase, better known as the Vampire of Sacramento.

I really didn't want to write about an unknown serial rapist and murderer. Such a book should be tackled by someone who has a great deal of interest; the kind of interest that would carry them through the monumental task of writing a book. That person is Anne. Anne Penn is not only an excellent researcher and story teller, but she's suffered a personal loss at the hands of the East

Area Rapist: Her uncle, Lyman Robert Smith and his wife Charlene Smith, of Ventura County, CA, were murdered on March 13, 1980.

Without question, the living victims of murder will carry what's happened to their loved ones for the rest of their lives; and in some cases, family members will channel that negative energy into something positive, and that's what Penn has done with the publication of her book. The author, who has spent years researching and living with this case – a case that covers numerous locations both in Northern and Southern California and spans some 13 years – has produced a work (I own the Kindle edition with some 500 pages), that is both large and bursting with information about these rapes and murders.

Indeed, within these pages you'll read about the Visalia Ransacker (1973-1976), Sacramento's East Area Rapist (1976-1979), and what is called the Original Night Stalker crimes (1979-1986), which is not to be confused with the crimes of another 'Night Stalker' Richard Ramirez.

Keep in mind too, that as Penn was writing this book, the killer, Joseph DeAngelo, had not been apprehended, she made a number of credible assumptions about the perpetrator that, since his April 2018 arrest, have been proven to be correct!

I highly recommend this book to all those who want a detailed look at this now discovered killer and the crimes he committed, from a person who not only was emotionally wounded by the killer, but who is more than qualified to tell the strange tale from her own unique perspective

Kevin M. Sullivan, True Crime Author

Preface before the preface!

Here is the thing..........

This is not a story told with beautiful prose or fantastic words where one has to stop to look up the meaning – it is not a tale – a fairytale that one can walk away from feeling lovely.

Sometimes stories that are real, raw stories can be told as in a conversation with real words and feelings, sometimes repeated as if to reconcile the story, to try to digest or comprehend things that are incomprehensible

This story is about something so brutal, so horrific one can find no words in the end, only silence that falls as we wait for answers. This story is about a man who went off the rails, one who used what he knew to protect us, in order to harm us. Not individually, but as a whole. He set out to make individual victims pay, and all of us as a society, our communities. He knew how to inflict pain and suffering on all of us.

I took this on to exorcise the beast, to shed light on the box carefully sealed in the darkest corners of my mind, to dust it off long ago covered, lid tightly sealed because what was in it, put there almost forty years ago was just too dark, too scary to touch.

Inside waited the details of murders of people loved by someone I loved as a father and friend, someone who meant a lot to me. Their loss was everyone's loss. All of the murders were all of our losses.

I do not know how one can ever get the visual of a crime so real, so brutal out of one's mind. Broken are we who hear it, never repaired, never the same. Eventually the images are shown on the internet for all to see. Less scary in some way from what lived in my mind. Broken and bloody fireplace log, pieces splintered, blood spatter, bed linens pulled up over bodies in their own home, in their own bedroom where they are supposed to be safe.

Some creep – stalking, watching, arrogant enough to get right up close. Peering in windows, hiding under bushes. Childish behaviors calling on the phone, terrorizing, breathing, whispering "I'm gonna kill you." Leaving after raping and bludgeoning if all goes as planned.

Soft, long hair bloody, not moving taking a last breath, never to laugh or sing again at the beauty of a day.

Studying the mindset of a serial killer soon after the murders. Trying to understand and somehow look at this in a clinical, logical way. Detach, desensitize, except for the FEAR – fear at how insecure one can truly be in our own home. Sticks in sliding glass doors, shades drawn at dusk. Worry at windows where one can see in, but one cannot see out. Who is watching? Who will see you and then decide.... Doors locked and checked again.

This book – designed to try and help find a killer of the most AWFUL kind, one who raises the spine in fear – determination to get the word out. Who do you know? Did you know him? Think back, this is how it was back then. How did we miss him? This book designed to heal my mind even if this monster is never caught.

Stay the fear, quiet the fight or flight response. And you are worried about the proper order of the words used, maybe a repeat of descriptors or worries? BUT WHAT ABOUT WHAT I AM SAYING? This is the story of a rapist and murderer who shattered a time, a place, and people. Lots of people. That's what some are worried about in this experience? Really? Not the gut wrenching horror and brutality one might have to wrestle with every day since the very beginning of these crimes?

Me telling my son when he was small that police were here to protect us. Many, but not all. How did I walk on the same streets as a man like this? One who hated so much.?

I could not ever get the images out of my mind, a man watching in the dark, watching private moments between a man and woman. Stalking, coming in looking around knowing he would be back. To take EVERYTHING from them. Everything, every drop of humanity, everything decent and good. All that is left is evil and hate until he exits taking everything once good. Leaving the shatteredness, the splinters, the drops of evidence, the silence. The sound had been loud enough to fill the room, your senses, the ugly brutal sound. Stillness left behind, two or three days, bodies found, the story told over and over into infinity. It's over now. At least for some of us.

Since publishing the first edition of Murder On His Mind Serial Killer I decided to share my specific experience with this story and my connection as a victim's family member. The advice given me previously by retired law enforcement was wise in that he told me I should be careful when giving information about my identity. The trouble with giving half a story is it left me feeling incomplete. I am one who usually tells the truth, the whole truth.

Every victim of the East Area Rapist Aka the Original Night Stalker has a story. Every family member attached to those affected by this man has their own story. Each person directly connected has a story that is unique and personal. The reality is this man has never been identified. He could well be alive and living among us. This story is written from the perspective of a person who was there in Sacramento in the beginning of this man's crimes. This story is about the perpetrator who so many in Sacramento and Northern California thought had been caught long ago. It is also a story about what it was like in the 1970's and what it was like to a community to wake up never feeling as safe again. Certainly when I first heard of The East Area Rapist there was no way I could know that in a short time he would be the one to move on killing family members in Ventura California

How could I not write about this experience? How could I not try to figure out who this guy is and was? How could I not talk about it? I kept this to myself for more than 35 years. I wrote this book to try and reach people that came from my neck of the

11

woods. This story is about how the East Area Rapist became the Original Night Stalker and about how he remains free to this day. Maybe writing about these crimes in the context of the times as they were and asking the public to think back to those times will be helpful in some way.

I took this project on in order to learn and to discover what looking at it would change for me. Doing this has had many benefits as I went back in time to many of the memories I have in life with Lyman Senior and Veonia Smith. What an unexpected gift to take the time to truly go back through my life as their granddaughter. They were very special to me. Love does not see pieces of paper or labels as definitions of who your family is.

Being with my grandparents throughout their lives and sharing so much with them over the course of forty years made it so that the experiences they had, the laughter and tears were also a part of how I felt, and what I witnessed as Lyman Smith Senior tried to come to terms with the extraordinary loss of his first born son Lyman Robert Smith. I am Lyman Jones Smith Seniors granddaughter and my name is Laurie.

FEAR

"You see what power is

Holding someone else's fear in our hand

And Showing it to them" – Amy Tan

Prologue

This is a story about The Original Night Stalker also known as East Area Rapist. It is also the story about how this person became intertwined with a family. This is how my part of the family was affected by this man's crimes and this is my part of the story. The East Area Rapist and The Original Night Stalker are in fact one and the same man. I began to write this story for several reasons. First I wanted to honor the victims of the crimes, especially those who were murdered at the hands of the Original Night Stalker. Because Lyman and Charlene Smith were members of our family they were a main motivation to put this on paper.

I wanted Lyman and Charlene in particular to be remembered more as the people they were rather than just the names of people who were attached to a serial killer. Families still wait after forty years for answers and for the person responsible to come to justice. I somehow wanted to make sure that the victims were seen as something more than the label "victim" as they all had their lives stolen from them. I needed to examine this case. I had researched serial killers since 1980. It was my hope that writing about this case could change how I feel about it. The memories were taking up space in the very dark recesses of my mind. I also thought getting the word out about the fact that this man has never been identified might also be of some help. If anyone out there especially those who were in Sacramento at the time like I was, if this helps to jog your memory during The East Area Rapists reign of terror and makes you think back to who you knew, who you may still know that sounds somehow like him it is not too late for justice to come for the victims.

The fact is that my Uncle Lyman Robert Smith was a murder victim along with his wife Charlene Smith in Ventura County, California. They were murdered on March 13, 1980.

Every book written about the unknown person who committed heinous acts such as serial rapes and then serial rapes and murders has listed this man's crimes, talked about each crime in detail, talked about the investigations and the missed opportunities. I admire Detectives Richard Shelby and Larry Crompton for taking the time to document as much of these cold cases as they have record of and memory of. They are important in shedding light on what happened in many communities forty years ago, from 1976 until 1986.

This unknown terrorist hurt and killed over sixty plus people. There have been a possible twelve murders or more with 10 confirmed, and over 50 rapes. If the Ransacker break-ins are counted in Visalia and if they are truly connected that adds over one hundred twenty-five plus more crimes from 1974 until 1976. One unsolved crime was the murder of Professor Claude Snelling in Visalia. We truly do not have information or proof to this point that the Visalia Ransacker is also the same man.

I suppose since the East Area Rapist and the Original Night Stalker are one and the same man and since he is still free and unknown to this point that he must be the focus of the story. I understand that detectives who have written about this unknown man's crimes have done so to document and get the word out there. They have put down on paper all of the circumstances about the East Area Rapist (EAR) crimes in Sacramento from 1976 until 1978. Then after tying the DNA to the Original Night Stalker the intent by Larry Crompton, who is a retired Contra Costa County Lieutenant was and is first and foremost to document these crimes and to hopefully have the help of the public to solve these crimes. The fact is that there have been several murder victims about whom we know little except mostly through speculation.

People have asked me anonymously and without knowing who I am why do you care about this case and who are you anyway? How could this case have actually affected you? Aren't you just some schmuck who wrote about this case because you are from Sacramento? I truly wish that these cases had never happened. I would not wish this story on anyone, on any family. There are tons of people who lived through the attacks in Sacramento from 1976 through 1978. Why should we care about what you have to say they ask? I wanted to help. My intentions have been stated about why I wanted to tell my part of the story. I wanted to work through some of the fear I have always carried with me through time. You will have to decide if you care or not because that certainly is ultimately up to you. There will always be those who condemn others no matter what, and there are thank goodness those who are supportive and kind.

This case, these serial rapes and then murders were personal. They are still personal not only to me and to the Lyman Smith family, but they certainly are to all of the other victims in these cases. These cases are personal to the communities, and in the communities in which they happened. If you lived in Sacramento through the attacks in 1976-1978 you will understand the terror that came into our town and you will understand the fear associated with this case that was felt by everyone. Especially felt by the young women and girls that were there for the two years of unrelenting attacks.

Consider being terrorized and then within about a year and a half after EAR seemingly stopped his attacks in that town you discover your grandfather's son and his wife are murdered. They were murdered by an unknown assailant who beat them to death with a log in their own bedroom. A murderer who may have watched as they were intimate for what would be the last time. Consider watching up close the absolute fallout that happens when someone you love loses someone they love. This was the case for me. I had to watch my grandfather try to live with not only the loss of his son and Charlene, but the way in which they were lost that one could not comprehend. A murderer is still free after all these years and he had an effect on many people.

I was born at Mather Air Force Base and lived in Sacramento all of my life. My family bought the house in South Sacramento in 1956 purposely buying this house in this neighborhood so that it and we would be close to my grandmother.

In February 1956 while my mother was barely pregnant with me my grandmother Veonia lost her husband of 17 years. He passed away from a heart issue, dying in my uncle's arms in their living room. By the time I was born that same year my parents had already purchased the house in South Sacramento which was off the 47th Avenue exit off highway 99. My grandmother lived just off the 12th Avenue Exit on West Curtis Park. She was alone there in the house her husband had purchased in 1928. The home had a very nice view of Curtis Park. It was close to Hughes Stadium and to Land Park. The Highway 99 freeway is one block away.

While my mother and father were busy adding children having my younger brother by March 1958 my grandmother was trying to get over the loss of my biological grandfather. She traveled; she socialized realizing that if she kept moving that she would somehow be able to get through her loss.

In 1956 Lyman Jones Smith lost his wife Wilma to cancer. He had one grown son and another teen aged son. Their names are Lyman Robert and Donald Roger. I am certain he was very devastated by the loss of his wife and it took him a while to process his grief.

I am not certain of exactly where Lyman Jones Smith and Veonia met, but both loved to have fun, loved to laugh, and by June 1960 they married one another having fallen in love. They were very happy. This is one of the first family events I actually remember because weddings are a big deal. I have included pictures of this event. Unfortunately, our group pictures were blurry, but what I can tell you is the wedding took place at the First Baptist Church in downtown Sacramento and the reception was at the Lanai off Freeport Blvd. in Sacramento June 26, 1960. I was three.

I am connected to this story like it or not. The story is certainly not one that a person would choose. It was never on my list to talk about much less write about. As a matter of fact, I never told anyone about the murders except my husband who wanted to know why I was so uncomfortable with shades not drawn at dark or sliding glass doors that did not at least have security locks or sticks in them.

Finally, I felt compelled to write what I think. As it turns out doing this has had a healing element in the process as I have looked back at my past and the really wonderful relationship I had with Lyman Jones and Veonia Smith. These two people were more like my own parents than grandparents. I do not know how I could have gotten through my childhood without them.

As I have said what motivated me originally to write about this subject was the fact that I wanted to pay tribute to Lyman Robert and Charlene as well as all of the victims including the ones who survived. At least the survivors were able to go on to write their own stories, have their own lives. The murder victims abruptly had their stories and what they were to become stolen from them by this serial murderer.

I have always had an innate curiosity about everything since I was born. I have always wanted to know why things are the way they are and why something happens. I have always asked why, but this particular subject and this particular story I had avoided like the plague. Too frightening, too dark it was a part of the past that I had tried to forget.

But then there is the part of me that never forgot, that looked at and studied serial killers. Since 1980 I have been researching serial killers, and studied the mindset of serial killers and others who commit murder more than once. Everyone who has ever known me has joked about this dark obsession. By the end of 1980 I began reading and researching information that we as a society knew about serial killers in particular. The murders of Lyman and Charlene appeared to be random from my perspective and it did not make sense to me that the murders would have been committed by someone they knew. Although Law Enforcement always looks at who the victims knew and those closest to them it just did not make sense to me. Especially when the Joseph Alsip case was dropped and the case essentially went cold as soon as they in Law Enforcement thought Alsip was the perpetrator in 1980. Alsip was released in 1982 after having been arrested in 1981. It is important to know and remember that the charges against Mr. Alsip were dropped and dismissed. The case never went to trial. They lacked any evidence. They spent an entire year of court time trying to determine if Mr. Alsip's Pastor was a reliable witness against him.

As a child I watched as everyone else did the story of the Manson murders unfold. This was my second experience learning about the bizarre behaviors of others who seemingly kill at random and in the most horrific of ways. The first experience was in 1963 when the murder of our President from a sniper's bullets' shook everyone. In 1968 Bobby Kennedy was murdered and so was Dr. Martin Luther King. We were in the middle of Vietnam, race riots and unrest in general. There were the Zodiac murders and that unknown assailant is still free. The craziness of the times became the norm.

The Smith murders to me seemed more like a crazed individual. The sheer brutality of how Lyman and Charlene were killed seemed more in line with a random act or a serial killer. I have written about my impressions about the man, the murderer, criminal, rapist, terrorist who is still unknown and free. The victims of these crimes were I think randomly picked by this criminal and were unfortunate enough to be picked at their most vulnerable. I am certain it was no accident that this criminal stalked all of his victims, chose them, watched them and set up the crimes so that he had the best chance not only of surprising them, but of obtaining and keeping control.

It was no accident that he waited until the couples in most cases had settled down for the night. I can picture him waiting and watching until these couples were asleep just long enough to have settled into a deep enough sleep to be the absolute most vulnerable that they could be. He wanted to make sure they were confused and hazy. When a man such as this comes into our awareness terrorizing and killing the people we love the stories do appeal to the fear in most of us. We should be afraid of the inhuman perpetrators of violent crimes.

There are many, many victims of violent crimes out there who have to figure out how to live every day, how to move on and how to live with such horrible memories and horrible visualizations of things that no one should have to experience or recall. Some people were lucky in the beginning to walk away from this madman. As this criminal fine tuned his game some were not so lucky.

In 1979 the East Area Rapist at last became the murderer he had promised to become. At least we can prove this man became a murderer by 1979. It may have been earlier if the Maggiore's were his victims or Professor Claude Snelling was his victim. He had finally worked up the courage or was it rages to finally kill several couples up close and personal by blunt force trauma, and then two more women who happened to be alone on the nights he struck. He began in Goleta which is in Santa Barbara County. He continued to destroy lives in Ventura, California and then in Laguna Niguel in Orange County, California. This was not enough. He went back to Goleta to murder three more people over the course of the next year and a half. He murdered from the end of 1979 until towards the end of 1981. Then, apparently the killing stopped.

Five years would go by before the next murder that we know of and the victim was back in Irvine California less than two miles from the murder scene of Manuela Witthuhn. Janelle Cruz would be the serial killer's youngest victim in May 1986. He would have the last word. As far as we know the killer has stopped for the last thirty years.

I have tried to piece together this puzzle. Many others also have tried to put this puzzle together. Some continue to work the case every day. This book was finally brought about because I grew up where I believe this man came from. I lived in Sacramento in many of the areas he struck. I was close by as this man grew from a boy into a young man. I was close by as he began to break in and terrorize many. I was lucky to have been missed along the way but shudder to think about the closeness to my geographic locations he would strike. I know there are many women that were in Sacramento who feel the same way. I know Sacramento well and I have been to all of the areas he struck. The descriptions given of neighborhoods in Sacramento I have been to having lived, worked, and played there. What are the odds that this killer not only came from where I did, but then eventually would kill people who were members of our family?

In March 1980 Lyman and Charlene Smith were brutally murdered. The fact is that Lyman and Charlene Smith were people. They had the right to live out their lives. Lyman should have been allowed to continue bringing up his children, to become a Judge if that was in the cards. Maybe Charlene would have had the children she so desired. Lyman Robert (Bob) had a real life with ambitions and plans. Lyman loved his family and he was loved. My grandfather Lyman Senior loved his son so much. When he was so viciously murdered for no apparent reason; my grandfather was never the same.

In February 1980 I was 23 years old. I had become engaged on Valentine's Day. My future husband and I set about planning our wedding. In March 1980 my grandfather's son Lyman Robert Smith was murdered. After this fact began to sink in my grandmother's reaction at first was that there was no way they could come to my wedding. It had been planned for May 10, 1980 a mere 8 weeks since Lyman Senior had learned that his oldest son was dead. A mere eight weeks since he was told all of the gruesome details about how his son and his wife had been murdered.

I can still recall my grandfather's words when faced with the idea of not attending my wedding. He said "Of course we will be there." We have to be there, and then they offered their punch bowl to use at my reception. Somehow Lyman Smith Senior found the strength along with my grandmother Veonia to come to my wedding in May 1980. They did not want us to postpone it, but wanted to move forward.

The last time my grandfather had sat in a church it was March 22, 1980 along with 350 other people to listen as the Rev. Leonard Dixon eulogized Lyman Robert and Charlene Smith. Somehow this man sat through my wedding listening to my cousins' sing as the rain came down on the roof of the church on this day. The wedding was in a beautiful old church in Auburn, California. After I walked with my new husband back down the aisle having just been married, in the vestibule my grandmother and grandfather were standing there. My grandfather was sobbing and sobbing and sobbing. He could not be consoled. He could not stop crying. There was nothing anyone could do for him. No one knew what to do. Somehow Lyman Senior managed to get to his car and drive my grandmother to my reception in Roseville. He was there having gathered himself together enough to talk to Bill Harvey (a local newsman of the time), and all of my relatives and friends. He somehow became the more pleasant and gregarious man he once was a mere eight weeks before.

My grandfather and grandmother came to my wedding because they knew that these events and these moments are important. I know my grandfather was thinking about his son, his family and the loss that they had all suffered. They were heartbroken and so very sad, and we were heartbroken with them, but they made it through my day for me and I hope for them.

Before this most horrible crime affected my family we loved each other the best we knew how. We got together every Thanksgiving with as many as 25 people showing up for dinner. My grandfather cooked for us all. He loved to cook. Most times when I think of Lyman Senior I picture him in the kitchen making biscuits or carving a turkey. During holiday's we had tables set up in every room. Before this tragedy happened my grandfather had been happy and more accessible than others in my family. He would let us sit on his lap as small children. He would take us as children every year to see the Singing Christmas Tree. We saw Lawrence Welk and Polish Dancers.

Every year we would stand out in front of the Memorial Auditorium in downtown Sacramento the first ones to be there. We would wait for more than an hour, waiting for the doors to open so we could get the best seats. It was a family joke really because when they finally opened the doors we always got any seats we wanted. No one was there but us. My girlfriend Kathleen was invited to come along and spend the night at my grandparents' house in Curtis Park. Kathleen was a guest in my grandparents' house so much that when she was married many years later my grandparents were invited to her wedding. My grandparents were the ones who consistently made our childhood and these events a lovely experience. I loved both of my grandparents very much.

My grandfather loved his sons Lyman Robert and Donald and the rest of his family, and our family. Lyman Senior's sons were the reason he sacrificed all that he had to raise them. Lyman Robert Smith and Charlene Smith had a life and then suddenly they did not.

All of the victims of murder were three dimensional people with lives, and purpose. All were very accomplished caring people who strived to make the world a better place. They were important to their families and to their communities. They all had the right to live out their lives. They were loved immensely and have been missed every day since this monster took them away from us.

Explanation of how this story is told in order to make it easier for the reader:

To make it easier to understand and negotiate the story what I have done is put in chronological order as much as possible news articles from when The East Area Rapist began his attacks in Sacramento. They are included in order to show his Method of Operation (MO) as well as show what the media and Law Enforcement were telling us as well as not telling us. I have noted when an article has been added and typed for clarity and also noted when it was the END OF ARTICLE. I have also added my comments about what was said and also about what was being done and also not done to stop this man.

In the writing of this story and in remembering where I was and what I was doing while all of the attacks were taking place I have interjected where I was and when, and placed that after the articles included. It seemed sort of a dance if you will to be in Sacramento during the attacks, continuing to live life, go to work, date, all the while travelling throughout Sacramento while this man was attacking and raping women at his will. It was nerve racking for everyone.

I also did not include all attacks in all the counties as my intent was to give enough information to the reader to inform what terror this man inflicted, how often he attacked and how much he got away with especially in Sacramento because this is where I came from. I also included information about the murders also in chronological order from 1979-1986.

In Sacramento in the beginning The East Area Rapist was part of my experience as a young woman who was already somewhat terrified by a society that especially in the 1970's still treated women as objects, humans to be stared at, whistled and yelled at every day. Also it is important to note that because society thought nothing of treating women in this way, and because the mindset had not changed yet to become more politically correct, many women put up with all kinds of hassles on a daily basis. It is also important to remember and to realize that back then there was no such thing as Sexual Harassment in the workplace either. If women complained typically it was she who lost her job. We were supposed to buck up and put up with these daily occurrences of sexism and harassment without complaint. If we did complain many times were seen as a bitch.

It was not really surprising that rape was not seen as a serious crime in the 70's and it is not surprising that women of the times felt nervous to begin with. Crime rates in the 1970's were very high. In 1968 in Sacramento California there were 5,744 rapes reported. Each year after 1968 the rates continued to climb. In 1974 the rate was 8,494. During the years of the East Area Rapist in Sacramento 1976 there were 9,614, 1977 there were 10,825 and 1978 there were 11,316 reported. I know there were many that went unreported. By 1981 the number had finally climbed to 13,566 forcible rapes. Finally, it began to come down in 1982. Add to that the penalty for rape was really not severe it was not very difficult to get away with it at the time. I have left all of the infinite details of each and every crime and each and every attack to Law Enforcement and others who just report the facts and who also ponder questions and propose that we ponder those questions as well.   It is my intent to ask the reader to ponder this question "Do you know him?"

The Beginning.......

A news blackout existed for the first several months. No one was warned no reports had been released so that the public could be aware and try to protect themselves.

This **news article** ran on November 4, 1976 by Warren Holloway a Sacramento Bee Staff writer:

Man Hunted As Suspect In 8 Rapes

Sheriff's detectives today disclosed an extensive hunt has been under way for a man who has attacked and raped eight women the past year in areas east of Sacramento.

Inspector Richard Shelby today said the same man is believed to have raped four women in Rancho Cordova, two in the Crestview area.

He said the first case occurred in October last year. He said the man did not strike again until June. Four of the attacks were last month.

Shelby said the man also is believed responsible for a case in which a woman was molested and another in which a rape attempt was thwarted. The sheriff's department has requested the rape cases be included in the Bee's Secret Witness program.

A reward of $2,500 is offered for information leading to the arrest and conviction of the rapist. Informants need not identify themselves. They are asked to telephone the private Secret Witness number, XXX-XXXX or to write, using instructions published on Wednesdays.

Sheriff's officials previously had asked the news media to hold back on reporting the case, saying publicity would ruin any stakeouts aimed at capturing the suspect.

But the series of rapes came to light last night at a Del Dayo Parents club meeting at Del Dayo School.

The meeting conducted by deputies, was to have been on crime prevention in general but the series of rapes was disclosed after questions about rumored rapes from some of the 500 persons attending.

Shelby said the suspect is white, has a pale complexion, may be between 5 feet 8 inches to 6 feet tall, of a medium build, 25 to 35 years old and has dark hair which hangs over his ears to his collar.

The attacks have been committed between 11 p.m. and 6:45 a.m. He frequently commits repeated attacks on individual victims over a period of three hours. He has entered the homes through a window. Investigators describe him as a "cat burglar" type who finds out if a husband is home.

He has worn a mask, but descriptions are vague as to what kind. He has worn military type boots and black tennis shoes. His weapons have included a revolver, knife, a stick and a club.

He has cut and beat his victims, but none severely.
END OF ARTICLE

This photograph was one of many taken at the meeting held at Del Dayo School where the discussion turned to the rumors of rapes that were occurring. It is believed that the perpetrator was in attendance along with about 500 other people. Many believe the guy wearing the puffy jacket has been identified and cleared and he is no longer a person of interest as well as the guy sitting in front of him. I have been unable to find out the facts behind how he/they may have been cleared, but it has been said by different sources that they were identified and cleared through DNA.

Man Hunted As Suspect In 8 Rapes

By WARREN HOLLOWAY
Bee Staff Writer

Sheriff's detectives today disclosed an extensive hunt has been under way for a man who has attacked and raped eight women the past year in areas east of Sacramento.

Inspector Richard Shelby today said the same man is believed to have raped four women in Rancho Cordova, two in Del Dayo and two in the Crestview area.

He said the first case occurred in October last year. He said the man did not strike again until June. Four of the attacks were last month.

Shelby said the man also is believed responsible for a case in which a woman was molested and another in which a rape attempt was thwarted.

The sheriff's department has requested the rape cases be included in The Bee's Secret Witness program.

A reward of $2,500 is offered for information leading to the arrest and conviction of the rapist. Informants need not identify themselves. They are asked to telephone the private Secret Witness number, 442-6221, or to write, using instructions published on Wednesdays.

Sheriff's officials previously had asked the news media to hold back on reporting the case, saying publicity

See Page B2, Col. 1

32

Rape

Continued from Page B1

would ruin any stakeouts aimed at capturing the suspect.

But the series of rapes came to light last night at a Del Dayo Parents Club meeting at Del Dayo School. The meeting, conducted by deputies, was to have been on crime prevention in general but the series of rapes was disclosed after questions about rumored rapes from some of the 500 persons attending.

Shelby said the suspect is white, has a pale complexion, may be between 5-feet, 8-inches to 6-feet tall, of a medium build, 25 to 35 years old and has dark hair which hangs over his ears to his collar.

The attacks have been committed between 11 p.m. and 6:45 a.m. He frequently commits repeated attacks on individual victims over a period of three hours. He has entered the homes through a window.

Investigators describe him as a "cat burglar" type who finds out if a husband is home.

He has worn a mask, but descriptions are vague as to what kind. He has worn military type boots and black tennis shoes. His weapons have included a revolver, knife, a stick and a club.

He has cut and beat his victims, but none severely.

Table of Contents

Introduction

In the early 1970's a young man or men began his/their journey into becoming an outlaw. What we now know about serial killers is they begin many times as angry, frustrated children who kill animals. It is common to discover that a serial killer's beginnings encompass voyeurism, peeping in windows, breaking into homes, burglary which progresses to rapes and then to serial rapists' who also murder their victims.

This book is about who and where this serial murderer might be. Because he or they are still free and because he still lives in the shadows I have written what I think, what I have studied, and where I came from. Why? Because I have had a gut feel about where this person or persons came from. I could be wrong. But, what if I'm not?

Trauma and fear predisposed me to putting this story out of my mind for thirty years. This book is my attempt to share with others what my impressions of this man's mindset has been and still may be. Because I have studied and worked at trying to understand the serial killer mind and watched the behaviors they have exhibited as reported to the public through the news media I am aware of the similarities in this type of killer. Dennis Rader aka BTK, Jeffrey Dahmer, Ted Bundy, The Zodiac, Son of Sam, David Berkowitz, John Wayne Gacy, Gary Ridgeway aka The Green River Killer, the list is very long. All are different yet they are the same when it comes to lack of empathy, lack of remorse and Narcissism.

I have been like a sponge over time, trying to look at and understand the motivations of people who feel compelled to kill. My interest in particular was about people who kill over and over. The same MO, the same signatures used by each and every one of the men I have mentioned. They seem driven to repeat the behaviors for periods of time. We now know that it is possible for a serial killer to stop for long periods of time. We also know that they may try to stop or control the drive to continue. Many have lived lives next door to and with people who think they are "normal" stand up citizens in their communities. Everyone is horrified to discover that not only were these men living among us, but that they were believed to be good leaders in the places they resided. Dennis Rader (BTK) was on the Board of Directors of his church, a scout leader with a wife and children.

Ted Bundy, a likable law student whose everyday persona was one of a man who had great potential and who cared about others as he voluntarily worked on a suicide prevention line. Ted's mother did not believe he was a serial killer until the day before he was executed. These serial killers are hard for us to wrap our minds around. Hard to believe that the monster within can be hidden behind a mask, a persona that is marketable to the world. They not only live among us they are a symptom of the countless mostly men and boys who do not receive the help they need as children and adolescents. We look the other way or fail to recognize the signs that show us what these young men will likely become.

Growing up in our societies there is tremendous pressure on our boys about who they should be, what they should be and how they should be. If any stumble or need help isn't it possible that not only do they not know how to ask for help, they are taught that they must not? So begins the metamorphosis into a young boy, and then a young man who becomes an unfeeling monster as an adult. There are signs, there are symptoms. I watched interviews with Jeffrey Dahmer's father and mother thinking, they must have known. They must have known something was very wrong.

Throughout this book I have abbreviated these three acronyms. EAR is referred to because when this criminal began his crimes he became known in Sacramento as the East Area Rapist. In the beginning his crimes were almost exclusively in East Sacramento. When he moved down to Southern California he was then called The Original Night Stalker because his crimes predated Richard Ramirez in the 1980's and included terrorizing and then murdering the unfortunate victims. I refer to him as many do as ONS throughout this book. VR is about the Visalia Ransacker who began his crimes prior to EAR. I and many others believe the three could be the same man. There is no proof that the Visalia Ransacker is connected to EAR and ONS. It has been proven through DNA that EAR and ONS are one and the same man. He is a prolific criminal.

I also feel it is important to make sure that when I talk about Lyman in this story that everyone knows **that there were two.** My grandfather's name was Lyman Jones Smith and he was Lyman Robert Smith's father. It can be confusing since I talk about them both to keep them straight. I call Lyman Jones Smith Senior although he never went by that, and I call his son Lyman Robert or (Bob).

Lyman Robert was the murder victim along with his wife Charlene. When reading this story to keep things straight this is also what needs to be known.

When Lyman Robert was a boy no one called him Lyman he was simply called Bob. When he was with family he was always called Bob. He called himself that until he was working as an attorney far from my grandfather in Santa Paula. So keep in mind in this story that Lyman Robert will also be referred to as Bob. His obituary and the stories written about his murder always have his proper name Lyman Robert Smith. My grandfather called him Bob.

Chapter One
South Sacramento – Getting right to it

I have spent many years not thinking about and trying not to think about a story that has had a profound effect on everything and every way that I am. I pushed this event and its' details as far from my current day to day life as I possibly could. It was a shattering event to my psyche as I tried to figure out how to reconcile the horrific events that happened. Like a scar that is no longer visible to the naked eye I can still feel it in me, sometimes around me, especially when I stand in front of my kitchen window at night. I turn off the light that surrounds me as quickly as possible most nights. When a murder happens up close and the fallout in a family is experienced and seen the damage that was done to my feeling of safety could not be undone. It is never the same.

Because the DNA that links the perpetrator to each crime, possibly 12 or 13 murders from the beginning until it appeared he stopped in 1986 and because his DNA profile is not matched in the system even though the crime labs have it no one has yet been identified as The Original Night Stalker and the very prolific East Area Rapist. Will we ever have closure? Closure? This is one of my least favorite words. Will we, any of us ever really know who changed our lives, how we thought, how we live and even what we do in some cases?

When these crimes of the East Area Rapist occurred in the late 1970's and then as he morphed into a serial killer into the 1980's I was nearby. So close by that it was a terrifying experience. Murders happen every day somewhere. Rapists commit these hideous crimes against women all of the time somewhere. Home invasions happen, robberies, stalking, and weird phone calls in the night, prowling in of neighborhoods where young men try to peer in windows to catch glimpses of women, girls or whomever they are seeking to get their rocks off. This case, this one has been of interest to me since it began. How could I ever have known, and what are the odds that as I read about and was afraid of the East Area Rapist that somehow eventually he would forever be connected to our family?

I grew up in Sacramento on the South Side. We moved there at the end of the 1950's just a month or so after I was born. My family for all intents and purposes lived there until I was 18. I attended all of the public schools there which included Nicholas Elementary, Fern Bacon Junior High and then Luther Burbank High School. I graduated from Luther Burbank moving on to Cosumnes River College and Sacramento City College.

Like the movie Back to the Future we lived in tract housing at the end of a street, across from a creek (Morrison Creek) which always made me nervous as I grew. All of the kids in the neighborhood would go there to play including me. Back then it was made out of dirt not cement yet. There were creatures living down there. Muskrats

41

and toads, pollywogs and crickets, we would make wooden rafts and float down this creek using long sticks and catch crawdads. The old rodeo rider, my neighbor who lived nearby had become surrogate grandparent to me and my brothers and to many of the neighborhood kids. When Richard Raymond (we called him Dick) heard that I was afraid of the muskrats in particular, he held my hand and walked me across the street on the short dirt path to the creek. He described to me what muskrats looked like and how I did not need to be afraid of them because they were afraid of me.

Who knows what kind of pesticides and chemicals were in there in the 1960's? Behind our house which was once at the end of the street behind the fence moved cows walking slowly by chewing the grass and their cuds softly mooing. It was lazy and somewhat comforting to live on the edge of the future and moved slowly enough to still feel safe, to live at a pace that was slow enough to build forts in the tall grasses behind the fence, to call back and forth to one another watching the blue sky and the very big white clouds as they slowly watched us back.

There was no fear to be found outside as we playfully would have dirt clod fights never really hurting each other as the dry, hot summers made it so our clods, launched at each other would hit nearby exploding and disintegrating into dust. We loved being outside with all of the freedom from all of our houses and what it brought us. We were very much like the rag tag kids that later actors would play in the

Goonies. We would be turned loose in the mornings by our parents playing together all day. Everywhere in Sacramento in the late 1950's and 1960's there were Larchmont living tracks of houses being built. The houses were very much the same in one neighborhood or another. The only differences were slight changes in floor plans. In the 60's there were so many children everywhere on sidewalks and playing outside. On our street within a two to three block area in every direction we all spent our days outside, away from our houses playing red rover, red rover or red light green light on our lawns. The house we lived in had a larger yard so it meant that most times we played there. There was little TV, no computers that we knew of yet, no internet, no cell phones, no devices of any kind. There was just each other calling out across lawns and yards to each other as it grew darker and darker until we could barely make out each other's outlines. We never wanted to give up the day. Until finally, our mothers would call us home. "Come in now dinners ready." This would be repeated everywhere, day after day from yard to yard until tomorrow.

The milk man would come early in the morning before the sun was too hot. He would leave several bottles on our porches inside a wire carrier. Because it would get to 110 degrees quickly in the summers we would hurry and bring the milk inside. The sun would stream up our driveway. Our kitchen window was right over the front porch. I could hear the milk man come and if I ran to the front door I would see him. The milkman wore a uniform and had a hat that made him look nice. When I feel nostalgic I have to

43

admit that I miss seeing the milkman come and go. The milkman and the guys running around your car at the Texaco gas stations. It really was like that then.

Every week the men who would come for our garbage were always all black men. They would carry beat up metal cans dumping our garbage into them before they would dump them into the big, ugly, dirty garbage trucks. I would always wonder why the men who came were always all black men. I remember thinking what an awful job they had and why would they ever want to do it? There was never fear, just a lazy way of watching them as they came every week.

All of the garbage men looked like characters that one could draw for a cartoon. Lines and creases in their faces, the very particular way they bent under the weight of the cans as they took turns dumping them into the big trucks. They were all safe to my way of thinking at the time. I would hang from my tricycle upside down in the driveway to try and get a different perspective on the world even then at the age of three and four. I liked it that way. There was no discrimination in our neighborhood, at least none that I was aware of. We had every ethnic mix of people there all in my two streets. Immigrants had come from everywhere. Germans, and Dutch people with accents, Japanese families who had been interned in camps during World War II, Italians, Portuguese and Mexicans. Asians who were at the time always called Oriental. Europeans and Black people who were not yet called African Americans.

We were a total mixture of what America was and is. It was 1959, 1960.

I felt that our neighborhood was a safe place to be. During the summers most times you could find me running barefoot down the street hopping from shadow to shadow so I wouldn't burn my feet on the hot pavement. My grandmother always would ask me "Where are your shoes?" I didn't like shoes. Year after year growing up in that place I would roam up and down the street in search of friends to play with. From the age of about three it seems I could go where I wanted. My best friend lived two houses away. She and I were introduced at the age of one. As soon as we could walk we became friends. We are still friends to this day.

I walked to school at Nicholas Elementary and sometimes I rode my bike at the age of nine with my violin hanging from one of the handle bars. I would visit the neighbors up and down the street, in particular the cowboy's house where I would help he and his wife do yard work picking up grass clippings and sweeping the sidewalk. My neighbor who had the coolest name for a cowboy, Richard Raymond Ratliff would tell me stories about his rodeo riding days in Texas, showing me scars on his hands and telling me what it felt like to ride an animal that didn't want you to ride him.

Sometimes Richard (nicknamed Dick) would make us lunch and then play his fiddle for us. The very first time I ever heard "The Orange Blossom Special" was when Dick played it for me as an audience of one. He played Blue Grass; he could play the Banjo, the Mandolin, the guitar and the fiddle. Back then no one thought it was odd or weird to have an extended family of the neighbors. Dick and his wife Evelyn really did become a part of my family and years later in a Christmas card I told them how much they had meant to me growing up. From then on when they sent me a card they added the word "Love" Dick and Evelyn. I would go back to my street now and again and visit until they died. It truly did take a community to raise all of us and we were grateful for the connection. Maybe that is how we were kept safe. We all knew who lived where – who belonged where. We were a small community and I knew and remember the names of all of the families I could see out of my kitchen window.

One day behind the fence where the field had always been the cows had simply vanished. There was a lot of noise as a whole new neighborhood was being built in the dirt. More concrete, more sidewalks. The workers would park their giant trucks on the dead end of the street. We would climb all over the trucks in the summer. I recall being in my baby doll pajamas in July the summer I was seven. I was sent to bed before it got dark. I had the chicken pox so I had spent the day in my PJ's.

Soon there would be another layout of Larchmont living homes; gone forever would be the field behind me. This must have been when I began to wish I could operate a bulldozer myself changing everything back to fields, dragging away all the new concrete which had buried our fields and our forts.

No more forts and dirt clod fights just new houses everywhere behind the fence. We would go inside them when no one was around sitting on the sheets of drywall. Walking on the newly created fireplaces where the sound of our voices would echo from room to room. I went everywhere the boys did. Sometimes it was close to dark so the insides of the houses half built were darker still. It always made me nervous because I was afraid we might get caught and might get in trouble. I knew we weren't supposed to be in the houses and to take pieces of drywall that we used to draw hopscotches with, but it was impossible to resist my curiosity of what an empty half built house looked like. I never wanted to miss anything. I would be the only girl with all of the boys many times. Eventually these houses were completed and put up for sale. One by one the rest of the newer part of the neighborhood became occupied.

As young kids in the spring and summer we would go to the creek to play but eventually there was so much gunk and trash down there that it was impossible to float on rafts anymore. They had put cement down there and then there must have been a drought because my last memories in my childhood where the creek curved were seeing a shopping cart trashed there and mucky muddy dirt.

Because it was so dried up it became easier to walk around from one end to the other. In the 1960's when we were children there was a path you could walk along the edge of the creek on both sides behind all of the yards and backs of houses. You could walk on the paths above the creek beds. Now it is overgrown with large bushes and all traces of the long forgotten paths are gone. They have since put up big blue fences by the bridge blocking any access we had long ago. You cannot walk back there any longer unless you want to walk in the creek. Personally I preferred walking down the streets. Once you get to Steiner Drive there is a little bridge there with a cool, shady spot if you cared to jump over the side of the bridge and go under it.

In 1968 they built the Florin Center shopping mall. My friends and I would walk there at 14. When we walked there we would jump over the side of the bridge on the opposite side going east because there was also a dirt trail that you could walk on beside the creek. The trail took you through the field until you got to the main drag or if followed the creek bed could take you all over Sacramento. A movie theater was built not far from Florin Center called The State Theater. I worked there at 17 watching Butch Cassidy and the Sundance Kidd over and over and over because Robert Redford and Paul Newman were really easy to look at. Who cared if they were outlaws? It was 1973 and 1974.

When I graduated from the sixth grade and moved on to Fern Bacon Junior High I had to walk through the new neighborhood they had built behind our street finding my way to the highway 99 overpass. Very close by there was a pump station which is at the very end of the neighborhood alongside the highway 99 Freeway. In descriptions of neighborhoods hit by the attacker there were many times pump stations mentioned because they are located very close to the freeway overpasses. Freeway overpasses could be found easily by locating pump stations and vice versa. A pump station is many times located relatively near the low point of the highway. If possible they are located so that a frontage road or overpass is available for easy access to the station. The station and access road should be located on high ground so that access can be obtained if the highway becomes flooded.

I mention these neighborhood markers because they were next to creeks. During floods especially in Sacramento with the river nearby we were very aware that when it rained the grown-ups would talk of floods. One of my biggest nightmares as a child would be about floods and water pouring into our house. I recall discussions about this – we were so close to the creek which ran through the neighborhood. I would picture it rising to the level that we would have to vacate our home in the middle of the night. (It never happened but those were my fears). There are levees all around Sacramento and the Morrison Creek ran twisting and turning through the streets I walked on.

Many times attacks were near an overpass in neighborhoods which can easily be seen by our suspect. The pump stations and creeks also go hand in hand with these neighborhood markers. This was important as the possibility existed that this was one way to escape from one neighborhood into another on foot. This was a brilliant move on EAR's part.

As a junior high student I had to cross highway 99 over-pass daily. Our neighborhood ended making it mandatory that I walk through another dirt field to the overpass. It was here I recall seeing my first real fist fight between boys. There were no parents around and no adults because it was a vacant field. The dirt was dry and as I came upon the scuffle the dust rose from the ground and from them. A group of children stood around watching them take swings at each other and then they were on the ground punching and tearing at each other. Their faces bleeding, corners of their mouths ripped from gaining access to a mouth pulling with dirty fingers. I was horrified. We stood stuck to the ground like people do when they see an accident. Staring and looking, doing nothing to intervene. And then we walked on. It was disturbing to me yet I don't remember who they were, what happened to them. They are frozen in time in my memory still there in the dirt.

Once we went up and over the freeway pass all of a sudden we were in another neighborhood where the houses were nicer called Bowling Green. I walked this way every day the entire time I went to the school 7-9th grades. There were times while walking on my way home near the overpass near Underwood Way that an older guy who could already drive would pull up next to me. (I am sure it was something he must have done all the time to multitudes of girls). He would roll down his window and ask, "Do you want a ride?" "I can take you home. I can take you anywhere you want to go." He drove an off white car (we used to call them boats) because they were big American cars. It reminded me of the car my Texan neighbor drove. Big like a Cadillac or Buick, maybe a Plymouth. All I know is I always tried to walk away fast never going up to the car. I would only say "no thanks I don't need a ride." This went on for the entire time I went to Junior High. In this day and age this boy/man would have been reported, gotten in trouble, but back then no one said anything.

By the time I got to high school and the tenth grade it was the end of 1971. The walk to school and back then included not only going over the overpass for Highway 99 into Bowling Green, but then it extended to having to walk up Franklin Blvd. Every morning I would walk inside the car dealerships always walking alone on the hard linoleum floors. I had tried the door one morning and finding it unlocked decided that this would be my own path to school.

I looked from left to right as I walked through every day. The echo of clip clop clip clop of my shoes in my ears was the only sound on the floors as I went through day after day. I carried my books against my stomach. There was no such thing as a backpack made for kids to carry yet. So we carried them in a pile against our stomachs. Arms tired by the time we got to school. Maybe this was when I began to walk fast and then faster. To this day I walk ahead of anyone I might be walking with. I never knew who was around or if anyone was. The offices and the building all seemed empty there was just me, clip, clop. The car dealerships were warmer than walking out in the fog, the rain and the wind.

Prior to getting my license to drive I would walk absolutely everywhere. From the area of 47th Avenue to Florin Road to Parkway, Center Parkway, Land Park, to Sutterville Road and Freeport to the Zoo. My travels encompassed Riverside and West Sacramento as well as Downtown. It did not matter if it was sunny or raining outside. I walked everywhere. The nuances of Greenhaven and areas mostly in the South part of Sacramento became very familiar to me. I walked and walked. I know how one can get from one neighborhood to another on foot through pathways and through parks.

I walked until at long last I became 16. I finally had a light green Volkswagen to drive to and from school. It had been my parents and then my older brothers. He went in the Army then and I inherited the car. I got a job. No more walking for me. All I wanted now was freedom from high school.

As soon as I could drive I recall discovering Goethe Park and then Paradise Park. When I received my license I then found my way to most nooks and crannies of every part of Sacramento. Downtown, North Highlands, Arden, Folsom, Rancho Cordova, you name it I found my way to the American River accesses and Sacramento River.

I would go to the Virgin Sturgeon on the river, water ski the Sacramento River and take a River Boat down it to the San Francisco Bay. I went on houseboats and speed boats through the Delta. I worked in Stockton, Galt, Yuba City, Sutter Creek and small towns around Sacramento in 1978.

You are likely asking yourself "why is she talking about this old stuff?" Because back then, in our neighborhood of what we thought were middle class families it felt safe and normal to walk anywhere and everywhere I wanted to go. I had no fear, no concerns, and no worries. It was my domain, our domain. All of the kids there seemed to feel free to move about. It was our space, our place to have fun, to play, to grow up and become contributing adults. Or was it?

Any fear I ever had was when I was inside my house at night. Like most kids I guess, the monsters or imaginary ones only came out at night as I was tucked safely in bed. The shadows would come out then. My bed was right under a window to our backyard. Eventually besides the wind that would blow on the trees and move the shadows and make the fence shudder at night there was more to be heard and more to be seen. To this day I cannot sleep well when it is windy. Wind has always made me uneasy.

I don't remember being truly afraid of anything that lived outside in the dark until I was about 14. In 1971 one night as I lay in my bed all of a sudden there was quite a ruckus outside. Dogs barking, people yelling and as my dad went to look into the backyard he was to catch a glimpse of the person who all of a sudden jumped over our fence, almost fell into our pool, ran around it and kept running to the other side of our yard to the fence where he again seemed to just leap over it. My dad chased him through the yard but as he went over the fence before my dad could catch him he was virtually gone. He moved very quickly and was a blur in the darkness as I watched out my bedroom window. I heard the fence clattering under the weight of this person's mad scramble to escape. It could be that I began to feel less protected at 14 because this was the year my father was to move out. The last summer he lived with us I had a terrifying experience.

It was July 1971. I had a first boyfriend that I rode part way home with on his banana seat bike. I got a little too far from home as he dropped me back on the sidewalk to make the walk back to my block.

I was not concerned at the extra few blocks I would have to travel. It was still light outside. I walked down my own block heading towards home. I wasn't very far away. I wasn't supposed to be off my own block as the end of the day was nearing. In Sacramento in the summer time it was light out until at least 9:00 at night. It was only about 7:30. I walked quickly to my own block now. My long blonde hair caught the breeze as I walked, barefoot. I was a blue eyed blonde heading into the 10th grade. I was enjoying my summer and heading home.

I was very close to my own front door when all of a sudden a red pickup truck came driving quickly towards me up the street. I heard it before I glanced behind me and saw it coming. I hurried up all of a sudden, feeling an instinctual foreboding. My entire being all of a sudden told me to run. As the pickup came along side me now a man jumped out of it and began to run after me. It felt as though I had known in that second before it happened that I was in danger. Trusting my instincts, I began to hurry and then to run. The man chased me and was getting so close I thought, oh my god I am not going to make it home. It is too far. What should I do?

I knew that if I continued to run that he would catch me. What about the other man driving the truck? He could catch me if I continued to run. One of my best friends that I had known all of my life lived near my home. I ran up to her front door and placed myself between the screen door and the front door. The man who was chasing me stopped dead in his tracks. I was pounding on the door of my friends' house and yelling help me. Please open the door. As I did this the young man watched and waited. He seemed calm as he watched me. Over my shoulder as I took a quick glance he seemed just to be waiting as I was to see if anyone was home before he made his next move. His demeanor seemed matter of fact. He was standing on the grass maybe 15 - 20 feet away next to the driveway. I felt the chill and the fear exploding inside me. What if my friend or her mother were not home? I don't know how long it took as I pounded and screamed but finally the door was being opened. I was so much in terror that I pushed my way into the door and ran over everything in my path as far into the house as I could go. I was screaming they are chasing me. Help me. Help me. They slammed the door shut and locked it.

The young man who had been chasing me got back into the truck. We watched out my friends' bedroom window as they decided to drive away. They did not seem to be concerned about the idea that someone might call the cops. They did not seem to be in a hurry either. It seemed they sat there deciding what their next move was. The men in the truck were young, white, and the one who chased me was wearing a white T-shirt and blue jeans. He was blonde and medium height. He looked like a student and he also looked something like one of my neighbors down the street. For the longest time I wondered if it had been him and another guy or my neighbor and his brother. I did not really notice the driver of the truck because I was too intent on getting away from the guy chasing me. The only thing I can tell you about the driver is that he was also white.

The truck they were driving was red but not bright and not shiny paint. It was older and the paint seemed more muted like a matte finish to it. I think it was a Ford because of the logo attached to the front. I know that if someone were to show me pictures of trucks from that era I could very well pick out exactly what they were driving that day. It was not a new model.

What has always puzzled me to this day is the fact that no one called the police, and the guys waited outside for a minute before driving away. The two young men appeared unconcerned about the possibility that someone would see the license plate, unconcerned about whether or not someone might call the police. They just sat there. I have no way of measuring the time because I was so afraid. They must have decided it was too risky to try and come into the house I had run into. They had no way of knowing who or what was inside.

In the 70's there was still a modicum of innocence everywhere. For those who think the children should have called the police about this incident I say to you we were innocent, shy and looked to our elders to protect us and to do the right thing. The adults that were there on this day did nothing to report this incident. My parents were more involved and concerned in July 1971 with what was to become their impending separation and divorce. We did not want to rock the boat and upset anyone. Lots of families back then did not discuss important issues. Families many times did not share information and in our case we were already walking on egg shells. By the time I started high school in the fall of 1971 my parents were separated. No one was paying attention to would be criminals, police reports and getting involved. Don't rock the boat and bad things happen to other people seemed a common way to think back then.

Society was a completely different animal than what it is today. Children truly were in many cases seen and not heard. Punishment typically was restriction for two weeks or more. Somehow when I was chased it seemed that I had done something wrong. I would have most likely been punished for not staying on my own block. We did not make a big scene; we did not talk about it. It was as if nothing had happened at all. But, it had. I was always frightened after that. I actually never spoke about this incident until the 1990's and was shocked to discover that when I did it made me tremble even after 20 plus years.

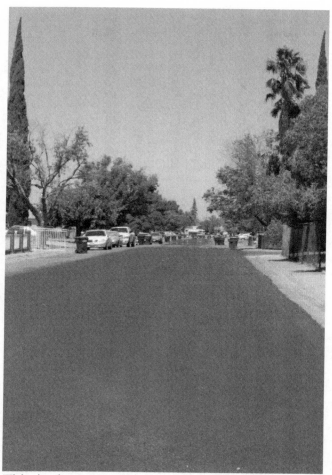

This is the street I was chased down in July 1971. Between the 47th Avenue area and Florin Road off ramps in South Sacramento, California. I was running toward where you can see the fence on the left. Back then the fence was not there only open driveway and grass leading up to the front door I ran to.

1960 Ford Truck as described by witnesses as used by EAR

The red paint job was a matte finish look (not shiny) Red Truck (circa) 1960 as seen by me when I was chased down my street in South Sacramento California

I called my mother and asked her to watch for me as I ran home later that evening. She sent my dad outside in the side yard to watch me run home. She never told him what had happened and neither did I. We wanted to keep the peace. This experience was to change my life forever. It changed how I felt about the world being safe. How safe can it be when you are chased down the street in your own neighborhood?

I have never before and never again been so afraid for my safety and my life. This was a fear that sent chills through my entire being. This was a fear, a terror that made the scalp on the very top of my head stand up. I never talked about it to anyone, ever. It was just something that I remembered and used on a daily basis since then to keep myself safe. No more carefree walks alone down the street. I have wondered in my travels through life about what would have happened to me had this person caught me. Did I narrowly escape Kidnap? Death? Rape? Would I have ever gotten to go to school? Would I have missed absolutely every joyful moment that I have had since then? It could be.

We will never know because I trusted my instincts that evening and began to run. It was that split second that saved me. I should probably mention so that no one thinks this young man was a slow runner or that I out ran him. I loved to run it was something I did a lot. I was on the track team in junior high running the 440 relay in competitions. Because instinct told me to run and the fact that I listened and immediately began to run, these are the only reasons I was able to place myself between the screen door and the door in order to get away.

This became a part of my being from then on. This one experience really is the one thing that almost happened to make me make sure my keys were in my hand in parking garages or parking lots even in broad daylight... Always ready for any threat, checking my back seats as I readied myself to get into the car, locking it as soon as I entered. I always walk fast and with purpose.

Not long after I was chased I began to babysit. I liked the idea of being paid to play with children, be the responsible one in someone else's home. What I found out very quickly though was that in another person's home I was unfamiliar with my surroundings, of the doors and windows, whether or not they had curtains or blinds at night. I recall babysitting one night in a home with hardwood floors that echoed every step. The curtains were up or maybe they did not have any. All I know is that I was terrified to keep the light on or turn the light off. I was afraid to stay awake while waiting for the parents and afraid to go to sleep. I remember standing in the room frozen and scared for the entire time I was in the home especially after the children I was watching went to sleep. I made myself as small as I could on the couch and waited for the parents to return. I do believe this was the last time I ever tried to babysit.

I was very young and had no one to talk to about my fears. I discovered I was too terrified to babysit anyone's children. I had even taken a CPR First Aid course in preparation to provide babysitting to earn money, but soon found I could not. I could not conquer my fear alone so I never babysat again.

I had no idea that this feeling would never really go away completely over time. I learned the value of knowing your surroundings and to be ready at any moment to escape from whatever might be looming in the darkness. I worked over the years to come to terms with my post-traumatic stress and most of the time the darkness is only the darkness.

Ironically, my father worked at the Preston School of Industry in Ione for The California Youth Authority. My dad was working with young men between the ages of 17 and 21 trying to get them back on track and to try to teach them that they could make better choices for their lives. One weekend I recall going to Ione on a very warm sunny day. The staff had decided to play each other in a football game. Our whole family went there to watch my dad play. All I can really recall of the day is walking across the lawn in the sun and being stared at like crazy. I did not take into consideration that day that these guys probably had not seen a young girl for quite a while.

I was stared at by these boys/men so hard and so much that it really creeped me out. I also recall going on a short tour of the inside of the facility seeing where these young men were locked up. The cells were small with nothing much in them.

My dad used to sometimes invite these young teenagers/men who had been released from custody to our house. I would worry because of the way that they stared at me. I was fourteen, almost fifteen. I could never tell my dad any of these things or express my feelings or worry. A long time after I was chased down my own street I wondered if these young men who knew where we lived, I wondered if they had come looking for me or if it was merely a coincidence. Were they the two men in the truck? We will never know.

Chapter Two
Building the Case

In the early 1970's while the East Area Rapist was just beginning to burglarize and then eventually graduate to raping women in 1976, I had not yet heard of him. By the time he earned the name EAR (East Area Rapist) I was 19. I recall hearing about this individual who was prowling around in Rancho Cordova, CA in areas I would drive through during the day. Later on I read the newspapers as this rapist moved about near the American River, Carmichael, Citrus Heights, and Orangevale areas of Sacramento. Finally, this man was in my neighborhood where I had slept at night in South Sacramento near Florin Road and Highway 99. I had lived in the area off the exit to 47th Avenue and Florin Road.

I had heard the news reports for the last couple of years and was appropriately frightened by the details I knew. While this man was possibly in Visalia in 1975 and 1976 I would drive my yellow VW Bug outside Sacramento to Davis where my best friend attended UC Davis. Her name is Marti. I was always alone on the road between Sacramento and Davis and invariably it was all hours of the day and night.

In 1974 I was 17, 18. My parents did not live in our home any longer because they were divorced. My mother would stay with her boyfriend near Florin Road and Sky Parkway. My father had moved to downtown Sacramento on 17th and L Street. This left me at home alone with my younger brother. I was 15 and he was 13-1/2 when everyone left. We had a sliding glass door out to the fenced back yard. We lived at the end of what once was a dead end street that was right across from the Morrison Creek access. You could jump the fence and get away rapidly if you desired to. I would stand in the middle of the hall in the dark of night watching each entrance. I would be frozen in my spot afraid to move, guarding and watching. I was obviously terrorized at the thought of being alone and afraid that if I slept I would be a victim of some kind. It was my worst nightmare. The idea of being so vulnerable I was certain I would not live to see my 21st birthday.

All of this predates news reports and activity of the East Area Rapist. My fear came from being chased down my own street in 1971. My brother and I were left alone in our house from the fall of 1971 until I was to turn eighteen in late 1974. No one in my family was to return to this house. In 1975 they would eventually put our house up for sale and I was forced to move to a home on Center Parkway along with my younger brother, my mom's boyfriend, and his two teenage kids. I was to go to college and work. This arrangement only lasted a year for me as I was to find I was living in the "Bad Brady Bunch movie" My mom said, "If you don't like it leave." And, so I did.

When I was 19 (it was 1976) I moved into my first studio apartment alone. It was perfect for me because in order to get inside you had to come into a long indoor hallway that was inside the building and then get to the apartment door. It was also on the second floor and the sliding glass door opened to my balcony. It felt safer that way and I loved it. I was attending Cosumnes River College at the time which is just off Center Parkway. This was the south end of Sacramento. The East Area Rapist had yet to make himself really known in Sacramento. Perhaps he really was in Visalia.

During the late 1970's and early 80's I must have moved almost 30 times. I lived in South Sacramento, Citrus Heights, Roseville, Orangevale, West Sacramento and many more addresses eventually landing in El Dorado Hills.

When I worked downtown in the beginning of my professional career at the age of 20 I was employed by a private investigator that would have me go out and serve papers on individuals until I realized how dangerous this could be for me.

In August 1977 I went to work downtown at 555 Capitol Mall for a computer company as the Executive Administrative Assistant. I started this job on the day that Elvis died. For the next three years I went to work in Downtown Sacramento. I was 20 almost 21. The East Area Rapist was known to look for targets downtown and in public places. I was there from August 1977 until 1980. EAR was known to be in Sacramento until the spring of 1978.

Elvis Presley dies: 'erratic heartbeat' blamed by doctors

By CRAIG SCHWED

MEMPHIS, Tenn. (UPI) — Elvis Presley, the gyrating king of rock 'n' roll who forever changed the face of music two decades ago when he growled "You Ain't Nothin' but a Hound Dog," died at his mansion Tuesday of an "erratic heartbeat."

The 42-year-old singer — Elvis the Pelvis" when he burst upon the world in the mid-1950s — died face down on the floor of a bathroom at his Graceland mansion.

He was found there by his road manager, Joe Esposito, at 1:30 p.m. But Shelby County Medical Examiner Dr. Jerry Francisco said Presley may have been dead since 9 a.m.

Francisco told newsmen after an autopsy that Presley died of "cardiac arrhythmia," which he described as a severely irregular heartbeat. He said it was brought about by "undetermined causes."

Bob Francisco and Dr. George Nichopoulos, Presley's personal physician, said there was "no evidence of any illegal drug use."

Efforts to revive Presley were abandoned at Baptist Hospital at 3:30 p.m.

More photos, stories, A2, A6

Rumors of his death raced from coast to coast. When it was confirmed, the mourning began.

Radio stations throughout the world played the King's music. Politicians and entertainers eulogized him. Record shops, which in his 22 years of recording sold 400 million Elvis Presley albums, were jammed.

Presley brought rock 'n' roll to the world with "Hound Dog," "Heartbreak Hotel" and "Blue Suede Shoes." Teenagers went into a frenzy and adults, seeing his long shiny hair, sideburns, hooded eyes, and most of all his grinding hip, went into shock.

He was, as Gov. Cliff Finch at his home state of Mississippi said, the "personification of the American dream." He rose from poverty to incredible wealth.

But one of his best friends, singer Pat Boone, said he lived as a "haunted man — an exile" afraid to try, afraid of the massive and frantic demonstrations that greeted him every public appearance right up until the last. He lived in seclusion, appearing only on his concert tours.

Francisco said at a news conference

8/17/77 — To A1, Col. 1

Clue to rapist at last?

By VEDA FEDERIGHI
Staff Writer

The Sacramento County Sheriff's Department is asking a letter-writer who signed himself "Afraid" to call the detective bureau to elaborate on inside information about the East Area Rapist.

It could prove to be the first break in a case that has stumped dozens of investigators since the ski-masked rapist began his attacks nearly two years ago.

"We've been given information, possibly valuable information," said sheriff's spokesman Bill Miller, "in a well-written, typed letter. It's not from a kook."

The information, which Miller indicated could only be known by someone familiar with details of the case that are not generally known to the public, "gives no clue to the identity of the suspect. We assumed the letter-writer knows the person he or she is writing about.

"Our detectives want to talk to 'Afraid,'" Miller said, adding that "Afraid" wrote that if detectives wanted more information, "you should indicate you do in The Sacramento Union or other local media."

Miller emphasized that the information may not necessarily mean a break in the case. "We're not sure of the information. It requires contacting all of the victims and taking time to check things out.

"But there is a statement in the letter of something that the letter-writer is aware of that is very, very interesting," Miller said.

Miller said that informants can be guaranteed anonymity and urged "Afraid" to call the detective bureau, 441-3441.

The man known as the East Area Rapist began his string of 24 unsolved known attacks on Oct. 31, 1975.

All but two of the rapes have been in the county, and until the last attack on May 28, the rapist concentrated in a huge, 70 square-mile section of the east area, encompassing the communities of Rancho Cordova, Citrus Heights, Orangevale, Carmichael, and the Del Dayo, Glenbrook and College Greens neighborhoods.

On May 28, the rapist, who had earlier broken an established pattern of attacking women alone by beginning to break into homes where two men were present, again changed his method of operation and struck in the south area. He has not struck since May 28, the longest hiatus since the first few attacks.

More than $33,000 in rewards have been offered, and police and sheriff's detectives have sifted through thousands of calls, followed up hundreds of leads and interviewed several dozen potential suspects.

The articles above show the time frame I mentioned. Elvis died, August 16, 1977. In the newspaper the following day August 17, 1977 the article about Elvis' death also shared the same page as an article about the East Area Rapist. I would imagine EAR

68

must have felt pretty famous on this day and did not mind sharing the newsprint with Elvis. I have typed articles for clarity:

News article: Clue to Rapist at last? August 17, 1977 by Veda Federighi Staff Writer Sacramento Bee

The Sacramento County Sheriff's Department is asking a letter writer who signed himself "Afraid" to call the detective bureau to elaborate on inside information about the East Area Rapist.

It could prove to be the first break in a case that has stumped dozens of investigators since the ski masked rapist began his attacks nearly two years ago.

"We've been given information, possibly valuable information said sheriff's spokesman Bill Miller, in a well written typed letter. It's not from a kook".

The information, which Miller indicated could only be known by someone familiar with details of the case that were not generally known to the public, gives no clue to the identity the suspect. We assumed the letter writer knows the person he or she is writing about.

Our detectives want to talk to "Afraid" Miller said, adding that "Afraid" wrote that if detectives wanted more information you should "you should indicate you do in the Sacramento Union or other local media.

Miller emphasized that the information may not necessarily mean a break in the case. "We're not sure of the information. It requires contacting all of the victims and taking time to check things out.

"But there is a statement in the letter of something that the letter writer is aware of that is very, very interesting." Miller said. Miller said that informants can be guaranteed anonymity and urged "afraid" to call the detective bureau.

The man known as the East Area rapist began his string of 24 unsolved known attacks on October 21, 1975.

All but two of the rapes have been in the county, and until the last attack on May 28 the rapist concentrated in a huge 20 square-mile section of the east area encompassing the communities of Rancho Cordova, Citrus Heights, Orangevale, Carmichael, and the Del Dayo, Glenbrook and College Greens neighborhoods.

On May 28, the rapist, who had earlier broken an established pattern of attacking women alone by beginning to break into homes where men were present, again changed his method of operation and struck in the south area. He has not struck since May 28, the largest hiatus since the first few attacks.

More than $30,000.00 in rewards have been offered, and police and sheriff's detectives have sifted through thousands of calls, followed up hundreds of leads and interviewed several dozen potential suspects. **END OF ARTICLE**

In the 1970's the $30,000.00 reward money was a huge amount of money. Now in 2017 the FBI is offering $50,000.00.

Apparently "Afraid" never contacted anyone again.

When I began working on Capitol Mall the parking garage was something that I was not used to. I had to be at work at 8:00 a.m. and I had my own key card to the gate. Although my space was right by the gate and very visible it has always been one of my least favorite places to be. I knew this was not what EAR did (haunt parking garages) yet his activities made me more aware of the fact that I needed to be more careful and I needed to take care of myself. This was in the middle of all of the reports and news articles about the East Area Rapist attacks. It was very frightening but it was also nothing that anyone could control. The awareness that EAR was continuing his attacks and that LE could not stop him was always in the back of my mind. At night alone in my apartment this awareness became extremely keen.

The people working in downtown Sacramento frequently went to lunch within walking distance of their offices. This was certainly true of our office. A group of us would walk a few blocks to a Chinese restaurant where the food was greasy and not so great. We would say "Hey you want to go eat at the choke and puke?" That was what we called it because the food was that good. There are downtown parks where according to Detective Shelby the criminal would visit. EAR went to public places where he could blend in like a campus, supermarket or hospital where he would select his next victim and likely follow them home. This is what Shelby thought anyway.

Downtown Sacramento is a very busy place to be. We would arrive ascending on the elevators riding to our floors in the fifteen story building I was to call home for the next three and a half years. These were the days when we all dressed up to go to work complete with ties and shined shoes. Business suits and business lunches were the order of the day. There were twenty-five people in our office. I think almost all of us smoked cigarettes. The fog was thick in our large office at the end of the hall back then. Our clients didn't mind because they smoked too.

The company was in the business of selling, programming, installing and servicing the first business computers. In 1977 the computers were large enough to sit on the floor, the entire console tucking around your legs as you pulled a chair up to it. The floppy disks were exactly what they say: floppy: and eight inches in size. The files and file sizes had to be created on the hardware, the programs to be installed within the file area were for medical doctors and insurance agents, and contractors. You name it we were some of the first to sell them. The company was called General Business Systems. One of our clients was Buzz Oates, a developer and contractor who still exists at 555 Capitol Mall today on the ninth floor. They also developed other areas in the State of California. The actual computer cost

$25,000 to $50,000 depending on the memory purchased. The software to run the programs was actually $10,000 or more as well. The commissions on selling these systems were huge and the sales people we worked with were hungry. It was most certainly better than selling cars for a living.

After my year first I was promoted and sent to Burlingame, California for training to become an installation analyst. My promotion and my new job would take me all over the Sacramento area and into Stockton, Yuba City, Marysville, Vacaville, Sutter Creek, and Placerville and even to Galt. From 1978 until 1982 my job was to set up the programs on computers we had sold all over the place. I loved driving to all kinds of businesses installing the software and training the computer operators. I wandered through this man's hunting grounds the entire time he was actively stalking, and raping women.

After work many times all of us as a group would stop by a restaurant or bar having drinks together at the end of the day. I had started going to Old Sacramento after it had been renovated and reopened with many bars and restaurants with different names like Fanny Ann's, Spyder Murphy's and the Gold Mine Shaft. As careful as I typically was I admit that I went to Spyder Murphy's many a night to dance all night, play pin ball and have a few drinks. Sometimes there were no parking spaces left that were as close as I would like so I would park in the alleys. This was when there were places in Old Sac that were still dirt. The late night walks to any parking garage after 2:00 a.m. was not in the cards for me. I would leave Spyder Murphy's alone most of the time, get into my car and drive the I-5 the short jump to Riverside Blvd. I was lucky I suppose as I never saw a cop on the way to my one-bedroom apartment. In 1977 I lived off Riverside Blvd. which is close to Seamas Avenue and close to Land Park. This is one of the many areas the East Area Rapist was to hit. The East Area Rapist struck approximately four blocks away from where I lived in April 1978.

This neighborhood where attack #32 took place reminds me of the area I came from. If one looks at what the rapist saw as he looked around it seems almost as if he is drawing everyone a map with which to find him. He had access to a waterway of escape, he attacked in a residential home adjacent to a neighborhood park, but what was most important as I have said in other parts of this book was what this criminal visually saw. This man had to recreate visually what reminded him most of where he came from, his home base, his neighborhood of origin. Everything else was almost secondary. Once he found a geographical location that was a replica (as close as possible) to where he came from, the next thing would be to pick his target.

In the 1970's this was a fairly easy task. Young families were everywhere in the 60's and 70's. After World War II the baby boomers happened. You could tell everywhere. There was a child explosion from the mid 1940's for the next twenty or so years. It seems that most families had at least three children or more everywhere you looked. In the 1960's when I was a child the sidewalks on Halloween were so crowded with children you sometimes would have to walk out in the gutter or street to get around because the sidewalks were packed full of children. By the time EAR began his attacks these children were his age and somewhat younger. Teen age girls and young women were a large segment of the neighborhoods he lurked in.

In many cases EAR would attack a corner home or the one next to it. The view of the park from the home was all a part of the necessary visual representation of what he knew in most cases. The view from the corner of Piedmont and Seamas in South Sacramento should tell you where to look for this man. The view from the home that Manuela Witthuhn lived in should tell you where this man came from. The view from the Fourth Parkway neighborhood and the neighborhood park called Sky Parkway which was next to the Morrison Creek should tell you where this man came from. That is why I say this man practically drew us a map in order to find him.

If detectives were to investigate each neighborhood this man struck researching who lived in the houses across from these parks in the 1970's or more so in the 1960's it would narrow their pool of suspects down considerably. It is my contention that this person came from a zip code farther south than the Carmichael neighborhoods and the zip code areas speculated to be his neighborhood of origin by

Professor Kim Rossomo in Larry Crompton's book, Sudden Terror.

I had always felt a presence of evil close by from the age of 14. I had no way of knowing who had chased me in July 1971. No police reports, no suspect caught he (they) were/was still out there probably terrorizing others. I had a description with no one to tell. There were two guys out there who apparently thought it was fun to chase down a girl walking alone. I wondered had the young men ever caught anyone and if they had what would happen next?

When I finally began to study the crimes of the East Area Rapist and the Original Night Stalker I had always felt this man had been nearby because of the descriptions of where this man attacked. The descriptions were exactly where in Sacramento I had come from. Even after all of the years that have gone by I still feel he is alive and watching his own story whenever his crimes resurface as an article in the local papers. Every now and again a reporter will drag this subject up and write about any changes or advances in DNA or hope that someone will call in a tip or talk to someone who knows anything. This has always been to no avail.

People speculate that these crimes will be solved. Over and over this has been repeated. As I look at these news articles with dates from the 1990's and then 2000, 2004, 2011 time moves on and now it is 2017. Some feel it will be solved; others do not want to talk about it anymore for many different reasons.

We are running out of time in our lifetimes to see justice done for these families of all of the victims and for the victims themselves. There are at least 50 women and young girls out there who will never forget what this man did to them. He took something of all of the people he hurt. He changed them all. This man's crimes were so far reaching with a ripple effect that lasts to this day.

On the following pages I have included pictures taken of where I grew up in South Sacramento as well as pictures from one of EAR'S target areas off Seamas and Casilada which was attack #32. This was also the last time EAR was to attack in Sacramento before moving to other areas and then moving down South. If you compare the neighborhood in South Sacramento where I grew up to the pictures of target areas where EAR struck you can't help but see the similarities.

Photographs from page 79-89 were taken by me, Anne Penn in the fall of 2016.

I intentionally did not take pictures of the fronts of houses here for privacy reasons.

Of note: palm trees always seem to be part of the landscape most of the time in neighborhoods of attack at least in Sacramento.

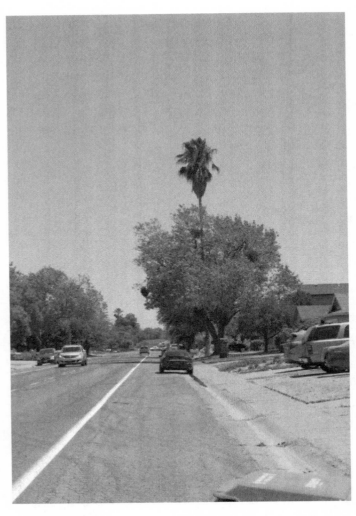

Morrison Creek runs behind this street on the right. South Sacramento. Between 47th and Florin Road this neighborhood is where the creek meandered through residential neighborhoods. Followed up to the stop sign it takes you to the corner of Steiner Drive and 53rd Avenue.

After the stop you turn right you will immediately see Morrison Creek bridge.

On the corner of 53rd Avenue, and to the right this picture shows the corner of Steiner Drive to the right towards Florin Road. This is the bridge over the Morrison Creek East side. Steiner Drive turns into North Parkway and then Sky Parkway. The park is just a couple of blocks from here.

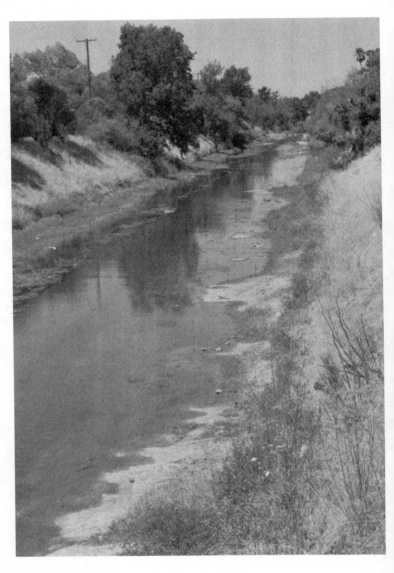

Morrison Creek West Side

The previous page shows the Morrison Creek view to the west once again. Children played back here throughout the neighborhoods. We played down there on rafts catching pollywogs and crawdads. The path used to run at the top behind all of the fenced yards that had their backs to the creek. It has since become overgrown and blocked on purpose so that there is little or no access.

In the 1960's and 70's it was easy to walk on the path above the creek right behind the homes. It would have been easy to peer into the houses and yards. Some backyards had traditional fences, some had no fence and others had a chain link fence you could see through. It would have been easy to peep at night. It would have been easy to break in and then escape. I believe this is may be where he began to fantasize, watch and peep.

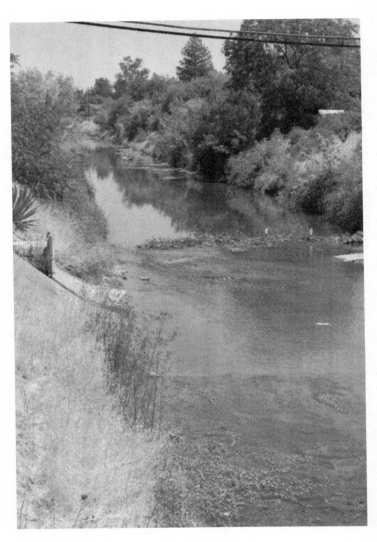

Morrison Creek to the **East** which runs out of the
neighborhood and to the east all through the Sacramento area.
In the 60's and 70's the path continued on the right upper side
to an open field which would eventually lead to Florin Center
and Florin Road. It was very close.

Morrison Creek Bridge which was not blocked by a fence in the 1960's and 1970's.

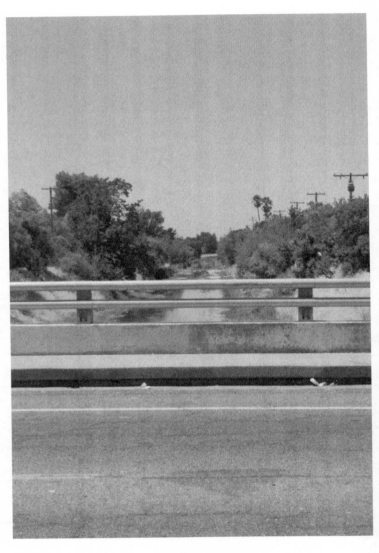

The creek runs behind 53rd Avenue to the West

The previous page shows the bridge over the Morrison Creek access that ran through the neighborhood which is between 47th Avenue and Florin Road and is near Sky Park, Nicholas Elementary School and 4th Parkway. This picture again faces west and this runs behind all the houses on 53rd

Above photograph taken in September. This is also Morrison Creek in the same South Sacramento neighborhood and shows that many parts of the creek access do not have water in them which makes it easier to get around.

Below photograph Sky Park

Sky Park is located just a couple of blocks away from
Florin Road and a block from Morrison Creek. I
played tennis here with my mother and heard my first
live rock concert in the park.

Another view of Sky Park which is located on the
aptly named Sky Parkway in South Sacramento

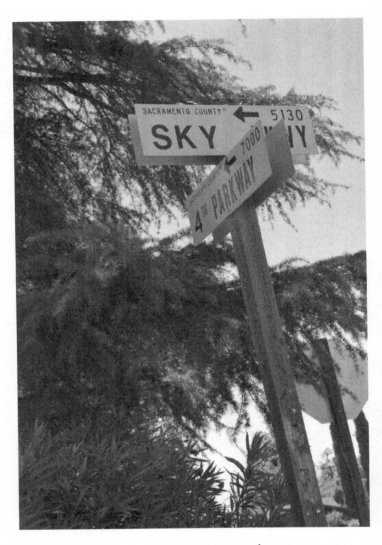

Fourth Parkway and Sky Parkway (4th Parkway was where attack # 22 happened on May 28, 1977 at approximately 1:00 a.m.)

Sunday May 29, 1977 Sacramento Bee **article** by Ted Bell **(His Headline stated this was EARS 24th victim) Other reports say this was EAR's 22nd attack**

The masked rapist who has terrorized Sacramento City and County neighborhoods for the past 19 months struck for the 24th time (there is a discrepancy on which attack number this was) early Saturday morning and for the first time his attack occurred outside of the east residential area.

The rape occurred inside a single family home in the **Sky Parkway** area in the southern residential portion of the county. (Sky Parkway is located east of Highwway 99 and north of Florin Road.) All previous attacks have been north of Folsom Boulevard and east of Howe Avenue.

Sheriff's spokesman Bill Miller said the rapist entered the house during the early morning hours after forcing his way through a sliding glass door. He then made his way into a bedroom where his 28 year old victim and her husband were sleeping.

The intruder forced the woman to tie up her husband and then took her into another room where the rape was committed.

89

The couple's young child was asleep in a separate room and did not awaken until after the rapist left the home shortly after 4 a.m.. The couple told deputies that the man was in the home for at least one and a half hours.

The rapist wore a ski mask and brandished a gun.

Miller said the rapist did not beat his victim but would not disclose what the rapist said during the attack. (This was continued on a second page of the Bee see below and continues:

During his last reported rape on May 17 in the Del Dayo area, the rapist threatened to kill his next two victims.

Miller said sheriff's deputies were convinced that Saturday's intruder was the east area rapist and not an imitator because "there are a lot of things about the rapist that are not publically known and thus would not be known to an imitator.

Why did the rapist move South?

Possibly it could have been due to all the publicity the EARS Patrol has been receiving, Miller said. The EARS (East Area Rapist Surveillance) is a group of more than 100 Sacramento residents with citizens band radios that has been cruising the east area at night since last Thursday.

EARS Chairman Ed Nannini said Saturday that up to 75 members of his group were patrolling Friday night.

Nannini said that the total reward for information leading to the capture of the rapist has been increased to $30,000 and issued an appeal for more volunteers with base and mobile citizen band radio units.

The sheriff's office has increased patrols using cars and helicopters and has been allocated $100,000 for overtime pay in the search.

A sheriff's spokesman said Saturday night that some extra manpower would be shifted south as a result of this latest attack. Besides the authorized overtime duty, the spokesman said, many deputies are donating their time for added patrols and some California Highway Patrol officers have volunteered their time. City police are also working on special details.

The rapist has been described as white, between 20 and 30 years old. Fear of the man has touched off increased sales of guns, guard dogs and alarm systems throughout the area.

END OF ARTICLE

Rapist

Sun. 5/29/[7?]/

Continued From Page A1

the rapist said during the attack.

During his last reported rape on May 17 in the Del Dayo area, the rapist threatened to kill his next two victims.

Miller said sheriff's deputies were convinced that Saturday's intruder was the east area rapist and not an imitator because "there are alot of things about the rapist" that are not publicly known and thus would not be known to an imitator.

Why did the rapist move south?

"Possibly, it could have been due to all the publicity the EARS Patrol has been receiving," Miller said.

The EARS (East Area Rapist Surveillance) Patrol is a group of more than 100 Sacramento residents with citizen band radios that has been cruising the east area at night since last Thursday.

EARS Chairman Ed Nannini said Saturday that up to 75 members of his group were patroling Friday night.

Nannini said that the total reward for information leading to the capture of the rapist has been increased to $30,000 and issued an appeal for more volunteers with base and mobile citizen band radio units.

The sheriff's office has increased patrols using cars and helicopters and has been allocated $100,000 for overtime pay in the search.

A sheriff's spokesman said Saturday night that some extra manpower would be shifted south as a result of the latest attack. Besides the authorized overtime duty, the spokesman said, many deputies are donating their time for added patrols, and some California Highway Patrol officers have volunteered their time. City police are also working on special details.

The rapist has been described as white, between 20 and 30 years old. Fear of the man has touched off increased sales of guns, guard dogs and alarm systems throughout the area.

To answer the question why did the rapist move South? I believe he moved South simply because he knew he could. The South area was not being patrolled like the East area was. He could move about on foot and did not need a car or bicycle because this was home base. Likely he moved South to show everyone that he could do as he pleased in response to so many people thinking they could catch him.

He must have loved proving that they could not stop him. He knew that patrols or not he could continue. He had a master plan. He knew that when it was time to move on he would do just that.

Nicholas Elementary School

This is where the mean sixth grade teacher worked when I went there. Could it be that we had had the same teacher although possibly a few years apart?

Nicholas Elementary School – Steiner Drive So. Sacramento. When reviewing pictures of this school you have to note that it is centered and surrounded by fields and playground much like a park.

The Morrison Creek is only about a block away from Nicholas Elementary School.

Photographs on pages 84-99 taken by Anne Penn Fall 2016.

Nicholas Elementary play area and fields that surround the school. All around the school on all sides are houses. This school is very close to 47th Avenue as well as encompassing the boundaries for school children attending which ends in Sky Parkway. When Florin Road is crossed to the south of Florin Road the neighborhood called simply "Parkway" had nicer homes and the entire area was a more socially acceptable class of families as they had more money. The homes cost more, the income was higher. All of the elementary schools from the area in South Sacramento fed into the Junior High called Fern Bacon which was located in Bowling Green.

Luther Burbank High School was located at the west end of Florin Road.   Lemon Hill, Pacific Elementary, Nicholas, Bowling Green, Parkway and others all went to the same Junior High and High School.

The corner of Piedmont and Riverside Blvd which
is close to my apartment 1977-78.

This is the corner of Casilada and Riverside Blvd. across from the overpass that crosses Interstate 5 in Sacramento, near where attack #32 occurred. EAR could arrive here having come across on foot. He left by way of the Sacramento River access road off Casilada running South past Minnow Hole and towards Greenhaven.

Park across from corner of Piedmont and Seamas
also in South Sacramento taken 2016

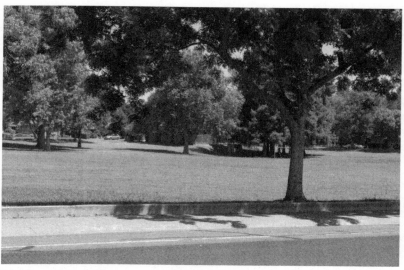

Piedmont and Seamas - Another view of the park.

Compare with park off Seamas – This is Sky
Parkway South Sacramento

All of the photographs taken of the neighborhoods
in South Sacramento were taken by Anne Penn.

Houses surround the park on all sides. Attack # 32 happened on Casilada near Seamas and Piedmont. The street directly behind where this picture was taken has the river access road.

There has been some confusion about where this attack occurred based on conflicting reports about where the victim lived versus where she was babysitting. This is how I think the story goes: EAR had scoped out the area and had found his target that lived on Piedmont. Also of note is there were sisters who lived in the home on Casilada. They were all out for the evening on the night of the attack. Piedmont is as the photographs show across from the park and close to the river access road.

He could have planned his attack at the location off Piedmont and Seamas. EAR scoped out Casilada and the entire area in prowling's previous to the attack. He could have planned to attack at Casilada and the sisters that lived there went out. The call came in asking the victim to babysit over on Casilada. It was a last minute arrangement. The victim was dropped off by her parents at the address on Casilada. The two streets are not far from each other. EAR was watching the house and realized his target was being left alone at another location which was also an easy escape if he chose to attack. OR if the targets had been the sisters at Casilada and they were gone he still had the babysitter as a target.

EAR had prowled in the neighborhood for a time prior to the attack. On April 11, 1978 prowling's were heard but no one checked the yard. On April 13, 1978 on Rio Lane not far from the attack a neighbor heard someone at their side window at 11:00 p.m. that appeared to be a scratching noise. When their dog began to bark the noise stopped. Another neighbor on Rio Lane noticed her side gate was open several times over the past two weeks. No one called to report anything.

On the night of the attack at about 9:30 a young woman on Casilada Way heard her dog barking in her backyard. Her husband was not home so she did not investigate. The attack occurred shortly after the babysitter was dropped off at Casilada. EAR had to have been outside waiting for everyone to leave.

This attack was the last one in Sacramento on April 14, 1978. The attacker was interrupted by the parents who rushed over to see why their daughter did not answer the phone. On April 16, 1978 an article came out in the paper with an enhanced composite of the suspects in the Maggiore murders. EAR left the area and began attacking to the South in Modesto, Davis, and Concord, Walnut Creek, Danville, San Jose and Fremont.

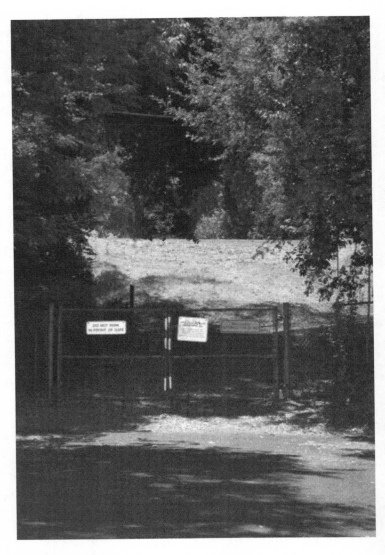

Sacramento River access road less than a block
from corner of Piedmont and Seamas and the park

The Sacramento River Levee Road runs parallel to the neighborhood and there are ways to gain access to the levee from Casilada and other streets. Apparently the perpetrator used an access road like this one to escape (shown on the previous page). If he turned right he would have been going towards Downtown Sacramento. If he turned left as he did, he would be heading towards what I think could be home base. Minnow hole which is off the Sacramento River access road is where witnesses saw a man running that night.

He did not use a car or bike here in my opinion. He merely had tested out his route on foot from where he lived to make sure he could quickly get away on foot. He knew how to blend in as he retreated from this neighborhood along the river access road. He most likely came out in another neighborhood possibly Greenhaven as he either walked the rest of the way home from here or he planted a bike along the route to get to home base faster.

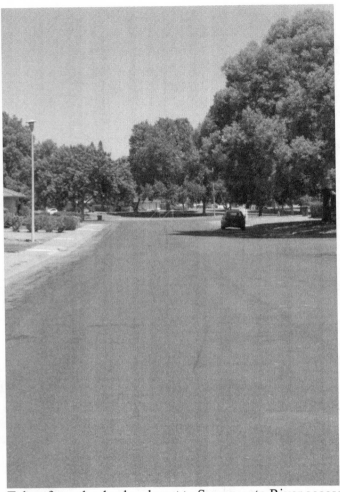

Taken from the dead end next to Sacramento River access road – on the right is the corner of Piedmont and Seamas and you can see the park across the street. If you turn around standing here, you are facing the fenced off access road to the Sacramento River. If you turn left in front of the park Piedmont takes you to Casilada going west.

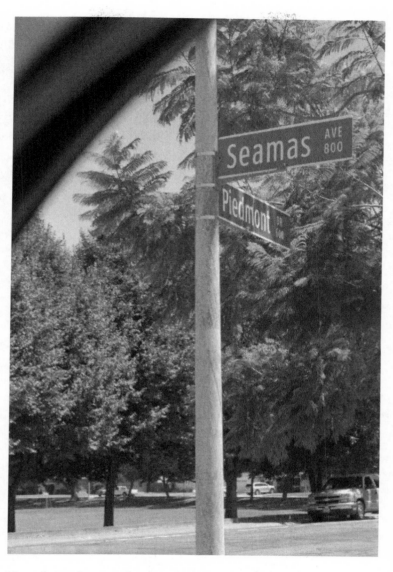

Near here the attack occurred. At the corner of
Seamas and Piedmont – you can see the park

Once again, The park at Seamas and Piedmont

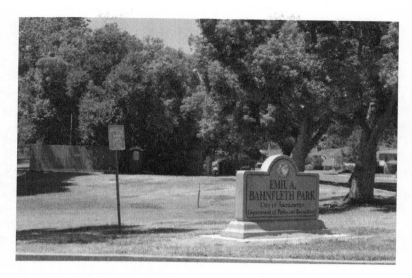

Photograph by Anne Penn

This is the opposite corner of the park. If you head west from this corner, you will run into Casilada. If you turn right from this corner, you will run into Riverside and also the I-5 freeway. The attack took place on Casilada. The victim lived on Piedmont. This is the marker for the name of the park which is the Emil A. Bahnfleth Park. This is not far (approximately a block) from the I-5 freeway and Riverside Blvd.

This is the neighborhood I used to ride my bike around on my days off to keep in shape. There are apartments there with pools up and down Riverside. It is close to the Sacramento River and close to downtown. I lived off Riverside Blvd. for all of 1977 and 1978 eventually moving to West Sacramento which is also close to Capitol Mall downtown.

By the summer of 1977 I had located to Riverside Blvd. The East Area Rapist had been active for over a year. In 1975 Lyman Smith married Charlene. They had not yet moved to High Point Drive. Lyman and Charlene's life was full of promise. Brian and Katie Maggiore were married in 1976. Brian was just 21 and Katie 20. All of the victims to come were enjoying their lives. Time was running out to catch EAR in Sacramento. The clock was ticking on the countdown to this criminal's ability to murder the way he envisioned it. After the attacks near Seamas and Casilada off Riverside Blvd. the East Area Rapist vanished from the area and began to move south.

Chapter Three
Victims

The thing about murder is that there is always a victim, a person who is no longer alive. The crimes are always horrific, the details always unimaginable. What is left are families, tons and tons of families who are also victimized, or lost or who always suffer the consequences of what the aftermath is. The criminal, the perpetrator we hope will be caught and made to suffer some kind of consequences for acts that are irrevocable. We hope that the right person is caught for the most heinous of crimes and made to pay in some way for something that cannot be undone, cannot be unseen or unknown. Sometimes, there is some kind of closure or forgiveness if we are lucky.

Thank goodness for forensic science and the advances in DNA technology today. These tools may make is easier to reopen old cases, look at DNA evidence through fresh eyes, and hopefully close more and more cases old and new. In the case I want to talk about the perpetrator has never been identified and he is now either dead, in prison somewhere or he was smart enough to take evidence with him as he realized that technology could someday find him and put him away if he were not careful enough. In this case the man responsible seemed and seems to always have been a few steps ahead of whoever was chasing him. In the 1970's all over the state of California this man is and was known by two names. First he was called the East Area Rapist and then as he moved and murdered he was named the Original Night Stalker. The two were not connected definitively until 20 years later. I have come to know his name as the Original Night Stalker. Some have added the name Golden State Killer way too long after the crimes. It had been stated that he needed more attention and the names attached were not very memorable. As though changing the name or rebranding the serial killer could somehow help in catching him?

The Original Night Stalker really did attack in clusters. He attacked in Northern California in certain areas and then attacked in Southern California in clustered areas. He did not commit crimes all across the Golden State from end to end. To me changing a name or adding another on to the serial killer 40 years after the fact is odd. The media seems to have picked up the name anyway. These cases can be confusing enough.

This story has been told in previous books published listing the crimes or the circumstances one by one. This story has been told by detectives who actively worked the case. Their focus was in documenting these crimes in order to enlist the publics' help in bringing this person to justice. What isn't told is the extremely high cost to the victims of violent crimes, but also to the families and to the communities that these things happen in. As I said, the crimes have been listed; the efforts to capture this criminal have been documented as best as possible. The victims of murder had remained a lessor focus by design I am sure because the murders are open cases.

All of the victims just wanted to live their lives. These are people who had the right to do this simple thing, undisturbed. In the end the murder victims were randomly selected by a sick individual to meet their end in the most violent way. At the other end of the log he was bludgeoned to death with was a person who did not care who Lyman Smith was who his wife Charlene was. He did not and does not care about who Cheri Domingo and her friend Greg Sanchez were and who they might have become.

He is proud of what he did in his own mind to Dr. Debra Manning and Dr. Robert Offerman, both who were in a helping profession. He thinks he got away with what some would call the perfect murder of Keith and Patrice Harrington and he has so far. Their potential to bring good into the world was snuffed out. Manuela Witthuhn came here as an immigrant and she was alone when this madman killed her. Her husband had been in the hospital on this day. The murders of the young just married couple Katie and Sgt. Brian Maggiore were completely senseless ruthless acts. They had barely begun their lives together.

The murder in 1975 of Professor Snelling in Visalia as he tried to stop an intruder from kidnapping his daughter, he was gunned down. A young girl left without her father. A young boy chasing the suspect in Sacramento was shot in the abdomen and was lucky enough to survive. And then finally Janelle Cruz was taken forever from her family. She was so young and had not even begun yet. Ms. Cruz was so full of possibility.

The list of rapes is too long and includes over 50 victims. He had the power to do these terrible things and did not care about anyone but himself. Even one couple lost was way too many yet here in these cases he struck again and again. This person remains free without consequence for his actions. That he has remained free all of these years is a crime in itself. This person is unknown and is happy to be free while those that want to bring justice to the families continue to methodically work on the case to apprehend him. He must feel very superior and very smug if he is still alive. In the 1970's when this man was in training to become a serial killer and honing his skills there were many mistakes made by everyone.

Mistakes were made because our society was still young, still naïve. When neighbors of intended victims heard prowlers they did not call the authorities many times. When something was off, or they saw a strange car or someone who did not belong in the neighborhood they ignored it and remained silent. There were so many opportunities to stop this man in the 1970's. Even when this man prowled before killing all of the couples in Southern California many never reported prowling's and break in's until it was too late. What was the silence about? Why did we not hear of the strange goings on until after the murders took place? That is when most from the areas of attacks reported strangers and strange cars, dogs barking at odd times, people jumping over fences, gates left open.

Why in God's name didn't more people report such things in order to try to help stop this man before he became the murderer that he was telling everyone he was working on becoming? Because back then many of us still lived in a bubble where we believed most people are like us and that evil and bad things that happen, happen somewhere else and to someone else. In many of the rapes he was working up his anger and his purpose. He repeated over and over "I'm gonna kill you" "I'm going to kill them." And then he did.

Those Murdered

Wedding photo of Sgt. Brian K. Maggiore and wife, Katie

Sgt. Brian Maggiore and Katie Maggiore murdered in Rancho Cordova 1978.

These murders have not been definitively connected to EAR by DNA or other evidence – we do not know if the Maggiore's were murdered by EAR or who murdered them.

The Maggiore's were married in July 1976

As of the time frame that this book was published we still do not have proof or a story that is consistent with EAR murdering this couple. The reports originally in 1978 described TWO men running from the scene, two descriptions, two composites were done. Sheriff Ken Clark has been interviewed on podcasts recently regarding the details of witnesses there at the time in 1978. He explains what happened so long ago.

I still find it difficult to reconcile the discrepancies in versions to the story. The story had changed over time to a (convenient)? story about EAR being the one guy who killed them? In Crime Watch Daily which aired fall 2016 it seems that the story changed from original reports in 1978 of two men being seen to one man and it was reported it was likely EAR. How did speculation almost become fact in the telling of this story? Details are now available form this interview. You will have to decide what you think.

Note - Update:

In 2018 Criminology Podcast by Mike Morford https://criminology.libsyn.com/ with Sheriff Ken Clark from Sacramento County . The interview is in great detail explaining why Joseph James DeAngelo was a suspect as EAR, and why he has been charged upon his arrest with the murders of Brian and Katie Maggiore on February 2, 1978.

Debra Alexandria Manning (Top)

Dr. Robert Offerman (Bottom)

Charlene and Lyman Smith

Lyman Smith (right) as a young man with little
brother Don at home long before the murders

Charlene and Lyman Smith

Keith and Patrice Harrington married about 3
months when killed

Manuela Witthuhn

Cheri Domingo and Gregory Sanchez

Janelle Cruz

Janelle Cruz was only 18 when she was taken from her family.

Claude Snelling

If EAR began as the Visalia Ransacker it is possible he murdered Professor Claude Snelling. If Claude Snelling is in fact a victim of the Visalia Ransacker aka East Area Rapist, he could be the first person murdered by the East Area Rapist in Visalia. This has never been proven. We do not know definitively if EAR is also the Visalia Ransacker and we do not know and have not connected the Visalia Ransacker to EAR or to ONS by DNA or other evidence. The murder of Professor Snelling is still an open case.

Professor Snelling was robbed of his ability to watch and enjoy as his daughter grew up. He did the most noble thing in giving his life to possibly save hers. He certainly was a hero in his final moments on earth.

Lyman Robert Smith

We called him Bob. In my case he was Uncle Bob. I had never heard him called Lyman until his murder. When my grandfather and grandmother talked about Lyman Robert they always called him Bob. When I was a little girl Lyman Robert and Marge came to visit everyone at the Curtis Park home. I was introduced to them as Uncle Bob and Aunt Marge. I was three and a half. Later after they divorced it was Bob and Charlene.

Lyman (Bob) was full of life, full of ambition and dreams. He had a family he loved and who loved him. When a person is killed by tragic accident or disease it is in some ways easier to bear the loss. When a person is murdered by someone, some unknown someone who feels it is more important to act out his or her perversions, anger, sickness and all of the other issues they have by savagely taking someone else's life, when they plan it and meticulously carry out the plan with deliberation and forethought this is the most difficult of things to bear and to resolve for the victims' families and friends. This is the most fear laden of acts of terror. The effects last forever and we can hope that the fear and grief are somehow lessened by the capture of the perpetrator. Yet, he is still free.

Lyman Robert was born in April of 1936. He was the first born son of Wilma Belle Shappart Smith and Lyman Jones Smith. Like any young couple they had many hopes for their son. The elder Lyman was willing and very able to work long hard days to provide for his new young family. He loved them both fiercely. Lyman Robert (Bob) was born in Pocatello Idaho where his father and mother worked the farm.

Lyman Senior was a very opinionated individual and was as stubborn as the day is long. Somewhere along the way Lyman Senior had a falling out with the church of Jesus Christ Latter Day Saints. He never spoke about what happened or why. I can speculate that it may have been that he would not allow any religious organization to dictate who he could or should marry. If by chance Wilma had not been Mormon that could have been the end of his affiliation with the Mormon Church.

Lyman Senior did attend the Baptist Church in Downtown Sacramento with my grandmother for years. When they came to Lake Tahoe during the summers they also attended the First Baptist church. Lyman Senior was a Mason who belonged to the Shriners Ben Ali Temple. He proudly did his charity work for the Shriners Children's Hospital once he moved to Sacramento. Lyman's (Bob's) dad believed in hard work and perseverance.

For most of his life Lyman Robert went by the name Bob. Bob's mother Wilma wanted there to be no misunderstanding of who she was talking to. From all appearances young Bob's childhood was happy. He worked hard at school to make his parents proud and he did all the chores his father asked him to do. He had an open and outwardly happy disposition and expression. Most days would find Bob with a twinkle in his eye.

Eventually Lyman and Wilma Smith moved to Citrus Heights, California living in the rural area it was back then. Eventually Bob was to have a little brother to follow him around. His name is Donald. Lyman Jr. was a good son. He often played with his new small brother, donning a cowboy hat and playing shoot em up with him. There were ducks, and other animals around to play with and life was really good for a little while.

Lyman (Bob) was to attend San Juan High School where he was a very active student. In 1953 Bob was a junior in high school. In every picture he could be seen with a big smile on his face and he looked so bright and happy. It was almost as though he had a secret, a good secret. He seemed to know that life was what you made of it and his attitude was positive and his energy was high. Lyman (Bob) was a member of the Boys League that year and his task was public relations. He was also a member of Hi-Y Club which had a reputation of being one of the "hustlingest service clubs on campus". Lyman Robert was already involved in the local annual Model Legislature meets in Sacramento and at Stanford. If this didn't keep him busy enough Lyman was also a member of Thespians. The production of "Our Miss Brooks" Lyman played the part of Mr. Wadsworth. On picture day for the year book Lyman must have had to run from group to group to be included in the photos because he was not finished yet. He was also on the Hi-Lites Staff. The Hi-Lites was the school newspaper and not surprisingly Lyman was their assistant business manager. When did he have time to date and fall in love? He must have met Marjorie Donald who became his future wife and partner in one of the many clubs he and they had participated in. Marjorie was one year behind Lyman in school.

In 1954 Lyman (Bob) was no less busy. This was his senior year and he was going to make the most of it. In the fall semester Lyman was the Vice President of the student body. In the spring Lyman was elected to Vice President again "They were chosen to rule" The yearbook says" The students played a major role in the functioning of our student body affairs. They plotted student policies and activities, sponsored our ever popular sock hop, and took active parts in the Student Leadership Conferences held in Oroville, El Camino, and Woodland. Lyman was also a Thespian and performed in the play "Drums of Death" as the character Cooper. Meanwhile his girlfriend was involved in in G.A.A. Lyman was on the Rally Committee (of course he was) this committee was charged with trying to keep up the gang's spirit for every game and worked hard to put on real pep rallies.

When Lyman graduated from High school he had a definite plan. He and Marjorie were going to be married. He was to attend UC Berkeley and then Law School. Marjorie worked to put him through school. They were young, ambitious and in love. They were a team. When they were married Lyman was 19 and Marjorie was 18. They were driven and had purpose. They did not have any thoughts of having a family until Lyman was through school. Their first child Jenny did not come along until 1962. Marjorie and Lyman were to have three children together Jennifer, Lyman Jay Smith and Gary Smith. They were married until 1972 when things began to break down. Lyman was so busy working to obtain his goal of moving up the ladder.

As I look at these pictures now from old high school yearbooks I cannot put the two stories together in my mind. It does not seem real or right that this young man did not have the time that he was to be allowed for this life to become what he was to become. We cannot know what good he would have done in the world because his choices and his life were taken from him. He actually did nothing to entertain his end.

This was a boy who had endless possibilities on what kind of man he would eventually settle into. This was a human being that wanted to do right by his family, his community and society. He wanted the best for anyone he knew. His murderer remains free without consequence for his actions. That he has remained free all of these years is a crime in itself. This person is unknown and is laughing at everyone who tried to catch him, to stop him. He must feel very superior and very smug. In the 1970's when this man was in training to become a serial killer and honing his skills there were many mistakes made by everyone.

Each of the people who were murdered at this criminal's hands were wonderful people. The Harrington's who had only been married a short time were busy working hard. Keith Harrington was in Medical school and was slated to graduate in December 1980. He specialized in emergency medicine and Patrice was a Pediatric nurse. "Brian Brenner, a friend of Keith said "Harrington was one of the most brilliant people I ever met; he was fun-loving, full of life, energetic, raring to go all the time."

The information on the internet, the reports written by countless reporters, crime writers and others did not contain much real information about the actual victims of the murders. One case in particular was scrutinized because the couple was somewhat high profile. The Smith murders in reports took on a life of their own from the beginning and over time that speculated about who the murdered might be. Conclusions can be drawn; rumors and half-truths can be repeated over and over again until the real essence of who all of these victims were is obliterated and forgotten. All that remains are the victims' pictures frozen in time, used over and over again to show who the "victims" were of this serial killer. As humans we need to remember that these 10 plus victims did nothing to bring this on to themselves. They were people like the rest of us who should still have been with us and with their families.

When I was very small some of my first memories have been filed away in my brain because they were important events in my family. It was a big deal the day my grandmother Veonia married my grandfather Lyman Senior. Everyone in our family was there.

I recall the sun streaming in the living room window at my grandmother's house. I was sitting on the floor playing with a Dagwood and Blondie puzzle. All I can see is the pant legs of my Uncle walking in and out of the room. Marjorie and Lyman Robert (Uncle Bob) had come to visit my grandparents. I knew that these people were going to be new additions to our family. We would see each other here and there when my brothers and I were small children at the house on Curtis Park in Sacramento. My grandfather had married my grandmother when I was three and a half years old in 1960. I was about to inherit two uncles.

Lyman Senior was the only grandfather I was ever to have and to know. He had two sons. Their names were Lyman Robert Smith and Donald Roger Smith. The two brothers were far enough apart in age that Uncle Don had not yet gone into the Navy. When his dad married my grandmother Don was 16 and still in high school. Right after high school Uncle Don did go in the Navy. He wore a white uniform and sailor hat. When he came home on leave one time he brought me a doll case that was blue with white stars on it. I was so excited to have it. I still have it to this day and it is stuffed with my childhood imaginations. Once in a while I open it and look at each piece. It was a great time back then.

Uncle Bob was a happy looking man from my perspective. I was always happy to add new people to my world.

Previous Page: Wedding photo of Lyman Jones Smith Senior to Veonia Lomax Hodgkin's June 26, 1960.

The left side of photograph is small blonde child (me) age three next to my big brother and our mother. Behind the wedding cake are my grandmother Veonia and her groom Lyman Senior. Next to him are Lyman Robert (Bob) Smith (age 24) Marjorie Smith (age 23) and Donald Smith (Age 16) The entire family – was there. Lyman Robert and Marjorie did not have children until 1962. The photographer took a very blurry group photo.

All of the family pictures herein are from my private collection. Anne Penn (Laurie)

Next page also wedding photos Mr. and Mrs. Veonia and Lyman Jones Smith

These were my grandparents June 26, 1960

Veonia and Lyman Smith Senior always looking for fun and finding it. (1961) Happy times

Family picnic Mother's Day 1961

My grandparents had been married a little less than a year. This photograph is my mom's side of the family as well as my aunt and her mom on the left side of photo. Left to right back row: My mother has the sun glasses on. Next to her are Veonia and Lyman Jones Smith and my uncle from grandmother's side of family.

All of the children shown are from my grandmother's side of the family. From left to right are my cousins (two young boys). The only little girl in the picture sitting is me (Laurie) age 4-1/2. Next to me are my two brothers. I was always the only girl until two female cousins were born in 1962. One was born to my uncle on my mom's side of the family and the other was from Lyman Robert Smith and his wife

Marge. Lyman Smith Senior treated all of the children as his own grandchildren.

Grandpa with my younger brother 1961, 62 at our house South Sacramento.

Laurie walking on the fence at home South
Sacramento 1963

This was the street I was chased down in 1971

Grandpa Lyman with Laurie and my two brothers.
Christmas 1966 South Sacramento. I was 10.

Lyman Senior Christmas 1966

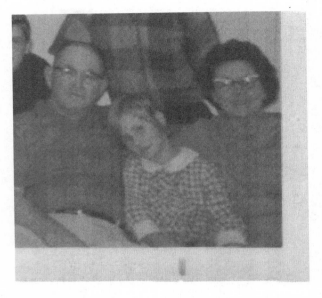

Another family picture – I have intentionally reduced the picture to only show Lyman Smith Senior, Laurie and Veonia Smith. I was 11.

Christmas time at our home South Sacramento.
Veonia and Lyman Jones Smith (Senior) 1974

I called the picture my grandparents laughing.

As a child I would stay with my grandparents
overnight. They lived in an old neighborhood in
Sacramento across from the park right off highway
99 near the Sacramento Children's home. I would
sleep in the room next to theirs in a large bed. I felt
safe there. In the morning Grandpa would get up
early and start breakfast. Grandpa would make
biscuits from scratch served with their homemade
jams of raspberry or marmalade. He would cut off

the top of a tin can and use it to cut out the biscuits on the cookie sheet. I still have one of his cans as I could not throw it away. Grandpa would make scrambled eggs with garlic in them (I never acquired a taste for garlic in eggs), but I ate them anyway as a child because that is what you did. He made coffee cake from scratch and pancakes and bacon. If I could go back in time one of the places I would go would be to that breakfast table with Lyman Sr. and Veonia.

When I was six years old Lyman (Bob) and Marjorie (Marge) came for a visit bringing their newborn daughter. What I recall of this particular day was that this was a pleasure visit because Bob and Marge wanted to show off their new daughter. I remember hearing the adults say that Uncle Bob's daughter's name was Jenny. Being from a family of mostly boys and my one cousin Catherine it was exciting to hear that the new baby was a girl. Jenny would eventually have the same thing going on with nothing but boys around her because she would have two brothers named Lyman Jay and Gary. Girls being few and far between I was glad to meet Jenny.

As children we see people come and go and don't really listen much to what the grownups say. I just know that they were now family. My grandfather Lyman Senior was the only grandfather I had. I have a memory from when I was 7 years old. Grandpa was a member of the Shriner's and they did many things for children. One day we all went to Elk Grove Park for a big Shriner picnic. It was a lovely day with children running about. The men in the Shriner club had put together a paddy wagon and dressed up as the Keystone Cops. They pretended to arrest my grandfather and it scared me so much that I recall it to this day. They had to reassure me that they were just kidding. I was not sure if I believed them. What struck me most about this memory was how protective I felt of my grandfather.

Picture below: Lyman Smith Senior and Laurie age about 7 with the Keystone Cops. Elk Grove Park South Sacramento California

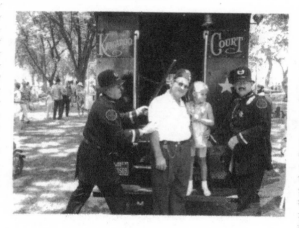

In a short twenty years one of my young uncles would already be dead. He only had just enough time to have three small children who would become step cousins and who would have the same grandfather I had. By the time he was 43 Lyman Robert would be dead. It is a good thing he lived as though he was in a hurry. Maybe he knew somewhere down deep that he was living on borrowed time.

When my grandmother became sick in 1990, right before she was to pass away I drove my grandfather to the hospital and back many times. On one of these drives to the hospital all of a sudden out of the blue my grandpa told me a story about when Lyman Robert was a child. He was talking about why he didn't like doctors. He said that when Lyman was a child he had gotten sick. He had a fever and could not get up out of bed. This was when he was about seven or eight and they were still living in Idaho. My grandfather had not wanted to take him into town to see the doctor from the farm they lived on.

He told his wife not to worry about it that Lyman (Bob) would be fine. Most of the time Lyman Sr. could say something and his wife Wilma would take him at his word, but this one time she finally insisted and made him take his son to the hospital. If she had not insisted, Lyman Robert would have died as a child because his appendix burst and he almost died then. I am certain that my grandfather was very relieved that he had listened to his wife on this day.

Lyman Robert did get to grow up and get married and have three children. He went to U.C. Berkeley and became a lawyer who was on Governor Jerry Brown's short list for appointment to one of two newly authorized Superior Court Judgeships in 1980. We will never know what Lyman's contributions to our society would have been. Lyman Robert was a man who wanted to help, wanted to make changes in our views, in our laws and in our people. He and Charlene did not get the opportunity to complete what they came here to do.

My grandfather never talked to us about his son until the trips to the hospital in 1990. This story came out of the blue during the three days we drove back and forth to the hospital. My grandpa was feeling stressed as he knew he was about to lose his wife Veonia. She had been diagnosed as having a stroke. The Doctors were trying to determine if she would live. I was with him as they told him there was no hope. I was with him when they had him sign papers to remove life support for my grandmother. We were both crying as he signed them and then we walked back to her room.

There was no one there but us. My grandpa said he could not bear to be there when they removed the tubes and the machines, I said "I have to be." My brother came and drove my grandpa home. He said he could not stay either. I was alone as the Doctors began to remove life support when all of a sudden my brother came back. It was 3:00 in the afternoon and all I wanted to do was crawl in the bed with her.

Somehow I managed to stand there holding her hand and rubbing my other hand on the lower edge of my shirt. It was the most surreal experience. We drove to Curtis Park to tell my grandpa she was gone.

Picture of Lyman Senior in 1944 Pocatello Idaho (Wearing a uniform as a security cop)

Photo from Anne Penn/Laurie's personal collection

These are my grandfather's siblings Marion Jones
Smith on the left Born November 18, 1907 and
Esther Jones Smith they called her Tessa – she was
born December 5, 1905. In the Smith family they
used the middle name Jones for at least three of the

children. My grandfather was born September 15, 1909. So he was the baby. The picture of Lyman's siblings shows how the family passed down the "Smith" look as well as the name Jones.

As a child I always wondered how a person could have two such common names Jones and Smith. Lol

Lyman Jones, Veonia, and Gibson (Adam) Everyone called him Gib. Lyman's older brother. August 1, 1975 in front of West Curtis Park home. Gib played Santa next page.

The Smith family definitely did resemble one another.

Grandpa's brother Adam Gibson Smith playing
Santa that year. I always thought Grandpa would
have been the perfect Santa and here his brother
played him perfectly with some of the Gibson Smith
grandchildren. Gib was born Nov. 1, 1901

Following pages: Pictures are from my personal collection given to me by Lyman Jones Smith (grandpa) of Lyman Robert Smith with little brother Don Smith at home in Citrus Heights California. Lyman Robert played cowboys with little brother Don.

Top Picture next page is of Don as a child with cowboy hat and (bottom picture) is of Lyman and cowboy hat. Even though Lyman was much older he took the time to play with his little brother on many occasions. The two lived in what Citrus Heights used to be in days past. It was very much in the country in the early Sacramento area. This place was complete with animals and ducks where Lyman and his family lived.

155

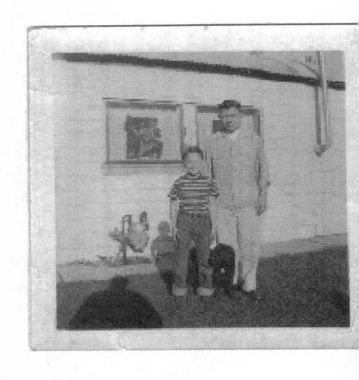

Lyman Robert (Bob) and little brother Don Smith at
home Citrus Heights about 1952.

Uncle Don and his mother (with her arm around Don) prior to her illness. I believe this is also Lyman Robert and Don's grandmother (far left) taken the same day as picture on previous page

Uncle Don in Citrus Heights

Photos on these pages are from my personal
collection as well and were given to me by
my grandpa Lyman Smith Senior.

Lyman (top) 1961 (bottom) Brother Don Navy 1963

G. Samuels, school reporter; L. Wadle, business manager;
L. Smith, assistant business manager

1953 Year Book picture of Lyman (Bob) as the
assistant business manager of the Hi-Lites staff
which was the school newspaper

Lyman happy to work on LBJ's campaign 1964

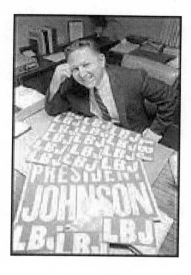

Charlene

What I know about Charlene Smith is mostly through Ancestry research and what I have read. I also know what my grandmother Veonia had to say about her. I met Charlene only once briefly at my grandparents' home in Curtis Park. I was coming to Curtis Park to visit my mother, and Bob and Charlene were leaving. I was reminded of this by my mother.

My grandmother Veonia showed me the picture of Lyman and Charlene that is now used as their victim photograph and said she thought Charlene was a lovely person. She had been so happy for Lyman Robert when they were married. My grandparents met Charlene Doyle sometime in 1973.

Many, many years after the murders of Lyman and Charlene had taken place I looked at the last guest book my grandmother had kept in their cabin up in beautiful Lake Tahoe. This particular guest book spanned the last twenty years of her life from October 1, 1970 until her death in October 1990.

They welcomed many, many friends there over the years. Many would stay and use the cabin with or without the presence of my grandparents. They all had to sign the guest book. That was the price of admission!

The book documents everyone who travelled to visit Lyman Senior and Veonia Smith which always included descriptions of where my grandparents had entertained their guests. Trips to the Clubs usually Harrah's or Harvey's were described. My grandparents and their guests saw Frank Sinatra, Lawrence Welk, Andy Williams, Jerry Lewis, and many other acts that were popular during the 1970's. I carefully went through this book to discover when the last visit of Lyman and Charlene was and what I might learn from their comments.

When Lyman Robert was married to Marge from the 1950's on Bob and Marge would vacation at Lake Tahoe. In the 60's they brought the entire family. Sheriff Hal Barker also made use of time off using the cabin and sharing time with his wife and children and the Smith family.

Years later in one of the guest books that I am so happy to have from those very happy times is an entry dated July 27- July 29, 1973. It says: Bob Smith and Charlene Doyle – thanks for a great time! Santa Paula California (You always had to write down where you were from as well). July 27th Lyman Senior, Veonia, Bob and Charlene took in the Phyllis Diller Show Camelot Room at Kings Castle. On the 28th of July – took the tram up Heavenly Valley and had dinner at the top. Bob and Charlene took in the cocktail show "Johnny Cash" at Sahara's – left for home Sunday morning about 10:00 a.m.

See next page for guest book entry: July 1973

7/27/73 ... Darlene & ... — Thanks for a
great time! Santa ... took
7/4 — Lyman, Leona, Bob & Charlene ... room,
... the "Phyllis Diller" show at Kings Castle — 28th took the tram up
Heavenly Valley and had dinner at the
top. Bob & Charlene took us in. Cocktail show
"Johnny Cash" at Sahara's. Left for home
Sunday morning about 10 A.M. and we stayed
at the cabin until Aug. 1, 1973 and had a visit
here over to Sparks Sept 3/ and took to Harrah's
with Anne & Henry. Came back ... the slots had 2 (75¢)
... good luck with the slots ...

The above notation is written out below:

Another entry from Friday July 19, 1974 says: Bob Smith (Lyman Robert) and Charlene Doyle came from Santa Paula California Saturday July 20 and spent time until July 26 when they left to go to Sacramento for Bob's 20th reunion from San Juan High School class of 1954. My grandma and grandpa called Lyman Bob because Lyman Senior was in the house. It also says they took in Sunday Brunch at Harrah's, Basque dinner in Gardnerville and Buffet dinner at Harrah's on Thursday. The couple's loved to go out to dinner.

July 9, 1976 Bob and Charlene Smith drove up from Santa Paula on Saturday July 10 and spent the week. We saw Englebert Humperdinck and Freddie Roman on Tuesday night July 13, 1976 at Del Webb's Sahara Tahoe – Humperdinck put on a very good show. Wednesday July 14, 1976 cocktail show at Harrah's South Shore Room – Lawrence Welk.

December 19, 1975 Bob and Charlene were married and now were visiting as husband and wife. They had come to Lake Tahoe for a short vacation.

The following was also written in the guest book in Uncle Bob's (Lyman's) hand for the same week in July 1976. He wrote: 7/10 to 7/17/76 Lyman, Max, Bob and Charlene enjoyed the Humperdinck show on 7/13. Bob and Charlene especially enjoyed the hospitality and great dinners prepared by Dad and Max. Thanks for the wonderful vacation – see you soon at 19755 East Telegraph Road, Santa Paula, California. Snapshot of entry next page:

This is the last entry pertaining to times shared with Lyman Senior and Veonia at the cabin. Lyman Robert was to become very busy and then the cabin was vacated for about a year while an extra bedroom and bath were added to it. Uncle Bob called my grandma Max because it was her nickname.

Bob and Charlene did not move to the High Point Drive Address until 1978.

From 1978 until July of 1980 there were no entries in the guest book. After the murder of Bob (Lyman Robert) and Charlene there is no mention of anything that had happened until I get to the next to last page of the book. All that is written in my grandmother's hand is this:

Charlene Doyle Smith

April 17, 1946 born – Died March 13, 1980 and the next line says:

Lyman Robert Smith born April 7, 1936 Killed March 13, 1980.

I found it interesting that she just entered the word died when writing about Charlene's death, but by the time she got to Lyman Robert Smith it changed to the word killed.

On the page across from these two birth and death dates my grandmother wrote: A quote from Rose Fitzgerald Kennedy.

A wonderful philosophy of Life about her grandchildren and I pass it on to my family:

"I hope they will have the strength to bear the inevitable difficulties and disappointments and griefs of life. Bear them with dignity and without self-pity knowing that tragedies befall everyone and that, although one may seem singled out for special sorrows, worse things have happened many times to others in the world, and it is not tears but determination that makes pain bearable."

My grandmother loved her husband Lyman. She quietly bore the pain of watching him be crushed by the loss of his son Lyman Robert.

Lyman Senior and Veonia would go to Santa Paula to visit Bob and Charlene as often as they could manage it.

Charlene was a very attractive young woman. Before my grandmother died in 1990 she gave me a pair of Charlene's shoes. Charlene had impressed my grandmother and she was glad for Lyman Robert when he married her. In November 1979 Charlene gave my grandmother a pair of deep wine suede heels. The reason I know that it was November of 1979 is because my grandmother always labeled things with dates so she would never forget any event. On the box in my grandmother's handwriting it says: November 1979. In less than four months Charlene would be dead. It was several years after Charlene died that I became the custodian of Charlene's shoes. My grandmother asked me to follow her to her bedroom. Whenever she wanted to speak to me privately or she had something she wanted to say that was important she would call me to the back bedroom.

On this day the thing on her mind was she wanted to be sure that if anything happened to her that she had given me Charlene's shoes. She did not want them to be some non-descript item in amongst her own very full closet. I suspect she had no idea what to do with them because she could never bring herself to wear them. I have never worn them either. I have wondered why I keep them. I suppose it must be because I found it touching that because my grandmother had admired Charlene's shoes Charlene had made them a sweet gift to my grandmother. When my grandmother Veonia gave them to me the look on her face as she told me what they were I knew they had meant something to her. That Charlene had meant promise and happiness to Lyman Robert.

My grandmother did not put these in a bag to the local thrift shop. She was telling me she wanted me to keep them because she could not bear to give them away. I suspect my grandmother knew I would take them out and look at them on occasion to remember the hope she had had for the couple. Every time I go in the closet and get to the back the box with the shoes is still there. Sometimes I pick it up and open the lid because I remember the place and time in a moment spent with my grandmother. The moment was in her master bedroom on Curtis Park. Such moments of absolute quiet and sincerity, reflection between people where one has died touch you in such a way that the picture is frozen in your mind forever there to look at to see and never forget.

This was my first experience in receiving items that had belonged to people who had died. My grandfather gave my husband two suit coats that had belonged to Lyman Robert. They could not bear to just package these things into a box or bag to be given to people anonymously. They gave them to family to remind us, and to appreciate the things that were left by the vacancy of their lives. The picture of Lyman and Charlene that has been used and posted everywhere to show who some of the victims were I first saw at my grandmother and grandfather's home on the dresser of the room that I had always stayed in. My grandmother was so pleased that Lyman had found such a beautiful spirited woman to share his life with. No one likes divorce that happen in families but as people we have to move on. My grandparents were very happy for Lyman Robert that Charlene had come into his life. Charlene seemed bright and cheery to my grandmother. She showed me the picture and told me the news that Lyman had married Charlene in 1976. I was exactly 20 then.

Charlene was born also in April as was Lyman Robert her third and final husband. She came into the world on April 17, 1946, exactly ten years apart from Lyman. She was born in Ventura California. Her birth name was Charlene Herzenberg. She was to marry three times. It seemed about every four years her name changed. In July 1966 her name became Charlene Clements. In January 1970 she became Charlene Doyle, and then she married Lyman Smith in December 1975.

As a child Charlene did not have an easy life. When Charlene was a very little girl her mother abandoned her. Her father remarried and then was killed not long after as well. As beautiful as she was it could not make up for the abandonment she must have felt. Charlene seemed to be very needy in her relationships with men. She needed much reassurance from them.

By the time Charlene met and married Lyman she was only 30 years old. Even though she married Lyman Charlene was to keep a lover the entire time according to reports I have read. This information has been passed on from early reports after the murders and perpetuated over time. People have many secrets for many different reasons. Charlene was young enough to still be trying to figure out who she was and what she wanted in this life. Apparently she like many others wanted security, love, a family. Lyman represented security and a lifestyle she could definitely live with. Charlene also had lacked parents herself. It is not surprising she would be attracted to an older man with much promise in his career. Lyman had been an up and comer to be sure. Charlene wanted the stability he gave her and she was contemplating starting a family with him. Yet, she needed attention when Lyman was so busy with his career and business ventures that Charlene was left alone too much. She contemplated divorcing Lyman and had a lover in Richard Atwood. When Lyman found out of course he was extremely upset. He loved Charlene about this there was no doubt.

For a brief time in her marriage to Lyman Charlene had felt alone because Lyman was gone on business trips frequently. She filed for divorce and moved in with her lover. After a while Charlene reconciled with Lyman moving back in with him.

The unfortunate thing about the murder of Lyman and Charlene was that there was much innuendo and speculation as rumors flew about who could have murdered them. Some of the speculation came in the form of wondering if either of them had done anything to or with someone that they knew to bring this murder on to themselves. It was as if by some stretch of the imagination that this couple had done something so that there may be some blame of the victims themselves. Business Associates were looked at, bad business deals, former or current lovers; there was even a quick look at one of Lyman's children. That was not logical at all (looking at one of his kids) and shows how much Ventura County was grasping at straws from the get go. Ventura County looked in all of the wrong places for the culprit of this horrendous crime. Unfortunately, it was to take a very long time to connect these murders with the Goleta murders and others.

This criminal kept changing some of what he did to try and confuse some of the detectives in some of the counties he would run through. It must have been extremely funny to him as the news reports came in speculating over and over. Sometimes ONS would use a gun and sometimes he bludgeoned and used a gun. He changed some of what he did on purpose. Because of the focus on one of Lyman's former business associates, the trail or case went cold. When it was suggested that the cases in Goleta or Santa Barbara were connected the different jurisdictions and counties denied that they really believed there was any connection. If the detectives

believed there was a connection it was usually denied
in news articles and stories at the time even until the
late 1980's.

Charlene's high school picture

Lyman Robert and Charlene

Hal Barker Lyman's (Uncle Bob's) Best Friend

Stories told to me by Hal

Hal and Lyman (Bob) met when Sheriff Barker ran across Lyman as a Deputy District Attorney. They had both arrived in Santa Paula at about the same time. The prosecutor and the cop hit it off. Lyman was a prosecutor working in the DA's Office. They hit it off professionally and personally. They both had young families and both men liked a good scotch. The two men would ask each other when they got together, "my scotch or your scotch?" Hal and Lyman were both married with young children. Lyman was married to his childhood sweetheart, Marjorie Donald. The two families would get together socially for many years. The two wives were very close friends until Lyman and Marge (Marjorie) divorced in 1972.

The cabin in Tahoe owned by my grandparents Lyman Senior and his wife Veonia was used for short vacations by Lyman Robert and his first wife Marge along with their young family. Lyman's best friend Hal along with the Smith family spent several weekends there over the years. On one of the visits to Lake Tahoe Lyman Robert made Hal mad. The cabin is small having one large room upstairs with 4 double beds in it. When people came up they were all forced to stay all in one room until years later when an additional room was added downstairs. Little did Hal know how noisy Lyman was as he

175

snored something terrible. Lyman said he didn't snore. Hal asked Marjorie how she could stand it and how could she ever sleep? Marjorie said she didn't sleep very well at all.

Hal; didn't get any sleep that night in Lake Tahoe and had to drive all the way home to Santa Paula the next day. It didn't stop him from coming back to the cabin again. Lyman and Hal had such a good friendship that over the years when Hal was in Sacramento for some law enforcement meeting he stopped for a visit in Curtis Park, South Sacramento to visit with Lyman Senior. He stayed for dinner talking about the railroad where my grandfather worked and Lyman Senior showed Hal his tools from being a Mason. As Hal said it "One old Mason and one young Mason talking about it." They also discussed some of the dealings that Lyman Robert was involved in with the business he had started transporting cattle overseas. Lyman Senior was concerned that his son may have gotten himself into a bad situation. As it turned out the murder had nothing to do with Lyman Robert's business dealings.

Hal described Lyman Robert as a sweet, sensitive kind of guy with no hard edges. They were running buddies even though Hal is a Republican and Lyman was a Democrat. Hal thought that Lyman was a Democrat because he wanted to be judge. He had a plan and he followed that plan. Lyman may have lived a life a little higher than where he was maybe a little beyond his means, and he always had the best things. He enjoyed his life. A week before Lyman's death at the hands of the Original Night Stalker Hal and his best friend Lyman met for lunch at the San Francisco Airport where Hal was the Police Chief. They discussed Lyman's possible appointment to Superior Court Judge. Lyman was excited about the possibility and he and Hal discussed that being a Judge would be great. Maybe Lyman could settle in and not worry about some of the types of business deals he had worked with in the past. Hal told him "Go do it." "Be a judge."

The two men enjoyed each other and frequently played golf together. They were both Rotarians and had both been President of the local Rotary club and both had achieved and been awarded the Paul Harris Fellowship in Rotary. Many barbecues were experienced and in the service club the two men were happy to serve the community. I asked Hal if he had spoken to Lyman's kids or Marjorie after the death of Lyman. He said he had tried to be an unofficial advisor to Lyman's kids after the murder until his own wife passed away.

Hal said "when Lyman's oldest daughter Jenny fell under suspicion about her father's murder because she had been angry with her father about the divorce she called Hal to ask "they want me to take a polygraph, should I do it?" Hal told her that since she was innocent she should do it. Of course Jenny passed the polygraph. Hal said Lyman's daughter had been angry because her dad had divorced her mother Marge and then married Charlene. Jenny did not get along with Charlene as her stepmother. According to Hal Lyman Robert's kids' likely saw their father more frequently after the divorce. What Hal had to say about Charlene was that she was a vivacious, good looking woman. He had asked Lyman "have you looked at this lady?" Lyman had kept his distance. He was a married man at the time. Hal said Marge did not leave her marriage to Lyman without a fight.

During Hal's career he was in charge of Patty Hearst's in custody for nine months. Hal has been a cop for fifty years and is still active in his retirement speaking recently at the California Rifle and Pistol Association of which he is a life member. At this event the sheriff of Santa Barbara County was recognized as Sheriff of the year 2016.

On the way back from Santa Barbara Hal was driving alone on the highway when I received a phone call from him. He had a great set up on the vehicle which I believe he said was a truck. I said Hal are you sure you want to talk on the phone while you drive? (it can be tricky down south) and he said sure I don't have anything better to do on the long drive we can talk for a while. I sure do like Hal.

To this day Hal would love to help find the perpetrator of his friends' murder. I spoke to Hal several times in 2016 and 2017 because he really wants to help.

I also wanted to include information about Hal's career because it shows what kind of man Hal Barker is. It also speaks to the caliber of friend he was to Lyman Robert. When Lyman was murdered Hal was so broken up about it he could not attend the funeral.

Hal Barker is a very well educated man who has served his communities and his State as a Police Chief. He was also an Honorary Lone Logistics Commander to a retired Colonel in the Army.

Sheriff Hal Barker has had a long and prestigious career in Law Enforcement. I want to include what was written about him even before 2000 from the FBI. Hal continued on for the next 15 years to serve and is still doing what he can.

"Harold N. "Hal" Barker was born and raised in Santa Paula California. Hal's father spent his career in Law Enforcement retiring after serving as a Ventura County Sheriff's Lieutenant and Marshall of the County. Hal began his career in law enforcement in his home town of Santa Paula in 1959, rising through the ranks to Captain. During this career period Barker earned an AA degree at Ventura College and BS degree at California State University at Los Angeles. He attended session 86 of the NA where he was awarded the J. Edgar Hoover Medal for study excellence for being number one in his class.

After running for Sheriff of San Mateo County unsuccessfully, Barker accepted a position as police chief of Folsom, CA (the prison town). After 14 years in Folsom, Hal Barker was appointed Sheriff of El Dorado County. He was later elected to a full term which he served.

In 1986 Hal was an honorary base commander at Mather Air Force Base.

Hal served as president of the Folsom Chamber of Commerce and was Folsom Man of the Year in 1995. He served Rotary as President and was named a Paul Harris Fellow, a life member of IACP, a Life Member of the California Police Chiefs Association, and a 40-year member (life) of the California Peace Officers Association. He served as CPOA President 1999-2000.

The sheriff has every post certificate awarded by Peace Officer Standards and training and graduated from Class 4 of the command college. Hal Barker served his nation as a colonel in the state military; as a master of his Masonic Lodge in 1997; and is active in the shrine.

Hal's wife Elaine and their children travelled to Washington D.C for the duration of the 86th Session. Elaine is deceased and son Russell is a graduate of the Air Force Academy and is a major in the US Air Force. Daughter Terri is a deputy district attorney in Contra Costa County.

Hal Barker intends to continue to serve the profession he loves until health indicates."

The career information was taken from the FBI National Academy book written by Randy W. Baumgardner

How We Were Told

Attorney, Wife Beaten to Death In Ventura Home. These headlines are taken from the Press Courier originally published on Monday March 17, 1980. Sometime in the previous few days of March 1980 my grandfather was to learn that his successful son Lyman and his lovely wife Charlene were bludgeoned to death with a fireplace log. Lyman's children and his ex-wife were to be shattered with this lasting image of brutality and horror. Charlene's family and friends were to feel the same shock waves of grief and silence.

How could anyone do such a horrific thing to another human being? When law enforcement came to my grandfather Lyman Seniors home in Sacramento to tell him that his oldest son was dead he was not home. So the cops went to his next door neighbors' home to ask if the Smiths were in town and when they might typically be returning.

The next door neighbors were Senator Al and Clarice Rodda. Mrs. Rodda told the detectives that the Smiths were likely out for the evening and would be home shortly. Mrs. Rodda called my mother and was so upset she did not want to say what was wrong; she only said that something really terrible had happened to Lyman Senior's son. She told my mother that the officers had come to her home. All Mrs. Rodda and my mother could do was wait until Lyman Senior came home to be told.

The officers waited outside across from the park for Lyman Senior and my grandmother to come home. What must it be like to sit in the dark and wait in order to shatter a family's world with news such as this? When my grandparents came home parking their car in the driveway they must have wondered who was parked on the curb. Knowing my grandfather, he was probably a little irritated by a car parked in front. People park in front of your house a lot when you live by a park.

All I could picture was their happy mood after having been out for the evening at an event that was fun and likely light hearted, and then suddenly the officers were there asking to come inside to deliver this irrefutable fact. To tell Lyman a fact that could never be undone, a fact that would crush him to his soul. One of the brightest lights in his life and his reasons for being on this planet was extinguished and in the most horrific way possible. I cannot fathom this. My grandfather was 71 years old when he received this news. He would live another 21 years after this moment and never know who killed his son.

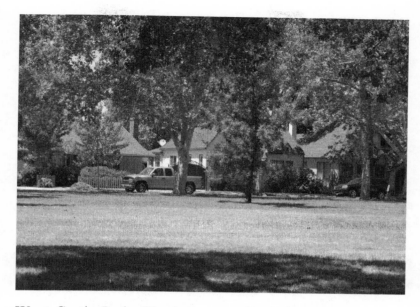

West Curtis Park. The house on the left with the small fence was Senator Al Rodda's home where the police detectives came to tell Lyman Senior. The house on the right was my grandparent's home. The detectives waited in front that night to tell them the news.

As a matter of information here is an article about when Albert Rodda passed away at the age of 97. The Rodda's lived on Curtis Park for at least 50 years and were my grandparents next door neighbors as long as I can remember. The following articles about Senator Rodda's passing are included in order to share with you the type of people my grandparents lived next to for all of those years. Senator Rodda took the time to say hello even to children.

Former Calif. State Sen. Albert Rodda dies at 97

The Associated Press (2010)

Former state Sen. Albert Rodda, a Democrat who represented Sacramento for 22 years, has died.

Rodda (ROD'-dah) died Saturday at his home in Sacramento at the age of 97, said his son, retired Sacramento County Superior Court Judge Steven Rodda.

He called his father "a servant of the community."

The Sacramento native represented his hometown from 1958 to 1980. Among other accomplishments, he wrote the bill that gave collective bargaining rights to California teachers.

He helped create Sacramento Regional Transit and the California Railroad Museum. Before he was elected to the Legislature, Rodda taught history and economics at Sacramento City College.

Senate President Pro Tem Darrell Steinberg, also a Sacramento Democrat, praised Rodda on Monday as "one of the great Sacramentans."

Following are quotes from an article that describe simply the man and his service to Sacramento. Obituaries were done all over the state of California when Senator Rodda passed away as he had always worked for the good of the State of California.

"Albert Rodda, considered one of the Legislature's intellectual leaders during his 22 years in the Senate, has died at age 97.

The Democrat represented Sacramento in the California State Senate from 1958 to 1980. He was involved in major state legislation throughout his long career.

Rodda helped guide the state through the Proposition 13 tax revolt and a historic state Supreme Court ruling, Serrano v. Priest that found poor neighborhoods were being unconstitutionally harmed by the state's school funding formula.

When he was elected to the Senate, Rodda was an instructor at what was then called Sacramento Junior College. Rodda Hall on the campus of Sacramento City College is named in his honor.

He also was elected in 1983 to the Los Rios Community College Board of Trustees, serving nine years."

I kept in touch with Clarice Rodda, Albert's wife for a time after my grandmother passed away. My grandmother had been an elementary school teacher and so the work that Senator Al Rodda had done on behalf of California teachers had made Senator Rodda a hero in my grandmother Veonia's eyes. Ironically my grandfather had worked for the Railroad for many years and Senator Rodda helped create the Sacramento Railroad museum.

Below: Close up view of my grandparent's next door neighbor's home where the detectives came. Clarice and Al Rodda were home that night. The driveway is my grandparent's driveway. The houses are close together. Photograph next page: My grandparent's home where the detectives waited to tell the news.

When my grandmother called my mother to tell
her this information and then when my mother also
called me I was so in shock I cannot remember the
exact words that were uttered out loud. This was one
of the memories I had utterly blocked out until in
2014 I asked my mother, how did I hear this news?
As she began to retell the story it all came flooding
back to me. To be told that a son or a child has died
is a terrible enough thing to know, but to then hear
the details of how he and Charlene had died, hearing
the words that they had been murdered, that they had
suffered indignities and been tortured in this way. To
hear that his son's life was over by way of a fireplace
log is just too much to bear.

I cannot imagine being Lyman's children and
hearing these words. Gary who was 12 at the time,
and who is included in each report, each accounting
of the gruesome crime scene as the one who found

his father and stepmother this way, I could not fathom this either. One article says: "We received a call from a hysterical child reporting the incident" said police Captain Paul Lydick.

I never heard my grandfather utter a word out loud about what had happened to his eldest son. The closet he ever came was in the car the day he told me the story about Lyman Robert almost dying as a child.

Any news I heard about the case in the beginning were reports from my grandmother who told about whom law enforcement might suspect had done this. Joseph Alsip had come up as well as the story about Lyman's eldest child being polygraphed and cleared.

I believe my grandfather did not speak about this because he could not. He could not say the words out loud. He could not retell the story or discuss it with anyone. This was too terrible to utter out loud or to repeat to anyone. I do know that my grandfather was never the same man again afterward. How could anyone love a child who grew into a successful man and then lose him in this most terrible of ways out of nowhere? The emotions, the depth of despair, the grief, anger and sadness were written all over his face. I have no idea how or if my grandmother could even attempt to console this man who had been gregarious and who had travelled through life with a twinkle in his eye until now.

My grandfather had had his share of hardships in life up to this point but who could ever expect a horrible nightmare such as this? How does one begin to try to live each day after this shatters your world?

I was close by and this was to have a long lasting life changing effect on me as well. When I was told about the scene, when I was told about what had happened to Lyman and his wife Charlene I almost could not comprehend it. I have spent many years since then trying to figure out how one supposed human being can do this type of thing to another. I blocked out how I had heard the news and where it had come from and only remembered the way in which they were killed.

I spent the next several years trying to process this story, this tragedy and also the fear that has never completely gone away. I put the information about the murders as far away in my mind as I could. Years later when I heard the voice recording of EAR it was too scary to listen. I tucked it all away for another several years.

Why does someone turn into a serial killer? What are we looking for and how do we find who did this? Always trying to understand and figure it out so I could try to begin to understand somehow. Of course there is really no way to ever really understand this. There is only the analysis of the behaviors and ideas about how each serial killer became what he became.

We have a description of this unknown man's many, many crimes. The perpetrator of my uncle's murder was connected through DNA to the prolific East Area Rapist and to many other murders. All of these victims' families are changed forever. All of these many years later this particular crime goes unsolved. This crime does not have a case number.

My grandfather and grandmother died never knowing who did this. My grandfather lived just long enough to find out that the person responsible for Lyman Robert's death and Charlene's death was not an acquaintance, not an old business partner, but a man who is a serial killer, a man who had terrorized Sacramento those many years ago. My grandfather found out that the DNA tied EAR to ONS and that the man had killed many others. He learned that it was most likely a random act.

Lyman Robert's kids are long grown as am I. Will this be the case that is never solved? Like the Black Dahlia murder will we really have to move on from this lifetime never knowing who did these terrible things to so many?

In books written about the different crimes Richard Shelby and Larry Crompton have shared mostly details about the crimes that happened when the east area rapist was getting started in the late 1970's. They have written about the rapist and terrorist and his MO. The rapist was operating in their jurisdictions and so they were there. They tried to stop this man before he had evolved into the murderer he became. Not as much is written about the murders. These detectives needed to get what they know about these crimes out of themselves and on to paper to document and possibly help solve the crimes. Discussing an open murder case is typically not done in great detail especially by detectives to the general public.

What were they like? Who were they really? They have been labeled victims and their pictures are stuck forever frozen in time where they stopped, where they ceased to exist. All of these victims were much more than that. The internet shows all of the murder victims and relates the story of their endings likely hoping that someone watching will help solve the crime. I get that. What I had trouble with though was the short pages of the crime descriptions that encased the victims, attached them to a serial killer with nothing said about the promise and the hopes that their lives were. This is my first reason for this book. The other reasons are empathy for the many victims of the rapes in the beginning. Empathy for the detectives who have not as yet caught the guy and who take it with them through life never satisfied because the case is still unsolved. Many have come and gone, many retired still wanting to help investigate this one last case.

Chapter Five
Official stance on release of information
Headlines

"Goleta Valley doctor, woman found slain."
"Attorney, Wife Beaten to Death in Ventura
Home." "Two found slain in Goleta case similar
to one in 1979." There were so many more
headlines I could not possibly list them all here.
Most likely the serial killer that was not recognized
as such had tremendous fun reading all about it.

How could anyone who loves a child, a mother or
father, people who were just beginning their lives
handle losing them this way? These people who
were not even half way through their lives had very
real relationships with family and friends. We lost
them in this most terrible of ways out of nowhere.

We have a description of this unknown man's
many, many crimes. The perpetrator of the rapes and
murders was connected through DNA to the prolific
East Area Rapist. All of these victims' families are
changed forever. All of these many years later this
particular crime goes unsolved. The murders do not
have a case number. Only a crime report number.
I was told a case number is only attached when a
perpetrator is charged and prosecuted with a crime.

**Note: The following was written prior to the
FBI announcement that they are asking for tips to
solve this case.** The FBI has decided to reinvestigate
the case thinking there could be a chance to solve it.
The announcement came in June 2016 marking the
40th anniversary of the beginning of the crimes in

Sacramento. It is relevant because of the frustration faced by the families that remain. This was written in February 2016.

After contacting a police commander in Ventura County one of the many jurisdictions that a murder had taken place and asking questions about the cases I was asked "what is it you want?" I replied "information, details." I was after copies of the actual crime reports. The detective told me there was plenty of information on the internet. He knew he was talking to a family member yet this is what I was told. Go read about it on the internet. I was told about the 80-page report (article) that Colleen Cason wrote more than a decade ago. I had read it already. I asked if there was a cold case unit in some of these jurisdictions and I was told there was not. I am told that any leads that come in on these cases would be investigated. That was all. I thanked him and went away as there would be no information forthcoming from this Police Department.

I know leads come in, but I have a hard time believing that anyone has the time or can provide the attention this case needs. (In February 2016 I believed nothing much was formally OR OFFICIALLY being done anywhere.) This case had been cold for quite some time. Keep in mind as well that originally Ventura County was so sure it had to be a business associate of Lyman Smith or that Lyman had pissed off someone he had known. Murder charges were filed against Joseph Alsip, a previous business partner of Lyman's. Ventura County eventually dropped the charges. They in this police department in particular went down the wrong path from the beginning because of who the victims were and who they thought they were.

When you try and get information from the medical examiner's offices such as records of autopsies, toxicology reports and anything else in the files because these are open murders no family members or the public in general can have access to these records even though it has been 40 years or 30 years in these cases. These records are typically a matter of public record UNLESS your family member or friend was murdered. In the case of homicides, it is up to the original investigating police department whether or not you can get any information at all about your loved ones. The California State law says that if the investigation is ongoing and this is an open case of murder they can use an exemption to the law and choose not to release anything to you because they say it could jeopardize a prosecution of the perpetrator in the future. Here is the disturbing thing – these cases are 37 years all the way down to 30 plus years old. The rapes are over 40 years old.

If these cases are never solved none of the families of the "victims" can have access to the reports or case files or any information pertaining to the details of the crimes ever. We could die ourselves never having access to what is in every other case of death a matter of public record. Because the detectives use the exemption to release the information to anyone who might ask for it we could NEVER have it because they may NEVER solve the crime. I doubt that the investigators have the funding or the time to investigate such an old case. Through no fault of their own they are working on current murders, current cases. They do not have the money to look at such an old cold case yet they will never release information that could possibly be useful to solving the case. Yet, they are following policy; they are following what the law allows.

I say again, this case is not new it is a lifetime ago and likely this case will be solved with a DNA match. The medical examiners reports and records will be of use when it comes to describing the wounds on each of the victim's bodies and when they likely occurred, but in reality once a DNA match is made it will be hard to refute that one single piece of evidence. That is really all they will need for all practical purposes. The information we may seek as family members or friends who just wish to know details in order to possibly help solve the crimes will not be what solves the case or brings this guy to justice. The exemption to the law to release records is outdated and does not make any real sense at this late date and in the case of crimes committed almost 40 years ago. Other states have different laws on this issue. It would seem there should be a time frame, (a statute of limitations) that release of this information especially to families should be done. Forty years is enough. Things have changed since these exemption laws were written. DNA matching should make it easier to convict without keeping the cases and the reports away from family after a lifetime.

It is protocol for the Medical Examiners offices to ask the investigating agency if it is ok to release the documents. Family members of victims must feel not only blocked from knowing details about their family members' death but are also left in the dark and left with their own desire to know more about what happened in their case. I empathize with any one of the families who may have already asked all of these questions from all of these agencies and who were blocked at every turn. Sometimes all a family has are the details about the stories of how their loved one died. The need to know details is common and universal to human nature. The victims' families are blocked from every angle by everyone even after 37 years. The ability to lay this story to rest (murder) many times lies in details. A victims' family want to know where the body is, they want their loved one found if they are missing. If the body is never found it is unsettling and there can be no peace. Once a body is found many people from the victims' family want to know the details of how they died, what their last moments were. They need to know the details. If the case goes unsolved no details are released to families or anyone.

I tried to obtain any information from different counties about these crimes. I am not able to even obtain a copy of the police report or crime report. I am told I cannot receive any information from the medical examiners' office because County Police Homicide Detectives prefer that I not see them. After 30 to 37 years? I know that other family members of victims in these cases feel that they should be allowed access to these records. The reason for my frustration is that after almost 40 years it would seem there would be a time limit on the exemption laws. That an update to this law and what can be released would change after 40 years. It would seem that the advancement of Forensics and the inclusion of DNA evidence would make it possible that this exemption list could be challenged and updated. I am certain family members have run into the same walls from the beginning.

When these laws were enacted (1968) there was no such thing as DNA evidence. There were rudimentary forensics, but there was no DNA. All they had in those days were pieces of paper, reports and records. The California Public Records Act (CPRA) under Government Code (GC) sections 6250-6270 were written in 1968. Things have changed tremendously since then in how investigations are done. I understand why it was written the way it was in 1968.

The definition of Public Records states: As defined in the Public Records Act, GC 6252 "public records include any writing containing information relating to the conduct of the public's business prepared, owned, used or retained by any state or local agency regardless of physical form or characteristics."

About Police Reports it states: "Based on this definition, the report of crimes and incidents written in the course of business of a law enforcement agency are public records and subject to release under CPRA with some exceptions." This information was retrieved from the Los Angeles Police Department regarding the Public Records Act and it does spell out Code 6254 and its exemptions list. What I have wanted to see is the official crime report on the day of the murder when the police department responded that tells what they found at the scene. It is that simple.

June 2016

I looked up the laws pertaining to the release of information specifically regarding autopsy – this is what follows:

Public, unless compiled by for law enforcement purposes and the prospect of law enforcement is concrete and definite, then, according to one appellate court case, the report may be withheld under the investigatory records exemption of the CPRA. Cal. Gov't Code § 6254(f); *Dixon v. Superior Court*, 170 Cal. App. 4th 1271, 1276, 88 Cal. Rptr.3d 847 (2009)(holding that an autopsy report produced by a coroner's inquiries into a suspected homicide where there exists the definite prospect of law enforcement is an investigatory file compiled for law enforcement purposes within the meaning of Section 6254(f)).

Dixon, however, arguably is wrongly decided. The court's decision turned on its determination that a coroner performing duties pursuant to an inquest into a criminally-related death is a law enforcement agency within the meaning of the investigatory records exemption of Section 6254(f). *Id.* at 1277. In so concluding, however, the court failed to cite or recognize the express provision directly governing a coroner's inquest, including those involving investigations into the cause of death in criminally-related cases that requires a coroner's inquest be open to the public. Cal. Gov't Code § 27491.6. Moreover, the court arguably applied an over broad interpretation of the investigatory records exemption by holding that the duties of a corner pursuant to an inquest under Government Code Section 27491 are performed "as a law enforcement agency" within the meaning of the investigatory records exemption of Section 6254(f) without any determination of whether the coroner is charged with the enforcement of <u>criminal</u> laws, as opposed to the enforcement of other laws, such as the issuance of subpoenas on witnesses or a summons of jury called to inquire as to the cause of death. *See*, e.g., Cal. Gov't Code §§ 27492, 27499.

Moreover, earlier courts, before the adoption of the CPRA, had held that autopsy reports are public records. *See People v. Williams*, 174 Cal. App. 2d 364, 390, 345 P.2d 47 (1959)("An autopsy report is a record that the coroner is required to keep (Gov. Code § 27491) and is therefore, a public record (citations omitted)."); *Walker v. Superior Court*, 155 Cal. App. 2d 134, 138-39, 317 P.2d 130 (1957); *see generally* Cal. Gov't Code § 27491 (setting forth duties of coroners); § 27491.6 (requiring inquests performed by coroner be open to the public). The Legislature was no doubt aware of these decisions when it enacted the CPRA, and could have expressly exempted coroners' reports from public disclosure, but did not do so. *See also San Francisco Examiner v. Plummer*, 19 Med. L. Rptr. 1319 (1991) (in a decision not certified for publication, a superior court judge held that a county sheriff's department was required to release autopsy records of victims of the Nimitz Freeway collapse during the 1989 San Francisco earthquake).

Here is what I was told after having an attorney review the above laws and issues:

"First of all, Dixon was factually similar to your case because it involved a very old murder, i.e. from 1971. The age of the case was not determinative. The trial court, the El Dorado Superior Court I might add, found that the "investigatory file exemption" within the meaning of section 6254(f) was applicable and refused to order release of the autopsy. On appeal, the Third District Court of Appeals dealt squarely with the issue of whether these circumstances qualified for the investigatory file exemption, and found that they did. It is significant that the decision came out of the Third District because that is the Court of Appeal for El Dorado County and is binding, not merely advisory."

During this same time frame I sent requests to all counties Medical Examiners involved just to see what they had to say about their policy in releasing records that are 36 years plus old.

Here are typical responses from medical examiner's offices.

Dear: (I have removed identifiers)

Our file contains toxicology reports, an investigation report, and an autopsy report. Since both deaths are the subject of an open homicide investigation, we needed to contact the investigating agency regarding your request. (The names of the officers are left out here for obvious reasons) Blank Police Department confirmed to us that the criminal homicide investigation is ongoing and requested that we not release any information in our files due to the pending investigation.

As a result, we must assert the exemption to the public records act found in Government Code section 6254 subdivision (f), which exempts investigation files from disclosure due to an ongoing criminal investigation.

Here is another:

I have received your request. Being that these reports were homicide deaths, we do not release homicide reports to anyone. Except other law enforcement agencies, so I will have to check with our County Counsel to see if this request will be possible. I will let you know the status as soon as I find out.

Thank you,

Removed name

Coroner's Bureau
Office of the Sheriff

I have to say that although everyone I spoke to in each medical examiner's office was cordial and patient there was nothing I could obtain to provide details. I only asked all of the jurisdictions to see what the responses would be.

I can only hope that by asking and by poking around, talking to detectives and others who have the reports in their files that maybe it will increase any dialog between them, maybe it will spark an interest to look into these murders further. If that is all we can accomplish at this late date, then at least something has been done to move this forward. I know that the medical examiner will take another look into the reports and into the files. Serial Killers and the crimes they commit are unfortunately somewhat more interesting than some of the other types of murders they may have, especially murders that have yet to be solved. Thank you for any help you can give to shine a light on this and to help catch the perpetrator. One small detail – one shred of information might help to find who is responsible. It is worth it to reread the reports, look at the information that each county has in the murder investigations.

The forensics has evolved since these crimes were shown to be connected by DNA by 2001 or sooner. (I have read a few different years about when this match occurred) Processes to lift fingerprints off the inside of a glove found in August 1980 have been tested in the past. Why not do it again – use new techniques? Give fresh eyes a chance to look at the files, the reports, the speculation and conjecture. Let new investigators' help to solve this once and for all. No victims' family should have to live with the feelings of things left undone to find this criminal. Just because this much time has passed do not think any of the victims or families of victims has forgotten this. It is a weight that they shoulder every day. They should not have had to carry this for so long. We are not meant to carry the pieces of a puzzle so long going around and around with it and over time lacking the piece that will finish the puzzle. This is what makes people crazy.

So we stuff it, stop talking about it or in some of the families come out from the shadows and start talking about it and try to build some sort of new momentum to get the case solved. Thank you so much to Larry Crompton for writing what he knew and knows about this case. This helps. Also thank you to Richard Shelby for the very same thing. Writing about what they know as much as possible in hopes of finding the one piece that remains missing.

I believe much of this testing has been done at this point, but Law Enforcement keeps what they know very close to themselves even after 40 years.

If cases are never solved the only information anyone has is about what happened in detail to their loved one. If there is no person to be held accountable the only things left to be told are what happened to the person in the commission of the crime. It is obvious to us that a family member died usually violently. Read John Walsh's book about the murder of his son Adam and you will find a man who needed to know. The frustration he faced with agencies in the investigation into his son's murder from the moment Adam went missing was horrible. Thank goodness he has chosen to fight for victims' families. Mr. Walsh's fight to help victims of crime has changed many things with his work through the National Center for Missing and Exploited Children. I want to thank Mr. Walsh and his family for their diligence and hard work.

Also, The Polly Klaas abduction and murder has called attention to what the families go through when a person is missing from their families and communities. Mistakes were made when Mr. Klaas' daughter Polly was taken from her home that might have saved her life. Mistakes were made when Adam Walsh was taken from the mall in 1981. Our society was more naive then. Mr. Klaas has fought for victims and has supported families of victims since his own child was abducted and murdered. The Polly Klass Foundation has worked hard for missing people for many years. Thank you to Mr. Klass and the Foundation for all of the support and hard work they provide to families that find themselves in the position he was in when his daughter Polly was kidnapped from her Petaluma home in October 1993. Both men have given and dedicated everything to changing how things are done in looking for missing children. They have helped to create change in our criminal justice system in the last 35 years. Their two cases were solved.

September 12, 2016 - I watched the program on Dateline this week about the unsolved murder case of Jon Benet Ramsey and was amazed to see that copies of crime reports, documents pertaining to the Grand Jury and low and behold autopsy reports showed up on the TV screen. I could see the report number, and all of the information pertaining to Jon Benet's autopsy conclusions. This is an open murder investigation. I have been told these documents are not to be released in California. It is ok to release such documents to a news investigative team so that they can report on an unsolved murder (although only 20 years old) to the American Public in Colorado.

The release of information and the laws pertaining to that release are different depending on the state you happen to live in. In California the law in this issue succeeds in excluding family and friends of the details of all of the open murder investigations of the 10 confirmed murdered by the Original Night Stalker. Plus, a possible 3 more murder victims if the Maggiore's and Claude Snelling are included.

If the law enforcement agencies were to release information on the case documents especially crime reports and reports including autopsy would that not be useful in helping to solve these many murders? I really do get that when a murder occurs information has to be withheld. My issue is with the length of time these reports are held. The fact is that DNA will be the key to solving the answer to the question who did it? (Not paper crime reports from the day the bodies were discovered once again, 40 years ago).

Each state has different laws pertaining to the release of information and public record as it pertains to people who were murdered. Colorado laws most definitely differ from California laws. I believe there should be a statute of limitations on release of information on cold cases that are more than 25 years old in the state of California. I would like to change this law.

Chapter Six
Detectives, Sheriffs, Law Enforcement

The detectives in this case and law enforcement in general no matter what state across the nation are most definitely the protectors of the people. These men and women are called to this position. They give everything they have and more trying to solve cases that are most of the time horrific and very evil. At great cost to themselves over a lifetime in this career choice they feel the cases they work and the people they protect. It never leaves them. In this case I know that the thought "what did I miss?" "How could I have stopped this man?" run through the retired detectives' minds. There were so many people involved in trying to catch this man, so many people trying to stop this man before he could fulfill his promise to kill.

The detectives and law enforcement officers see things, hear things, and discuss things every day that are the worst that the human race has to offer. Yet they go to work every day knowing that this is the case and will be the case. They are our protectors as they form a network in every county and city, in every state watching and listening, working to find the evil that lurks and that menaces us threatening to take away everything dear to us, our lives, our way of life, and our loved ones. These men and women try to take care of us and stand guard. We ask them to do this and to also track and find the perpetrators of evil and to help bring them to justice. We don't really have to ask them to do this as I am sure they would do it anyway, but they must feel doubly purposed with these tasks because we do ask them to stand guard and to figure out who has committed the crimes so that they can remove them from among us. They want to keep us safe to enforce our freedoms to live whatever kind of life we have chosen for ourselves and our families. They choose to do this for us, not so much is it about a pay check or a "lifestyle" it is truly about protection. They are driven to protect us as it says "To Protect and Serve." It really is about that. I have nothing but great respect for the all of the people who work in this profession.

If you look and listen to these detectives, these men and women especially as they retire from this life you can see the pain in their eyes, and feel the heartbreak. Their regret is that they feel they could have done more. There is a feeling, an expression on their faces that holds a lifetime of the cost, of the care for the families of the victims and for the victims themselves. They more than most feel the cost of the losses to us as their families, and the loss to our communities of the potential that has been lost. These victims of violent crimes had more of a legacy to leave everyone but because of the sickness and the illnesses of our societies' and of the individuals who commit murders the victims lives have been cut short.

In the case of the East Area Rapist aka The Original Night Stalker he has left a trail of debris and destruction that is felt and moves in waves over time and space. His actions have left holes in lives and left a legacy of darkness that is to be borne, buried, and in many cases the victims fall silent as a way to cope with the losses. There are so many victims in this case who will never be the same. In California ONS struck in so many different counties that it became easy for him to hit, move and disappear.

The murders took place in Santa Barbara County, Ventura County, Orange County, and Sacramento County and possibly Tulare County (Visalia, California). This scenario is repeated over and over in our country. One of the things that these older detectives have in common is the one case that they never forget. The details are engrained in their minds as they check and recheck them trying to figure out a way to find the one detail, the one thing that will ultimately solve the case. The Original Night Stalker has murdered at least ten people that were confirmed and connected as well as a possible three more that are known:

Professor Claude Snelling, Visalia, California
September 11, 1975 (Crime of Visalia Ransacker)
Tulare County, CA (There is no proof and no
evidence that these crimes are connected)

Sgt. Brian Maggiore, age 21 and Katie Maggiore
age 20 February 2, 1978 (Sacramento) Also
speculation that EAR committed these murders.

Dr. Robert Offerman, age 44 and Dr. Debra
Alexandria Manning age 35, December 30, 1979.
(Goleta) Santa Barbara County

Lyman Robert Smith age 43, and Charlene Smith, age 33, March 13, 1980 Ventura (Ventura County)

Keith Harrington age 24 and Patrice Harrington age 28, August 19, 1980 (Dana Point) Orange County

Manuela Witthuhn, age 28, February 6, 1981 (Irvine) Orange County

Cheri Domingo, age 35 and Greg Sanchez, age 27, July 27, 1981 (Goleta) Santa Barbara County

Janelle Cruz, age 18, May 4, 1986 (Irvine) Orange County

As far as we know there were at least 50 rapes of women and young girls in Sacramento and in neighboring counties from 1976 through 1979. Fifty women who have people that care about them. Fifty women including teens who were never the same after this guy who was just practicing moved about wherever he pleased. The ripple effect of the carnage left in communities and the cost was staggering. Back in the 1970's the penalty for rape was not as severe as it is today. The way these crimes were investigated was also different then.

The Northern California rapes of the East Area Rapist are too old to prosecute because the statute of limitations has run out in 1981 – 1984. However, there appears to be an exception to this. I have read that because the statute of limitations has run out on these crimes that EAR could now only be charged with murder in several counties and possibly for kidnapping in Sacramento because he dragged victims out of their homes to the drainage ditches behind their houses. Obviously if he is ever caught being prosecuted for murder will be enough to put him away so in the rape cases that will never be prosecuted this should satisfy the victims and the communities. The laws in some states have evolved so that the crime of rape has no statute of limitations and charges can be brought and the crimes prosecuted long after they were committed. This is not so in California. I have included what I have found in researching the crime of rape below. Apparently aggravated rape (involving a weapon) can be prosecuted without a time limit. EAR it seems should be able to be charged with aggravated rape because his assaults always involved a weapon. I do have to say I find it interesting that the word "Normal" sexual assault was used in the description which is the law that has the limitation of six years to file charges. See below and next page:

"For criminal cases, a prosecutor may file a charge of aggravated rape at any time, with no limitation (in California, an aggravated rape is rape that involves a weapon, more than one person, or seriously injures the victim). Prosecution for **"normal sexual assault has a statute of limitations of six years. Nov 17, 2015"** **California Statute of Limitations on Sexual Abuse | Legal Match Law...**_www.legalmatch.com/law-library/.../california-statute-of-limitations-on-sexual-abuse.ht..._

The punishment provision for rape is contained in Penal Code Section 264. The penalties for rape in 1976 were "3, 4, or 5" years in State Prison. Prior to 1976, it appears that the punishment was not less than 3 and no more than 50 years in prison unless great bodily injury was inflicted in which case the penalty was 15 years to life in prison. In 1978 the punishment section was amended to "3, 6, or 8" years in prison.

The penalties for Rape law did change after 1978. Rape used to be seen as not so serious a crime compared with today. Women many times would not report the crimes for fear of being blamed themselves for what had happened to them. Many times these types of crimes were not really followed up on the way they are today. Many are not solved today because of the expense and backlog of rape kits yet to be tested. I have included here an article about DNA testing of rape kits. It is important to note that a lack of resources to enable testing and many times prosecution of these cases is why there are not more rape convictions. If rapists understood that they would really be held accountable the statistics on rape would drop.

This article is about why the backlog on testing rape kits exists:

DNA testing of rape kits:

"A rape kit backlog starts for several reasons. One reason is **lack of resources**. On average, it costs between $1,000 and $1,500 to test one rape kit. As crime labs have grappled with limited capacity and state and local law enforcement budgets have tightened, untested kits have piled up across the country.

- **Crime lab resources.** While public crime labs throughout the country have struggled to maintain sufficient funding and personnel in recent years, technology has advanced and the demand for DNA testing has grown dramatically. In addition to rape kit evidence, crime labs receive DNA samples from hundreds and in many cases, thousands of crime scenes each year. The result has been exceedingly long turn-around times—sometimes years—for testing.
- **Police resources.** Many kits never make it to a crime lab in the first place and instead spend years—even decades—sitting untested in police storage facilities. Law enforcement agencies often lack the technology to track untested rape kits and the personnel needed for shipping or transporting untested kits to a crime lab in a timely manner. These agencies further lack resources and staffing to investigate and follow up on leads resulting from rape kit testing.

Another reason behind the backlog is **detective discretion.** In the majority of jurisdictions, the decision whether to send a rape kit for testing rests solely within the discretion of the officer assigned to the case. Several factors can affect the officer's decision, including:

- **Whether the department prioritizes sexual assaults.** Law enforcement agencies often fail to dedicate the time and resources that other crimes receive to sexual assault cases. More than with any other crime, members of law enforcement frequently disbelieve or even blame victims of sexual assault rather than focusing on bringing the perpetrator to justice.
- **Whether the case is likely to move forward.** Due to a lack of understanding about how trauma can affect a survivor of rape, officers often misinterpret survivors' reactions and choices in the immediate aftermath of the assault as being "uncooperative" or "not credible." In addition to the biological and emotional impact of recovering from the direct trauma, survivors also may be hesitant to participate in the criminal justice process for a number of reasons, including fear of retaliation, being treated poorly by members of law enforcement, shame and not wanting others, such as family and friends, to know about the assault.

- **Whether the identity of the perpetrator is known.** Many jurisdictions only test kits in cases where the assailant is unknown in order to attempt to identify a suspect through DNA evidence. It is important to remember, however, that rape kit testing has significant value beyond identifying an unknown suspect, including the ability to confirm a suspect's contact with a victim, corroborate the victim's account of the attack, link unsolved crimes to a serial offender and exonerate innocent suspects. Testing every rape kit booked into evidence ensures greater access to justice for survivors and signals to perpetrators that they will be held accountable for their crimes.

Jurisdictions that are deeply invested in bringing justice to survivors and preventing future crimes have dedicated the necessary resources toward addressing their backlogs and moving cases forward. New York City served as a model for the rest of the country when it committed to testing every rape kit in its backlog and aggressively following up on leads and prosecuting cases. Detroit is now working to pull together the resources needed to test every kit in its backlog of more than 11,000 untested kits and to investigate the resulting leads. In Cleveland prosecutors have initiated cases against hundreds of perpetrators as testing has begun on a backlog of nearly 4,000 kits. And in Memphis nearly 6,000 kits have already been tested as the Memphis Police Department addresses their backlog of 12,164 kits. http://www.endthebacklog.org/backlog/why-backlog-exists **END OF ARTICLE**

Change will only come through us as we voice the importance of funding for Rape kit testing as well as DNA testing on cold cases so that perpetrators especially in crimes against women will know they will be held accountable. We need to make sure this is an issue that receives attention now and in the future to ensure there is funding allocated to police departments and investigators.

For how long can DNA forensic evidence be kept?

DNA is relatively stable. It is most likely that forensic samples collected from a rape victim will yield results: however, time factors, chemical factors (such as washing using soaps and detergents); external factors (such as temperature and humidity) and internal factors (other bodily fluids) may affect the validity of a sample. The earlier samples are collected and tested the higher the chances of yielding solid, reliable results. The following are just some guidelines as to how long different DNA samples may remain viable:

o   DNA from fingers in vagina — up to 12 hours.

o   DNA from a penis — most likely to obtain a profile from the victim within the first 12 hours.

o   DNA from skin to skin contact (e.g., on bruises, or from kissing) can be detected up to two days. This includes detection of body fluids, cellular material and lubricant. If by chance, the person has not bathed or showered then the Forensic Science service says that the relevant area can be swabbed up to 7 days after the incident.

- Fingernail scrapings — two days.
- Oral (saliva and mouth swabs) — two days.
- Lubricant from a condom — up to 30 hours.
- Anal — up to three days.
- Vaginal — up to seven days.
- Fibers of anything put on the head can last up to seven days.
- Semen can be detected on clothing despite washing.

In some cases of assault, the assailant may not have ejaculated, meaning no semen will be present on the victim's body, and genetic evidence from semen cannot, thus, be extracted. In such cases all semen tests will fail. Alternative genetic evidence linking the perpetrator to the victim could be collected, including saliva samples from places where the assailant has licked the victim or cells from the perpetrator's penis that have been left behind in the victim's vagina. **END OF ARTICLE**

https://www.forensicmag.com/article/2015/01/dna-forensic-testing-and-use-dna-rape-kits-cases-rape-and-sexual-assault

Cold Cases

In my research into these cases I ran across an article from the National Institute of Justice that discusses the fact that every day across the United

States investigations slow or stop completely and cases go cold. Homicide and sexual assault units are backlogged.

"The National Institute of Justice's Solving Cold Cases with DNA grant program helps states and local governments' identify, review, investigate and analyze violent crime cold cases – homicides and rapes – that have the potential to be solved through DNA analysis."

"The goal of NIG's cold case grant program is to analyze or reanalyze evidence using modern DNA technology. In 2005, NIG awarded a total of 14.2 million to 38 state and local agencies." Another 8 million was awarded in 2007 to 21 state and local agencies. This is a very informative article about how funding has helped reignite investigations on previously unsolved crimes. "More than 30 unsolved crimes have been solved with DNA hits in the FBI's Combined DNA Index System (CODIS), which operates local, state and national databases of DNA profiles from convicted offenders, unsolved crime scene evidence, missing persons and arrestees (if state law permits the collection of arrestee samples)."

"The Sacramento (Calif.) Police Department is also having success with funding from the NIJ grant program. In 2003, an unknown male offered a woman a ride home, sexually assaulted her and held her captive for hours. Evidence in the case was recently reexamined, and DNA was found. A DNA profile entered into the state DNA databank matched the profile of Timothy Foy, who was subsequently arrested for the crime and convicted in August 2007. He received 65 years to life."

"Like many agencies the Sacramento Police Department continues to face challenges, particularly on cases in which the murder victim's identity is unknown." **END OF ARTICLE**

There is never closure for families only resolution as the above article states.

DNA Phenotyping - A case example of use:

NEW ARTICLE

"Sometime over that winter night in Colorado, the unknown male burst into the Bennett family's home. He had a hammer, and he had something sharp.

The killer murdered 27-year-old Bruce Bennett, his wife Debra, and their seven-year-old daughter Melissa with the weapons. He raped mother and daughter. Only the younger daughter, three-year-old Vanessa, survived the blunt-force trauma he left in his wake.

The Aurora Police Department has investigated the case since the bodies were discovered the morning of Jan. 16, 1984. The last in a series of attacks over a two-week period, the killer has never been found. Some hope in solving the cold case was mustered when a DNA profile from the Bennett crime scene was developed in 2002. But no match was made in any database. The case stayed cold.

Now the police have turned to DNA phenotyping, using some of the clues in the genetic profile, to estimate the look of the killer, they announced last week.

Parabon Nano Labs, a Virginia-based company which specializes in phenotyping, put together a "Snapshot" predictive sketch of what the murderer would look like at age 25 and age 55 – an estimation of what he would look like today, if still alive.

"This is the first time we have had some idea of who we're looking for. He is no longer invisible," said Steve Conner, the Aurora detective leading the investigation into the Bennett killings. "With release of these Snapshot composites, we hope people familiar with the case and the area at that time might be reminded of something or someone significant to their investigation."

Phenotyping has been used in a handful of cases where traditional leads have been exhausted. The first investigative usage was announced in January 2015, with the double-homicide of a mother and daughter in Columbia, South Carolina.

Aurora and other agencies warn that the phenotyping images are "scientific approximations" – and are not exact replicas of the person's appearance. Notable disparities can be created by environmental factors outside of the genetics, including drug use and drinking, smoking, weight gain, facial scars, and facial hair." **END OF ARTICLE**

The articles are published for educational and informational purposes only in the interest of this book and I am using them as set forth under Section 107 (the Fair Use doctrine) of the U.S. Copyright Act of 1976.

By Seth Augenstein 8-30-2016

In this case The Original Night Stalker is still invisible. Even if we use Phenotyping technologies and I am sure LE has this technology it also has its limitations. It could be that ONS will remain like a phantom in the night. I hope I am surprised sometime by resolution in these cases, but I have to be realistic about the possibility that these cases could remain unsolved.

I have been talking to retired LE mostly by phone for the last year and a half. From the first moments I identified myself he has always taken the time to talk to me until I was satisfied with whatever questions I had for that day. He was and is kind enough to listen to my thoughts, to tell me what he thinks and is a very, very good man. We met in February 2016 to talk in person as I felt that this detective in particular has a good gut feel about the case and he still has the hope that we will find out who committed these crimes. He wishes more than anything that they had stopped this man before he got to Southern California to commit the murders.

Investigating crimes, even cold case crimes are a long and methodical process. Patience is a skill that must be mastered. I would have thought that the FBI would be involved in trying to at last nail the guy who did these terrible things. I am told that when it comes to cold cases everyone has way too much to do that are current crimes and that they do not have the resources or the time to truly investigate crimes that are 30 plus years old. (Once again I wrote this before the announcement of the FBI stepping back in to investigate the case in June 2016. Prior to this it has been many years since they were involved in active investigating on these cases).

Ann Rule said this of detectives. "Every experienced homicide detective knows that if a case is not resolved within twenty-four hours, the chances of finding the killer diminish proportionately with the amount of time that passes. The trail grows colder and colder." It must seem at this late date that to investigate this particular serial killer would be like banging your head against a stone wall. It feels so good when you quit. Yet, there are those who have not given up. Since Ann Rule's time there is now the hope that DNA brings.

There are those in several counties in California who are still working from a list of suspects waiting patiently for DNA to clear people one at a time. At least the testing process has been refined and sped up. It is not as long and tedious a process that it once was.

Chapter Seven
Study of Serial Killers
Causes? Possible Diagnosis and Profiles

After this crime occurred, after I was told what few details about the method by which Lyman and Charlene were dead I have to say that sliding glass doors have always made me nervous. I cannot stay in a hotel that does not have an inside hallway inside the building that takes you to the room. The idea and the fact that this stalker came into a house prior to attacking, bludgeoned people to death with a fireplace log horrified me. Just the visual images this creates took a long time to try and push to the back recesses of my mind. I was not Lyman Robert's child, but I was his father's granddaughter. I watched my grandparents struggle with what to do, how to feel, and how to go on. After this happened I tried to study every story, everything that had anything to do with murders. I watched for the next twenty years as my grandfather struggled to deal with not knowing who had done this to his son.

In 1980 Ann Rule wrote a book called The Stranger Beside Me which is about serial killer Ted Bundy. Mr. Bundy killed at least 36 women that he admitted to. It was the first book I had read about a serial killer. I studied it in 1980 pouring over the pictures of the victims empathizing with the families of these women. Ted Bundy had some similar characteristics as the man depicted in the profiles of EAR/ONS. Ann had met Ted Bundy in 1971. In a relatively short period of time Mr. Bundy had committed many murders and had been caught. By

1989 Ted Bundy would be dead, executed in a Florida Electric Chair. Like EAR/ONS Ted Bundy was young, could fit in to his environment, and likely no one would ever think this man could be capable of murdering young women. The East Area Rapist aka The Original Night Stalker was also young, seemed to fit in and not seem out of place in a neighborhood. From the composite sketches shown he seemed nice looking and athletic. But what makes him scarier by far is the fact that he was not caught, we don't know who he is and we do not know if he will repeat the behaviors. Like BTK and others who lie dormant for years at a time, we do not know if the Original Night Stalker will wake up again, if he is dead or incarcerated. The answer still remains a mystery.

For me, back in 1980 when I first read Ann Rules account of Ted Bundy's crimes there had not been a connection yet made to the murders in Southern California through DNA of EAR and ONS. No one really knew that this was the work of a serial killer. In my gut it seemed the only plausible explanation of what this perpetrator was and is. It makes sense to me that ONS would travel throughout the State through multiple jurisdictions, counties. Back then the communications between counties and crime units was somewhat limited. This is probably what Ted Bundy counted on as well as he worked the Northwest and eventually moving on through Colorado and then Florida. If I were a serial killer who wanted to live I certainly would not have gone to Florida. I think that subconsciously Ted wanted to be caught, he wanted to be held accountable, and he wanted the media attention. Now that cell phones with camera's, video capability, and many other things have come along it would seem much harder to get away with as many crimes.

In the 1970's because technology was still evolving to what we know today, and because forensic science still had a long way to go the defense lawyers that Mr. Bundy had at the time tried to cast reasonable doubt to the jury. All they had to convict Mr. Bundy in Florida were bite marks that they could not be 100% sure were made from his teeth, hairs pulled from his mask that were probably his as they were "like" his hair, an eye witness who wasn't 100% sure. There was nothing definitive that could say for certain that Ted was the one who committed the Chi Omega murders. Ted had no alibi and no one to step forward to produce one. In today's world the DNA collected from the scenes would have convicted him. The bite marks and the hair would have been proved to have been his. Forensic Science had not evolved yet and could not definitively match Mr. Bundy to his crimes. Mr. Bundy was smart enough at the time to wipe down the places he stayed and the murder scene's so that he left no fingerprints.

Mr. Bundy's defense team asked the jury to not compound the tragedies of the murders by convicting the wrong man. They also stated that "the state's evidence is insufficient to prove beyond a reasonable doubt that Mr. Bundy and no one else, is the person that committed these crimes. How tragic it would be if a man's life could be taken from him because twelve people thought he was probably guilty, but they were not sure." Another of the defense team said "There are basically two ways for the police to investigate a crime. They can go to the crime scene; they can look for clues to their logical conclusions and find a suspect. Or they can find a suspect, decide on the suspect, and decide to make the evidence fit the suspect and work to make the evidence fit only him." In the case of the Original Night Stalker there will be no reasonable doubt when he is caught. His DNA will match. The rest of the case which involves making sure the suspect was in the areas at the times of the attacks and murders, and all of the circumstantial evidence and the story that is told about this man and his crimes will come after his DNA matches the samples of the East Area Rapist and the Original Night Stalker. There will be no reasonable doubt. There will be no doubt at all.

Now that it has been 31 years since the Cruz murder, 37 for the Harrington's and Smith murders, and about that same time frame for the Domingo, Sanchez and Offerman and Manning, Witthuhn murders, and since other victims also perished at this criminal's hands if we don't solve this case soon it will pass into our history. The Original Night Stalker could become and remain one of the most successful and smartest serial killers of them all. Many serial killers rack up more murders in numbers but most of us are happy and feel comfortable with the fact that they get caught. I have studied serial killers since the 1980's not knowing that those murdered in Southern California by this man were murdered by one. I studied serial killers in an effort to try and understand the mindset of such a man. I wanted to know why and how they became killers. Son of Sam, The Zodiac, Jeffery Dahmer, Gary Ridgeway, BTK, you name it I listened to every detail. Somehow trying to figure it out and studying it helped me live with it.

It is terribly unfortunate that the murders of the Smith's, and the young Harrington's were to become what one profiler said was one of two perfect crimes. The Smith and Harrington murders were essentially identical. I am still shocked by the idea that one human could do something so horrible to others. The Harrington house in Dana Point had an identical floor plan to the Smith House in High Point Drive in Ventura. Both homes had a view of the ocean. So many horrific crimes happen like the murder of John Walsh's son, the murders committed by Jeffrey Dahmer and so many others. In this country we appear to be a breeding ground for the most serial killers in one place.

After all the years of looking at and reading about serial killers, and then currently in present time reading books about the crimes of EAR and ONS, watching reports from various television programs, listening to detectives discuss the case, and finally talking to a detective who even in retirement wants to solve this case it is my opinion that this is where this criminal is today:

On February 7, 2016 I called retired law enforcement to ask a few questions and to firm up a time and date to get together to discuss this case. I wanted to tell him what conclusion I had come to about this perpetrator. I said "I believe that this man is still alive and that he is not incarcerated and he has never been locked up. I think he is like BTK and is sitting back having stopped doing what would get him caught. I think he is enjoying his life thinking he has gotten away with raping and murdering. And he has. I think he is likely from Sacramento and that if we go back to Sacramento we will likely be more able to solve the question of who did these things."

He agreed with me completely. I came to these conclusions independently after weighing the crime reports from news articles, the brazen way this man was, and also the fact that he was aware enough of forensic science and the advances coming that he should stop what he was doing hoping the trail would go cold. I think that at this point he does not think anyone will truly take the time to track him down. **(This was also written before the FBI announcement in June 2016) I** believe this man grew up in my neighborhood or very close by. Possibly he went to my schools for the entire time he and I were both just a short distance away from each other. This is possible. After telling this to the retired detective within an hour he had a volunteer who works on the case call me.

I am certainly not an educated profiler, but I have my theories about this man's mindset. The following are my speculations. One needs to have an open mind to consider the many possibilities. If one is to believe that this serial killer really is the author of the poem sent to the newspapers and radio stations in December 1977 I would say that he likely wanted to be an outlaw of some kind from the time he was a child. He did not like rules and certainly did not feel that they applied to him. He thought that a "normal" life and what it involved were too boring and tame. He wanted to be special somehow, wanted to be noticed and be famous. How does one become famous as a serial killer and not get caught?

I think this person had a fairly normal family and childhood at least from what others could see from the outside. What went on at home behind closed doors is anybody's guess. Likely he had issues with both parents. Possibly his father was a very, very strict disciplinarian and he had a mother who watched without doing anything to stop what discipline was handed out. It could be that she too was rather harsh or just did not really connect with her son. I also think that this child's birth order is that he was the oldest son and likely had at least two siblings that consisted of a sister and brother. He probably shouldered the brunt of his parents' anger throughout his childhood. I would also imagine this person likely felt inferior because he never could please his parents or anyone. At least this would have been his perception.

The notes he wrote (if in fact these were written by EAR) about how angry he was at his sixth grade teacher, how terrible it made him feel when he was punished by writing the same thing over and over again speaks to a frustration level that was phenomenal. He did not know how to deal with his frustration. He had no one to talk to about his feelings which continued to grow into rage.

This child likely began killing animals as young as 10 to 12 years old. He did not fight at school or with others because the cost to him would have been too great. He would have been subjected to punishment at home. But, in secret he found release by stalking and killing animals. He likely played in creeks and waterways as a child fantasizing about the people in the houses he could see behind the fences backing the creeks and waterways. He thought about what it would be like to live in some of these different houses. He was a spy and then a "peeper" as he got older. For a while this seemed to satisfy him.

He spent more and more time in his head fantasizing about different ways to live. What conclusion he came to was that he did not fit in. He did not believe he would ever fit in. He fed his anger and his frustration and his disappointment. He decided at a young age to thumb his nose at traditional society. He would take from some what he would never have, a "normal" life. Combine all of these things with a very deep hatred of women and you can get a man who kills women, over and over.

I also think that this child was extremely smart and that it is likely his teachers did not realize it. Perhaps he has ADHD. He may have had Oppositional Defiance Disorder and was feeling misunderstood by everyone as well as feeling frustrated on a daily basis in school. He had no one to talk to, no one to turn to. He put on an amicable, amenable face for the world all the while simmering underneath at his rejection of a traditional way of living. He would not be boring.

I have included the definitions a couple of disorders that may be very relevant at the end of the chapter. Conduct Disorder is one as I feel that this person could have had this issue combined with a couple of other behavioral issues that I explore. Likely he was left to his own devices to deal with his feelings. Certainly in the 1960's and 70's discipline was used to try and correct behavioral problems. Sometimes very strict discipline was handed out. Without parent or teacher understanding and help with the issues he may have been experiencing while growing up he truly would or could have been made worse.

This child who would grow up to commit terrible crimes would have the excitement he craved as well as one-day becoming known to the world. Maybe at some point he wished he would be caught so that he could take credit for his deeds. He counted on the law enforcement personnel to not be as smart as he was and is. In some ways it must be disappointing to him to not be able to step forward to take responsibility for his crimes.

The Original Night Stalker likely stopped killing in 1986 as far as we know. If he didn't really stop he likely committed crimes when he travelled, but not often. I have not heard of any killings in the United States with the same MO. Because this perpetrator learned as he went in the commission of his crimes I would not be surprised to learn that he evolved and changed his MO if he decided to commit further crimes after 1986. Some crimes in the country I have heard about were close or similar, but the perpetrator was caught. This man was so young when he committed these crimes that by 1986 he was probably 31 – 38 years old. He likely got married, had a family and tries to live within that context. I think he may still be experiencing difficulties having any real long term relationships. He has most likely been divorced more than once because the woman leaves him. Hard to say though depending on the woman he chose. If he chose a wife who is rather subservient and compliant and if he is the one in control and in charge, then this marriage might be working for him.

In the definitions of possible issues this man may have I have used **bolded type in** the descriptions in particular that I think may apply to this suspect. The definition of Oppositional Defiance Disorder as defined by Mayo Clinic about children:

Frequent and persistent pattern of anger, irritability, arguing, defiance or vindictiveness toward parents and other authority figures, he or she may have oppositional defiant disorder (ODD).

Oppositional defiant disorder is a complex problem. Possible risk factors for ODD include:

- **Temperament — a child who has a temperament that includes difficulty regulating emotions, such as being highly** emotionally reactive to situations or having trouble tolerating frustration

- Parenting issues — a child who experiences abuse or neglect, harsh or inconsistent discipline, or a lack of parental supervision
- Other family issues — a child who lives with parent or family discord or has a parent with a mental health or substance use disorder

ODD may lead to problems such as:

- Poor school and work performance
- Antisocial behavior
- Impulse control problems
- Substance use disorder
- Suicide

Some have mentioned in reports that the perpetrator wore very light jackets and not heavy clothing as he stalked and prowled in the winter. There have also been reports about bloodhounds picking up on the criminal's scent and law enforcement thinking there is some kind of chemical imbalance that the man may suffer from. I have experienced people with ODD and ADHD that always think it is too warm even to the point of opening windows in the middle of winter. Perhaps this individual also suffers from being too warm as a part of his chemical imbalance which could be caused by a hormonal imbalance which could explain his tolerance to cold. This hormonal imbalance may also be a part of why his voice seems high as reported and possibly why his penis is described as small.

Since the first edition of this book I have removed the information about Intermittent Explosive Disorder because I do not feel it applies to this perpetrator. I believe Antisocial Personality Disorder and Conduct Disorder are more likely.

The definition of **Conduct Disorder as defined by Web MD. This is the diagnosis that speaks to what I think is or was one of ONS' core personality issues:**

Conduct Disorder is a serious behavioral and emotional disorder that can occur in children and teens. A child with this disorder may display a pattern of disruptive and violent behavior and have problems following rules.

Aggressive behavior: These are behaviors that threaten or cause physical harm and may include fighting, bullying, being cruel to others or animals, using weapons, and forcing another into sexual activity.

Destructive behavior: This involves intentional destruction of property such as arson (deliberate fire-setting) and vandalism (harming another person's property).

Deceitful behavior: This may include repeated lying, shoplifting, **or breaking into homes or cars in order to steal.**

Violation of rules: This involves going against accepted rules of society or engaging in behavior that is not appropriate for the person's age. These behaviors may include running away, skipping school, playing pranks, or being sexually active at a very young age.

In addition, many children with conduct disorder are irritable, have low self-esteem, and tend to throw frequent temper tantrums. Some may abuse drugs and alcohol. **Children with conduct disorder often are unable to appreciate how their behavior can hurt others and generally have little guilt or remorse about hurting others.**

I think that it is quite possible that at the time of the rapes the criminal responsible was possibly trying to throw off law enforcement by bringing and leaving beer cans at the scenes. It is my opinion that this man was stone cold sober especially during the attacks. He wanted to have his wits about him and the only high he sought came from his own actions in trying to have control over others. He was trying to find a path to what he really craved which was murder, destruction or obliterating others. He knew he could not fit into "normal" society. He had to obtain power and control over whomever he chose to destroy.

When discussing the Ted Bundy case Ann Rule talks about Anti-Social Personality Disorder. It is my opinion that there are varying degrees of this disorder or a wide spectrum of disabilities with the disorder. As there are degrees of disability in Asperger's or Autism I think that holds true for those with personality disorders and in this case Anti-Social Personality disorder.

What are causes and risk factors of antisocial personality disorder?

One of the most frequently asked questions about antisocial personality disorder by both professionals and laypeople is whether or not it is genetic. Many wonder if it is hereditary, just as much as hair, eye, or skin color; if this were the case, children of antisocial people would be highly expected to become antisocial themselves, whether or not they live with the antisocial parent. Fortunately, human beings are just not that simple. Like all personality disorders, and most mental disorders, antisocial personality disorder tends to be the result of a combination of biologic/genetic and environmental factors.

Although there are no clear biological causes for this disorder, studies on the possible biologic risk factors for developing antisocial personality disorder reveal that, in those with the illness, the part of the brain that is primarily responsible for learning from one's mistakes and for responding to sad and fearful facial expressions (the amygdala) tends to be smaller and respond less robustly to the happy, sad, or fearful facial expressions of others. That lack of response may have something to do with the lack of empathy that antisocial individuals tend to have with the feelings, rights, and suffering of others. While some individuals may be more vulnerable to developing antisocial personality disorder as a result of their particular genetic background, that is thought to be a factor only when the person is also exposed to life events such as abuse or neglect that tend to put the person at risk for development of the disorder."

Psychiatrist Dr. Herve Cleckley who interviewed Ted Bundy and who was an expert on the anti- social personality acknowledged that standard tests do not reveal this problem. "With Anti-Social personality disorder the observer is confronted with a convincing mask of sanity." Dr. Cleckley said "we are dealing not with a complete man at all, but with something that suggests a subtly constructed reflex machine which can mimic the human personality perfectly." "The anti-social personality does not evince the thought disorder patterns that are more easily discerned; there are few signs of anxiety, phobias, or delusions. He is, in essence, an emotional robot, programmed by himself to reflect responses that he has found society demands. And, because that programming is often so cunning, this personality is extremely hard to diagnose. Nor can it be healed."

Finally, it is my lay person's opinion that for this perpetrator the place, the geography was as important to him as all of the other elements of his crimes. He had a particular way of stalking, breaking in, tying up and terrorizing his victims. He had a way he liked to rape and then murder. But, one of the most important aspects of this MO so that everything else would work for him was the place in most of the cases. The similarity of place to where he grew up. The neighborhood he came from. He had to have the same type of geography. The creeks and waterway's had to be an element and the nearness to the homes, and the highways. The most important visual aspect was the neighborhood park. It is interesting to note that the East Area Rapist attacks as well as the murders where they called him the Original Night Stalker were most times next to creek beds, near neighborhood parks, were close to main areas and then main highways.

Not only did this location allow for easy escape, conveniently it is and was part of where he felt compelled to kill. These types of areas did allow for easy escape, but I do not believe that was his main motivation. First and foremost was the familiarity to his own neighborhood. The fact that these areas allowed for easy escape was actually secondary or even a coincidence. He seems to be a visual type of person. When he sees the right geography, the right neighborhood he recognizes it and it feels familiar, he feels at home there. He needs this element as much or more than all of the other elements of his MO. The visual representation of the place was an integral part of the entire event.

ONS was possibly mentally killing some female that had rejected him that came from or stemmed from his home base at a time that he was young and impressionable. It is also my opinion that this person had a traumatic event or events during his childhood that he ends up trying to obliterate the entire past or people from existence and that his main focus of hatred was definitely female. I think that when he began to take control of the man and integrated the man along with the female into his MO he found that this element made his victory even sweeter. He had power and control over both victims, but controlling the man and then eventually killing the man first, and then the female made the fantasy and then the reality and the rush of power and control feel even better. The houses, the neighborhoods, the actual reminder of the feel of this place that he recalled from childhood were all part of the act. I can see him going through neighborhoods near creek beds and he would have a feeling of familiarity in the ones he

239

killed in. He was at home here. He could feel it. Now all he had to do was find his target. He would scope out the neighborhood looking for empty houses or houses for sale. He would sit in his car or walk through the neighborhood looking for the human target that went with the right house. It wasn't too hard to find.

When I look in particular at photos of the neighborhood that Manuela Witthuhn lived in it strikes me as familiar to where I grew up in South Sacramento. It is startling really when I looked at her neighborhood my thoughts were "holy ---." This looks like the neighborhood I grew up in. Eerily familiar. (No this was not intended as a pun) The geography is part of the attraction and part of his story. Something happened to him in his neighborhood of origin. I emphasize and repeat my comments about the geography so that maybe someone will think about where they lived and who they might have known there.

ONS many times would enter houses next to his target that were empty. It is an amazing thing how well he planned, how much he scoped out the neighborhood, the houses surrounding a target, and to the extent that he was in the neighborhood sometimes for a couple of weeks prior to his attacks that no one appeared to notice him. I believe this man is and was hyper vigilant. In his home as a child he learned to be. He had to anticipate and know what might be coming at him. He was very aware of his surroundings. While he scoped out a neighborhood if someone went by him he would turn his head away. If anyone noticed him in a car, he again would turn his head away. This truly is why he was a phantom. It was almost as though he was invisible. If noticed at all it was not enough to make a lasting impression in the daylight.

Chapter Eight
My Fictional Speculation
Comparison to Ted Bundy

Serial Killer in the Pacific Northwest and other States

Over time as I have read about this case in depth I have the distinct feeling that the Original Night Stalker was long fascinated by the idea of raping women and then as he learned more and more about Serial Killers, in particular Ted Bundy he became enamored with the idea of doing it better than Mr. Bundy. His goal was to evolve into a serial killer, but he would not be the one to get caught. He decided somewhere along the way that he would do anything it took including gunning down people walking their dog in the street in order to be free. I am certain that once these unfortunate victims saw the rapists face he was prepared and knew what to do. He had already made the decision to kill if he had to.

In what I have read about the Maggiore murders in Rancho Cordova, CA there seemed to be some reporting differences in the story line. Most reports I have read said there were two men that witnesses had seen and described. There were two separate composites done and distributed. What if there really are two suspects in these hideous crimes? I know it seems farfetched in some ways. What if it were true? Go along with me for a minute on this ride. The two composites and also the many other composites done over time show two different types of facial structures yet they are similar. Much like they could be related. The descriptions given by witnesses over time talk about the range of height and weight. All descriptions have the man (or men) as not too tall – 5'6" to 5'9" at the short end and up to 6 feet tall. I believe the correct height is likely 5'9" or 5'10" as it was the height mentioned the most. I believe he is 5'9". The men or man has blonde hair and then dark blonde hair and blue eyes. In Richard Shelby's book there are descriptions of one of the victims of rape talking about two different men, two different weights on her, two different penises' during the same attacks. There are voices heard talking to someone, horns honking outside and then banging on the door. This is only mentioned briefly in his book, but the idea that there were two men at least some of the time does repeat. I had come to these conclusions prior to reading Mr. Shelby's book, Hunting A Psychopath. My thoughts about two men were confirmed after I read his book and especially when reading the following:

"On October 7, 1978 an attack came in Concord California. A security officer's badge was found that could never be traced to the killer. More importantly on this date was information given by neighbors. "A woman living very near the victims reported that two nights before the attack they had experienced a prowler. It was about midnight when she and her husband heard someone inside their house. Turning on the light, her husband went downstairs to investigate. Seeing nothing downstairs, he stepped outside. She, still upstairs, heard someone leave the house by way of the dining room door. She ran to the window just in time to see two people running through her garden. They ran to a fence, which they quickly jumped over, disappearing into the neighboring churches' parking lot. The woman witness could only say they were white. One was about 6 feet tall and dressed in a white T-shirt and Levis'. They were both estimated to be in their 20's."

When I was chased down my street in 1971 it was by two men in a truck. One got out and actually chased me while the other followed in the truck. I did not get a good look at the driver but I did see the guy chasing me. He was young, and he was definitely white with blonde hair. I thought he might have been a neighbor from my old block near 47th Ave and Florin Road. The guy I thought it might be had a brother. He was two years older than me and went to the same high school. We had many guys at school growing up that were of Scandinavian descent or European. Is it too farfetched to think that since I grew up in South Sacramento that the East Area Rapist came from my neighborhood or went to the same schools I did? He had to come from somewhere and he had to live in a house in a neighborhood somewhere. Like EAR I had a sixth grade teacher who was mean as well. This teacher got into some trouble with the principal at our school because he was so harsh. He had actually cussed at me because I was talking in the back of the room.

This teachers' kids went to all the neighborhood schools I did until we graduated. The last time I checked this teacher was still alive at the age of about

95. Could the idea that two men who are brothers know what the other one did and they have kept silent all of these years be feasible? Would this or does this explain why rapes and murders occurred in Southern California? Did one of the brothers stay with the other as he moved on to college and then came back and forth between Sacramento where they grew up and a University down South? This guy or guys were young, just out of high school if you believe the ages mentioned in the 1970's. Between the age of 18-30. I would bet that this guy was probably about 21 when he started the rapes in Sacramento. It is possible that prior to that he was just learning his craft as it were.

Maybe he went out of town away from Sacramento to commit the Ransacker burglaries in Visalia. He was honing his breaking and entering skills. Likely he was peeping and stalking as well. Just like some of us when we study a subject in school this man or men were studying how to become an outlaw, a man or men to be feared. He would show us all in the end that he is and was smarter than the rest of us. I think this man or men have relatives in Southern California, in Visalia and in Sacramento and likely Stockton. I say Stockton because there was a lot of activity in Stockton by this night prowler. He was college age and could travel, staying with friends but more likely relatives.

What is mentioned over and over by reporters, authors and storytellers is as this criminal lurked in Sacramento during the commission of the crimes and prior to the attacks he used waterways and trails, river access roads as much as possible. When I talk about my old neighborhood in South Sacramento I have talked about the creek right across the street from my house. If the perpetrator grew up near the Morrison Creek could he have honed his skills following this creek all over Sacramento? It was ripe for someone to look into backyards and into windows. The Morrison Creek across the street from my house is built right behind backyards. Back in the 60's some yards had fences of wood, some had chain linked fences. As children everyone in our neighborhood played back there. At the end of the street there was a bridge that crossed over to another small neighborhood. Then the creek continued east on and on throughout Sacramento.

Is it possible that this rapist got his start peeping as a child or teen as he found his way down the creek areas to see where they would lead? In Sacramento the Morrison Creek has tributaries all over the areas this man travelled. Morrison creek crosses paths with every main road throughout Sacramento. It crosses or intersects with the 65th Expressway, Power Inn Road. The creek runs behind the US Naval Reserve recruiting and the US Marine Corps US Naval and Marine Reserve Readiness Center. The Army National Guard Military Recruiter is back there.

The creek runs parallel to Florin Perkins and then crosses South Watt Avenue, parallels Alder Avenue and runs into Bradshaw. Eventually it appears to stop behind Mather Regional Park and Mather Lake. When you get out there, there is the Folsom South Canal which parallels Sunrise Blvd., crosses White

Rock Road that goes into the City of Rancho Cordova. The Rancho Cordova attacks have the Jedidiah Smith Memorial Trail which crosses a ditch that leaves Dolcetto which is one of the neighborhoods EAR attacked in. On August 1, 1974 near Dolcetto Way and Dawes Street a dog was beaten to death with a log. Was this EAR early on before the rapes? Later on EAR raped and terrorized here.

Then finally, the ditch runs across trail to the American River. This criminal learned in great detail how the rivers and creeks got him around the area leading to easy escapes. If he had to he could actually find his way home from wherever he might be on foot. He did not need a car. The reason he was like a phantom in the night as he has been described was because he was brilliant about how he committed these crimes. While he was searched for after one of these crimes, there was no road he was on, no area he travelled like the rest of us. He was simply gone in the night. Young, quick on his feet and agile, he could jump fences and obstacles and out distance anyone who tried to keep up. If a person who chased him caught up, if he was followed he would simply shoot the person following. He was ready to do whatever it took to get away.

I have included the newspaper articles and composites drawn from the Maggiore murders in Chapter Ten. You can decide for yourself if you think it is truly feasible that two brothers committed these crimes, at least in the beginning before it got so serious.

Ted Bundy was already creating havoc in the early 1970's in the Northwest. Since there was no internet and news did not travel rapidly as it does today it is interesting to me to think that this young man got information about Ted Bundy by way of regular newspaper articles. I think ONS tracked the stories printed in newspapers about Ted Bundy. Ted Bundy was a serial rapist and killer of the most sadistic kind. He not only raped and beat women to death he was a Necrophile. He dismembered at least twelve of his victims. In Ted Bundy's own words, he warned against the dangers of showing horror movies and media that show graphically torture, rape and murder of women.

What they say about whatever you give energy to or feed can or will manifest itself is true. In Ted Bundy's case he watched pornography and studied with fascination these types of crimes as he fed it and morphed into a very prolific serial killer. The sheer numbers of women he murdered in a relatively short time were many. Before he was caught and electrocuted he had confessed to at least 36 murders. He was active from what they know from 1974 through 1978. Some believe he actually started his crimes prior to that. "Circumstantial evidence suggests that he abducted and killed 8-year-old Ann Marie Burr of Tacoma in 1961 when he was 14, an allegation he denied repeatedly. His earliest documented homicides were committed in 1974 when he was 27 years old. By then he had (by his own admission) mastered the skills needed—in the era before DNA profiling —to leave minimal incriminating evidence at a crime scene." Ted was known to be a peeper and a thief prior to upping the ante to rapist and murderer.

What is said about Ted Bundy in a short version is that he chose to become a monster. The way he lived with a nice guy persona as well as his monster serial killer persona is that he was very able to compartmentalize his behaviors. He would likely tuck the monster away while he was a student at the University of Washington graduating with a degree in Psychology as a 28-year-old. Make no mistake Ted Bundy was a very scary, angry serial killer who bludgeoned his first known victim with a crowbar. He also took a bed rod that had come off the bed during his vicious attack of an eighteen-year-old University student and rammed it into her vagina.

In Ann Rules' book as they were trying to determine who "Ted" was Dr. Richard B. Jarvis, a Seattle psychiatrist specializing in the aberrations of the criminal mind, drew a verbal picture of the man known as "Ted". What follows is his description of the assailant.

"Probably between the ages of twenty-five and thirty-five." Jarvis felt that Ted feared women and their power over him, and that he would also evince at times "socially isolative" behavior. A sexual psychopath according to Dr. Jarvis is not legally insane, and does know the difference between right and wrong. He is driven to attack women. There is no deficiency in intelligence, no brain damage, or frank psychosis. Jarvis saw many parallels between the man they now were looking for and a twenty-four-year-old Seattle man who had been convicted of rape involving other girls. He was designated a sexual psychopath and was currently serving a life term in prison. The man Jarvis referred to had been a star athlete all through school, popular, considerate and respectful of women, but he had changed markedly after his high school girlfriend of longstanding had rejected him. He later married, but began his sexual prowling's after his wife filed for divorce."

It seems that this type of rejection may have been the catalyst for many a serial killer. This was the case for Bundy. The frustration, the lack of self-esteem he had when rejected were a major trauma. He could not deal with the feelings he had. How dare his girlfriend reject him and leave him with feelings of inferiority and loss of any power or control? He would never allow anyone ever to have any power and control over him again. He would always be the one with the power from then on. It was no accident or coincidence that Ted Bundy began killing a short time after his girlfriend Stephanie rejected him.

In early discussions about who "Ted" was Ann Rule and the detectives she knew from writing True Crime stories said "He obviously had to be quite intelligent, attractive, and charming." "He's got to be someone who seems to be above suspicion." "Someone that even people who spend time with him would never connect to "Ted." It is speculated that Ted eventually would want his story told so he kept in contact with Ann Rule writing to her while eventually being caught and while he was incarcerated. Ted was likely an exhibitionist. He ultimately wanted to take credit for his crimes. He appeared to take perverse pleasure in the publicity about him.

In comparing the time frames of the East Area Rapist and then the Original Night Stalker with what he could have been reading about Ted Bundy in the early 1970's I find it interesting. The Original Night Stalker was younger than Ted Bundy and likely was a quick study. I believe he chose to follow in other serial killer's footsteps learning from their mistakes. Ted Bundy achieved notoriety and was arrested in 1976. If you compare timelines with the East Area Rapist, Original Night Stalker there are some interesting similarities in my opinion. EAR started raping in Sacramento in June 1976. Ted Bundy was convicted on his first trial June 30, 1976. His trial had begun in February 1976. Bundy escaped in December 1977. He was rearrested February 15, 1978. His second trial began June 25, 1979 with his second conviction July 30, 1979. He had a third trial which began for yet another murder January 7, 1980 with the third conviction on February 7, 1980. Ann Rules book The Stranger Beside Me was published in 1980 and was about Ted's crimes. Ann personally knew Ted and was as amazed as everyone who knew Ted that he could possibly be so evil.

Anyone who has known the serial killer BTK was also shocked at the two sides to this man. From all reports BTK began killing women in Wichita in 1974. He wanted recognition from the start and began talking to the media and the police immediately. Dennis Rader aka BTK, Serial Killer was not arrested until 2005. Dennis Rader had stopped killing for quite a long time. Because Dennis wanted so badly to be given credit for his crimes he could not let it go. He began contacting law enforcement again in 2004 and because he could not resist the communications and because he was contemplating killing again he got himself caught. Subconsciously he really must have wanted to be infamous much more than he wanted to remain anonymous. BTK named himself because his MO was to Bind, Torture and Kill. Not so unusual for a serial killer. He had not invented anything new.

In biographies' I have seen about Dennis Rader it is amazing to me that a person could be so completely disconnected from "normal" human emotions that as he talked about his crimes he lacked the ability to understand that this was not all about him. He had no idea that he had harmed the victims', their families and society. He had no connection to the idea that what he had done was horrific. He talked about his victims and tried to pretend to empathize or connect somehow. It was one of the strangest things I have ever heard. BTK talked about how he would troll for a victim. After he picked out the person he was interested in he would truly then begin stalking them and then of course he would strike fulfilling his very sick fantasies. His MO included strangling, stabbing and shooting. BTK was one of the first criminals to have his DNA run in the United States. Because investigators did not want to give Dennis a heads up that they were looking at him as "the" suspect they did not ask

Dennis for his DNA. They had his daughter DNA tested to see if she was a part of the family that was related to BTK. This was done by subpoenaing her DNA from a Pap smear medical test she had done at a medical facility. They compared it to semen left at crime scenes. This way the detectives knew they were going after the right guy. BTK's daughter matched a familial match to the semen left at the crime scenes. Detectives had their guy. Dennis Rader was arrested February 26, 2005. Is it possible that he may never have been arrested if he had kept his mouth shut and resisted the temptation to have conversations with the detectives after being silent for so many years? Yes, I think he may never have been caught.

Police in Wichita, Kan., could not ask Dennis Rader for a DNA sample in order to confirm he was a murderer known as BTK. During the interview with Dennis Rader the FBI asked Dennis, "Would you be surprised to know that the father of your daughter is BTK?" "There was a stunning silence," Agent Foulston says. "The FBI agent said, 'Tell us who you are.' And he said, "I'm BTK. You got me.'"

Back to Ted Bundy: Most compelling for me are the dates of publicity, book releases and movie releases about Ted Bundy in relation to the crimes of The Original Night Stalker. Consider this: On August 17, 1980 the book The Stranger Beside Me was published by Ann Rule about Ted Bundy and his crimes. In particular chapter 29 which talks about the Chi Omega murders in Tallahassee Florida. Keith and Patrice Harrington were murdered on

August 19, 1980. I think that by this time ONS was reading any news he could about Ted Bundy. In reports about the crimes at Florida State University Ann Rule talks about the crime: "In the Chi O house itself, room 4, 8 and 9 were littered with the debris left by both the killer and the paramedics, the walls sprayed with droplets of scarlet, the floors and beds full of blood and bits of bark from the death weapon. One of the Officers found a pile of oak logs in the back yard of the sorority house. It appeared that the killer had picked up his weapon on the way in."

News articles about the Chi Omega murders in Florida appeared in newspapers across the country. Is it a coincidence that it was written in articles from reports that a pile of oak logs was in the back of the sorority house and that the killer had picked up his weapon on the way in using a log to bludgeon young women to death and that in the Smith murders the exact same thing occurred? ONS scoped out the house, planned his attacks of the Smith's and then how perfect that the log pile was just outside the master bedroom? Descriptions of some of the murders committed by ONS are very much like what occurred in the murders committed by Ted Bundy. And then also in Chapter 29 of Ann's book the description of how he left one of the victims that he had bludgeoned to death Ann says, "The man who attacked Lisa Levy as she had lain asleep had struck her, strangled her, torn at her like a rabid animal, and then ravished her with a bottle. And then, apparently, he had covered her up and left her lying quietly on her side, the covers pulled up almost tenderly around her shoulders."

In her descriptions of the scenes Ann tells about the horrific injuries suffered by these several young women. Broken Jaws, teeth knocked out, facial bone fractures and cuts. When this story broke it was front page news in the Sacramento Bee and probably all over the country. What strikes me is by the time ONS got to 1986 and his murder of Janelle Cruz he used exactly the same technique when he bludgeoned her. It was complete overkill as he knocked out her teeth and demolished her very lovely face. Janelle's dental records had to be used to confirm her identity. How can one not think that he followed Ted Bundy in committing crimes that were so similar in execution with the exception of the game he played in tying up the victims and in actually raping them in most cases? The way some of the bodies were found was also a signature I am certain. Ted left women lying diagonally on the beds he killed them in, so did ONS in the murder of Janelle Cruz. The murder of Janelle Cruz was text book Ted Bundy. How could one not see the connection?

On May 4, 1986 the movie "The Deliberate Stranger" was on television starring Mark Harmon as Ted Bundy. Is it a coincidence on this Sunday that ONS picked this exact date to stalk and murder Janelle Cruz? Is it because ONS saw this movie that he could not contain his overwhelming urge to again feel what it was like to kill? If this is true and if it is not just a coincidence, then what it tells me is that ONS was near Irvine at the time of the killing. He did not have to drive very far from where he stayed to get to Janelle Cruz's home.

He had to be in the area because Janelle Cruz was killed that same Sunday night. ONS had time to drive over to where he had surveilled this neighborhood five years before. The distance between the Manuela Witthuhn murder and Janelle Cruz was very close – less than two miles. He knew where his target was, he knew the way of escape from this neighborhood and this house. He had scoped it out five years before when checking out the neighborhood that Manuela Witthuhn lived in. This man likely always had a second target in mind in each instance if the first one did not work on the night he planned an attack. The pictures of the access at the end of the street to the path and canal leading away and helping him to escape were already known to ONS. He could not resist the temptation to murder on this particular night. After five years of silence why now? Why this date? Had ONS seen the movie about Ted Bundy and not been able to control his urge to kill this one last time? At least this one last time that we know of?

Was he in his own mind still paying homage to Ted Bundy his larger than life folk hero? He modeled himself into a serial killer that he hoped would make him worthy and then better to the likes of other serial killers. In particular Mr. Ted Bundy was still alive in 1986 although he was locked up in Florida awaiting his execution. Wouldn't it have been interesting to know if ONS tried to send Mr. Bundy mail in 1986 with articles of deeds done by ONS? No he wouldn't have tried that because he was too smart. Perhaps Ted did hear about ONS and his crimes all the way out in California.

Items found in Ted Bundy's car in Utah 1975 –
Ted's "Kit" By Source, Fair use,
https://en.wikipedia.org/w/index.php?curid=25967414

Ted's MO. I have **highlighted in bold the similarities** between Bundy and The Original Night Stalker aka The East Area Rapist.

"Bundy was an **unusually organized and calculating criminal who used his extensive knowledge of law enforcement methodologies to elude identification and capture for years.** His **crime scenes were distributed over large geographic areas; his victim count had risen to at least 20 before it became clear that numerous investigators in widely disparate jurisdictions were hunting the same man.** His assault methods **of choice were blunt trauma** and strangulation, two relatively **silent techniques that could be accomplished** with common household items. **He deliberately avoided firearms due to the noise they made and the ballistic evidence they left behind.** He was a "meticulous researcher" who **explored his surroundings in minute detail,** looking for safe sites to seize and dispose of victims. **He was unusually skilled at minimizing physical evidence. His fingerprints were never found at a crime scene,** nor was any other incontrovertible evidence of his guilt, a fact he repeated often during the years in which he attempted to maintain his innocence."
https://en.wikipedia.org/wiki/Ted_Bundy

This sounds very familiar doesn't it? Differences are that ONS and EAR invaded homes and those were his crime scenes. He controlled them as he learned. The Original Night Stalker changed his criminal behavior as the result of media reports and to try to keep law enforcement guessing. During the time that he was known as the East Area Rapist only news reports stated that he targeted women who were alone. So taking it as a challenge apparently EAR began to target couples. When the Sacramento Bee highlighted on their front page the Chi Omega murders in Florida many believe this spurred the Original Night Stalker to begin murdering his victims to achieve the same notoriety. The Chi Omega murders were committed January 15, 1978 by Ted Bundy who was later convicted and sentenced to die in the electric chair. He was put to death January 24, 1989.

Not much seen pic of serial killer Ted Bundy.

Didn't he look like a nice friendly guy? Ted Bundy

In learning about these cases, and researching, and reading posts and theories, coincidences and farfetched ideas it is amazing but not surprising that one can connect the dots in many, many different directions here. What makes sense to one person is completely ridiculous to another. In my case there are so many incidental connections and small coincidences merely because I lived in Sacramento. I wanted to share this as a side note just to show how connected we are; how small the world really can be when living on the same planet for a length of time.

So here goes. I was born at Mather Air Force Base. My grandmother worked at the Sacramento Army Depot for a time, but her full time career was as a teacher at Ethel Phillips Elementary school and also at Mark Hopkins in Sacramento for over 25 years. She taught mostly the fourth grade, but on occasion had taught the sixth grade. My grandfather worked for the Southern Pacific Railroad out of Roseville California and had lived in Citrus Heights. EAR attacked in Citrus Heights and Rancho Cordova among other places. My grandparents lived across the street from a neighborhood park in Sacramento near Highway 99.

In 1980 my Uncle and Charlene were murdered by ONS formerly The East Area Rapist. An article appeared in Sacramento March 13, 1980 in the Sacramento Bee about how inept the attacker was in some cases. EAR may have seen the article. I would bet that he did. He attacked and murdered The Smith's sometime that night. I listened to how the

261

investigation was going over time and heard about it when Joe Alsip was arrested. I did not believe it could have been someone my uncle knew because of how the scene was and the fact that Charlene had been raped and so on. I mention this again because it seemed like a random act by someone who enjoyed killing. It made sense to me that the guy was a serial killer when this fact was later confirmed. This information did not surprise me. Murders are not always committed by someone the victims knew. Like in the crimes written about in Cold Blood the murders were committed by strangers.

I read the book by Ann Rule about Ted Bundy in 1980 after the Smith murders. I had the book on my shelf at home when my stepfather and mother came over for a visit. This was still in 1980-1981. My stepdad whose name was James saw the book on my shelf and said, "I know Ann Rule, she and I were very good friends. We both attended Washington State University a long time ago." How much of a coincidence is that right? When Ann heard that my stepfather was ill in 2005 she sent him a long letter talking about old times when they gone to college together. It turns out she had a crush on my stepdad that long ago time as they were both finding their way into the criminal justice field.

I told my stepdad what I thought about the Smith murders being random. I said I thought they had been killed because the guy had stalked Charlene. Maybe he had seen Charlene in Sacramento when Lyman Robert and she had gone for a visit at Curtis

Park. Since the perpetrator was known to stalk victims who lived adjacent to a neighborhood park near avenues of escape like the highway he could very well have seen Lyman and Charlene at my grandparents' house anytime between 1973 and 1980.

Speculation, coincidence? Or farfetched theory? If there was a Sacramento connection, I would not be surprised if this could have been one. Or... there was a real estate connection as Lyman had been in Sacramento the week before his murder looking for or meeting with potential investors for a new project. There are avenues to follow in investigating this particular idea. At least it should be looked into.

One of the men in Lyman Robert's address book that he had when he died coincidentally worked with us at 555 Capitol Mall in Sacramento as well as lived off Salmon Falls Road right off of Highway 50 in Folsom during 1977-1980 while I was also there. The man who ran the computer company and was my boss in 1977 at Capitol Mall also knew Buzz Oates who was a developer in Sacramento. My boss also had a building company putting up houses in the Folsom area 1976-1981 and he lived off Salmon Falls Road in Folsom.

There are many more coincidences that occurred because we are all in the end connected in some way and it is a small world.

Bits and pieces taken from a letter written by Ann Rule to my stepfather James (Jim) in 2005 when he was extremely ill. The letter was 8 pages long, and Ann in typical form told Jim stories and recollections from when they were in college together. I did not include the entire thing of course for privacy reasons.

ᗩNN Rule

View   auᴛhor/lecᴛurer

January 22, 2005

Hi Jim,

I've heard from Betty May Crites-Settecase and Hugh Nelson that you are facing more health challenges, and I am so sorry to hear that. I'm coming down to Salem in about the third week of February to visit Betty May, and we have plans to come and visit you if that's o.k. She told me that you live in West Salem now. I remember when I was talking in McMinnville about ten years ago that you were living in Amity--if I remember correctly. And we had a short time to visit then. I hear from some of the old Willamette crowd once in a while, and it doesn't seem possible

I cut to the end of the letter next page.

Jim, I want you to know that I am thinking of you, and I never forgot about you. I'm sure your wife won't mind now that we are both so old! Betty May and I will call you up when I'm heading down to Salem and see if it's o.k. for us to come and visit. We both look just a little bit older than we did in 1951. It's funny how that happens. And both Betty May and I have arthritis so that we can tell what the weather is going to be before the weatherman knows. Sigh.

I'm pulling for you and hoping you will beat the illnesses that have you down--but not out. I used to think it was dumb when

I cut to the end of the letter here.

Love,

Ann Rule

P.S. I am enclosing one of my "show-off" cards with my Willamette
Ph.D. on it. :*)

AUTHOR
P.O. Box 98846
Seattle, WA 98198
email: AnnieR37@aol.com
Webpage: www.annrules.com
206-246-0811
FAX 206-241-5542

Ann had an honorary PhD from Willamette she included for Jim to see. The letter came in January 2005. My stepdad passed away less than two months later from a brain tumor.

Chapter Nine

Timeline – Sacramento attacks

What follows is a timeline for EAR and then the Original Night Stalker

East Area Rapist attacks begin Rancho Cordova, California

June 18, 1976   Rancho Cordova

July 17, 1976   Carmichael

August 29, 1976 Rancho Cordova

September 4/5 1976 Rancho Cordova

October 5, 1976 Citrus Heights

October 9, 1976 Rancho Cordova

October 18, 1976 – two rapes one in Carmichael one in Rancho Cordova on the same night

November 10, 1976 Citrus Heights

December 18, 1976 Fair Oaks

There were 20 attacks in 1977 in and around Sacramento.

There were 14 attacks in 1978. Only two appear to have been in the Sacramento area while the other attacks were in Stockton, Modesto, Davis, Concord, San Ramon, San Jose and Danville, California.

In 1979 there were 7 attacks – only one in Rancho Cordova, California while the other six occurred in Walnut Creek, Danville, Fremont and then Goleta. All of the attacks were rapes and assaults. Obviously the EAR suspect had become more mobile. What was going on in his life that he began to travel outside his known hunting grounds? If he was 18-30 (It is my belief, he was about 21 when the attacks began) he was now older and possibly transferred to a University in Southern California. I am aware that this is more speculation on my part, but it seems logical that this could be a reason for the change in areas.

Many have considered the possibility that this man worked in construction and this could be the reason for his mobility. I do not wholly agree. His hands were many times described as soft or not calloused. I suppose it is possible that he was working part time in this endeavor, but he was not seriously working full time in any career yet in my opinion. I think either he or a sibling (his brother) possibly moved to a University in Southern California and so he was able to move about freely in the night time. This enabled him to have time to stalk his victims. If he wasn't in school, it is my belief that he or they had a relative who lived in Southern California.

Also I think that a real estate connection can be made based on his MO and his interest in homes that were for sale. I think he had access to real estate listings and knew which homes were occupied as well as more information that real estate agents would know if they were to show a house. They had the ability to know who might be staying in the home or if it was empty, what hours to show the home, when there might be an open house and a number of other details about the property. I think he either worked for a real estate firm or possibly was the child of someone who either worked for a real estate company in the late 60's and 70's or possibly his parents were brokers and owned a real estate agency. There are lots of theories.

Rather than discuss all of the attacks in Sacramento, and because there were so many there are three areas that stand out in my mind because of where I was and when. First are the attacks off Sandbar and in East Sacramento near Paradise Beach. In the summers of 1977 and 1978 I would drive there to hang out with friends and strangers alike. I could drive up in the summer at almost any time of day and there would be a volleyball game going on. Young people the same age I was were there enjoying the day. I am certain the neighbors were really tired of all of the cars parked there in the neighborhood, but it was not a deterrent to any of us. I was 20 and 21 those two summers. I have an old friend that that I still speak to as an adult who was one of those on the beach with a volley ball back then. I recently asked him, "Hey do you remember when we went to the beach in Sacramento? What was the name of that park?" He said the words at the same moment I remembered it. It was Paradise Park off Carlson Drive. There were four attacks off Del Dayo in 1976 and 1977. The East Area Rapist struck July 17, 1976 (attack #2) Very early on in his game. He also attacked on October 18, 1976 Del Dayo attack number 7 and 8.

There was attack number 21 on May 17, 1977 as well. I would imagine that it is entirely possible that this young man could have hung out with us in Paradise Park those two summers. Perhaps his car was among those that were towed from the streets. I am not kidding myself, I am certain this man had many different vehicles with many different license plates if he in fact ever actually drove a car there. He could have ridden his bicycle to the park as well. Bottom line he knew the neighborhood well. These are the attacks and these are the neighborhoods that I cannot shake from my mind.

The second area that I think about frequently is the one off Seamas Avenue. As I have mentioned previously I lived in this neighborhood in 1977 and 1978. My apartment is on a corner along a row of apartments. Mine, a smaller complex only had about 6 to 8 apartments in them. My small one bedroom was on the corner bottom floor and a woman lived above me. I was right next to the managers live in apartment. We were right on the corner of Riverside and Weber facing the residential street. My kitchen window faced out onto Riverside Blvd. The bedroom also had a window on the Riverside Blvd. side. I would sit in the yard sometimes on a blanket under the shade tree relaxing on my day off. The attack off Seamas/Piedmont on Casilada was only about 4 blocks away.

April 16, 1978 **ARTICLE**

East Rapist Kicks In Door, Attacks Sitter In South Area

The east area rapist is believed to have struck again — this time, his 33rd, in the South Area within the city limits.

The attack took place about 10 Friday night in the general vicinity of Seamas and Riverside Avenues and the victim was a 15-year-old babysitter.

According to sheriff's spokesman Bill Miller, she was looking after an 8-year-old when the rapist kicked in a rear door, attacked the girl once inside the house, then took her into the back yard and raped her again.

The second attack was interrupted, according to Miller, when the girl's parents arrived at the house to check on her safety. The man fled, Miller said, when they drove up.

Miller said the 8-year-old was in a bedroom all the time and never saw the rapist.

The victim herself, Miller said, was so shaken by the incident that she was unable to give a very good description of her assailant, but "there were several M.O. (method of operation) fac-

See Back Page A20, Col. 5

The East Area Rapist is believed to have struck again – this time, his 33rd, in the South Area within the city limits.

The attack took place about 10 Friday night in the general vicinity of Seamas and Riverside Avenues and the victim was a 15-year-old babysitter.

According to sheriff's spokesman Bill Miller, she was looking after an 8-year-old when the rapist kicked in a rear door, attacked the girl once inside the house, then took her into the back yard and raped her again.

The second attack was interrupted, according to Miller when the girl's parents arrived at the house to check on her safety. The man fled, Miller said, when they drove up.

Miller said the 8 year old was in a bedroom all the time and never saw the rapist.

The victim herself, Miller said, was so shaken by the incident that she was unable to give a very good description of her assailant, but "there were several M.O. (method of operation) factors similar to those of the east area rapist.

Miller said the rapist wore gloves and had his head covered "but the girl was unable to give a good description of his ski mask." She thought he carried a gun, Miller said, but wasn't sure.

The east area rapist got the name because most of his 32 confirmed victims live in the vicinity of Carmichael, Fair Oaks and Rancho Cordova. Before Friday, his last attack was on March 28 in Rancho Cordova. He has also struck twice in Stockton.

If this proves to be by the same suspect, Miller said, it will be the first time he is known to have surfaced in the Riverside - South Land Park neighborhood.

According to Miller, the girl's parents arrived and frightened off the rapist because the people who had hired the teenager had not been able to contact her by phone.

The mother of the 8-year-old, Miller said, called the girl's house when she failed to get an answer, thinking the sitter, who lived nearby, had gone home.

The girl's parents subsequently tried to call, Miller said, only to have her answer "Hello" and immediately hang up.

The worried parents hurried to where their daughter was, arriving about 10:30 p.m., Miller said. "That's how we know the attacker was on the premises for only about a half hour." Miller said.

The girl told officers that the rapist allowed her to answer when her parents phoned, then made her hang up immediately. It was then, according to the girl, that she was ordered into the backyard and again sexually assaulted.

The teenager was interrogated Friday night and again Saturday in the hopes that time would allow her to give officers a better description of her attacker. **END OF ARTICLE** tors similar to those of the east area rapist."

Miller said the rapist wore gloves and had his head covered "but the girl was unable to give us a good description of his ski mask." She thought he carried a gun, Miller said, but wasn't sure.

The east area rapist got that name because most of his 32 confirmed victims live in the vicinity of Carmichael, Fair Oaks and Rancho Cordova. Before Friday, his last attack was on March 28 in Rancho Cordova. He has also struck twice in Stockton.

If this proves to be by the same suspect, Miller said, it will be the first time he is known to have surfaced in the Riverside-South Land Park neighborhood.

According to Miller, the girl's parents arrived and frightened off the rapist because the people who had hired the teen-ager had not been able to contact her by phone.

The mother of the 8-year-old, Miller said, called the girl's house when she failed to get an answer, thinking the sitter, who lived nearby, had gone home.

The girl's parents subsequently tried to call, Miller said, only to have her answer "Hello" and immediately hang up.

The worried parents hurried to where their daughter was, arriving about 10:30 p.m., Miller said. "That's how we know the attacker was on the premises for only about a half-hour," Miller said.

The girl told officers that the rapist allowed her to answer when her parents phoned, then made her hang up immediately. It was then, according to the girl, that she was ordered into the back yard and again sexually assaulted.

The teen-ager was interrogated Friday night and again Saturday in the hopes that time would allow her to give officers a better description of her attacker.

Second page of the **article typed previous page**

I was working downtown now on Capitol Mall. This was my first real job. There were victims EAR chose that worked downtown near Capitol Mall. As time went by there were weird things that happened in our apartments off Riverside Blvd. In 1978 during the correct timeline of the attacks off of Riverside someone had come into my apartment, and the woman upstairs apartment having gone through our underwear drawers. Nothing seemed disturbed except for the fact that it was obvious that someone had been in our bedrooms and had rifled through our underwear drawers. This creepy fact happened during the correct time frame when EAR attacked off Seamas and Piedmont.

My friend Melanie, who would eventually marry Bill Harvey the newsman from KCRA, lived in the apartment above me. She and I suspected it was the manager of the apartments. We thought he might have used his key to get in and into our underwear drawers or was it someone else? We will never know. The man who was the manager of the apartments at the time was in Law school at McGeorge. Not long after the underwear incident in 1978 in 1979 I moved to West Sacramento and became roommates with Melanie the woman that had lived upstairs on Riverside. We are still friends to this day.

The third is the attack on 4th Parkway which was not far from the home I grew up in near Steiner Drive. This attack was in my old neighborhood for all intents and purposes – it is .5 a mile from my house. This is why it stays on my mind. This neighborhood if in fact it is the rapists' neighborhood of origin is perfect in terms of the geography. He is extremely comfortable being in a neighborhood with a creek bed, neighborhood park and schools. This is a neighborhood he knows intimately and because he attacked so close to home must have been very exciting to him. The fact that he may have known the couple prior to their moving to 4th Parkway made it even better. According to Detective Richard Shelby, the couple of Fourth Parkway (Cindy and

Fred) was a top level supervisor at a water treatment plant for Sacramento. The attack prior to South Sacramento was the one off Sandbar Circle near Paradise Park.

Rather than repeat and reflect on the rape reports one by one in Sacramento, and because there were so many from 1976 until 1979 in several counties, **I have included the information from just a few articles from local news of the time.** It is my intent to familiarize those who may not know the style of EAR or ONS, and his MO by telling about some of the attacks. The first several months of the attacks were not reported in the media; they were essentially blacked out. I can surmise that they did not want to panic the public and then there is another reason which could be partially true. Back in the 1970's rapes were not yet seen as the serious crime that they are today. The penalties were more of a minor offense and sometimes the leads were not followed as intently or as voraciously as other crimes of the time.

Unknown to everyone at the time these crimes were committed is that it is common for peepers to turn into rapists and many times serial rapists turn into serial killers.

Lurker Shoots Youth

A prowler shot and seriously wounded an 18-year-old youth who was chasing him in a residential neighborhood in east Sacramento at 10:30 o'clock last night.

Rodney Richard ████████, who lives on Ripon Court, was in critical condition when he was admitted to Sutter Memorial Hospital. He was shot in the abdomen.

A hospital aide today advised Detective Jay Pane that the youth emerged from surgery in a stable and alert condition.

The prowler, described only as male, white and long-haired, escaped despite a police cordon on the neighborhood.

The neighborhood is near the Glenbrook District. Detectives are considering the possibility the prowler might have been the east area rapist who has sexually assaulted 15 women in 18 months, including one last Jan. 19 in the Glenbrook area.

The youth's father, Raymond, told investigators his son just had entered the house from the garage when they heard a noise in the back yard. Miller said he and Rodney went into the yard and saw the figure of a man in shadows.

The father said the man ran, and he and his son chased him across the street.

Crimes
276

Crimes of the East Area Rapist – I have only included a small portion of articles as examples of EAR's MO.

February 17, 1977 **ARTICLE**

A prowler shot and seriously wounded a 15-year-old youth who was chasing him in a residential neighborhood in east Sacramento at 10:30 o'clock last night.

Rodney Richard (Blank) who lives on Ripon Court was in critical condition when he was admitted to Sutter Memorial Hospital. He was shot in the abdomen.

A hospital aide today advised Detective Jay Pane that the youth emerged from surgery in a stable and alert condition.

The prowler, described only as male, white and long haired, escaped despite a police cordon on the neighborhood.

The neighborhood is near the Glenbrook District. Detectives are considering the possibility the prowler might have been the east area rapist who has sexually assaulted 15 women in 16 months including one last Jan. 19 in the Glenbrook area.

The youth's father, Raymond told investigators his son just had entered the house from the garage when they heard a noise in the back yard. Miller said he and Rodney went into the yard and saw the figure of a man in shadows.

The father said the man ran, and he and his son chased him across the street. **END OF ARTICLE**

November 6, 1977

East Area Rapist Attacks Girl, 13

The East Area rapist broke into a Sacramento condominium early today, raping a 13-year-old girl after he awakened and tied up her mother.

The 27th attack in 17 months occurred on La Riviera Drive near Watt Avenue in the College Greens section of the city about 3 a.m., said sheriff's Chief Deputy Fred Reese.

The rapist spent about two hours in the home, raping the girl, then fondling her as she sat tied in a chair.

He entered the condominium by forcing open a sliding glass door, Reese said.

Once inside, the rapist awakened the mother, tied her in her bed, placed china on her back and said if he heard the dishes rattle, he would cut off the daughter's fingers, police said. The rapist then led the 13-year-old into another room and attacked her.

After the ski-masked, armed man left the home, the girl and the woman screamed until neighbors heard them. A neighbor then followed the screams into the home and untied the two victims. She was the youngest victim in the terrifying series of attacks, police said. In his last 10 rapes, he has victimized sleeping couples in cases where he has tied the men in bed, then led the women to other parts of the homes for sexual assaults.

The East Area rapist last struck Oct. 29 north of Whitney Avenue.

After this morning's attack was reported about 5 a.m., sheriff's deputies took into custody a possible suspect in an El Camino Avenue restaurant. The man was questioned, taken to the scene of the rape and held in custody about two hours before he was released.

City police simultaneously

See Back Page, A26, Col. 5

Crosses mark the sites of the East Area rapist's attacks.

Rapist

Continued From Page A1

11/6/77

broadcast a description of a suspicious car that had been spotted in the area at the time of the rape. The car was described as a 1966 blue Chevrolet with Arizona license plates.

The rapist has struck 25 times in the East and North Areas of Sacramento County, once in the South Area and once in Stockton since his first rape was reported June 18, 1976.

He has been the subject of the most intensive manhunt in the county's history, police have said. Detectives have checked out in one fashion or another more than 5,000 men reported as possible suspects. Still, they have no idea of whom they are looking for or what kind of man he really is, detectives say.

The rapist was described in the spring as a man in a "homosexual panic" caused by feelings of sexual inadequacy attributed to his having a small penis. After talking to several more victims, however, sheriff's deputies Tuesday revised the sexual description of the rapist to say he has an average size penis, neither abnormally small nor large.

His strikes are punctuated by silence in what sheriff's Detective Carol Daly has described as "mental torture on the victims, not just physical attacks."

"His big thing is being master over their minds once he gets them tied up," she said. "That's his big trip."

279

The East Area Rapist broke into a Sacramento Condominium early today, raping a 13-year-old girl after he awakened and tied up her mother. The 27th attack in 17 months occurred on La Riviera Drive near Watt Avenue in the College Greens section of the city about 3:00 a.m. said Sheriffs Chief Deputy Fred Reese.

The rapist spent about two hours in the home, raping the girl, then fondling her as she sat tied in a chair. He entered the condominium by forcing open a sliding glass door Reese said.

Once inside, the rapist awakened the mother, tied her in her bed, placed china on her back and said if he heard the dishes rattle, he would cut off the daughter's fingers, police said. The rapist then led the 13-year-old into another room and attacked her.

After the ski masked, armed man left the home, the girl and the woman screamed until neighbors heard them. A neighbor then followed the screams into the home and untied the two victims. She was the youngest victim in the terrifying series of attacks, police said. In his last 10 rapes, he has victimized sleeping couples in cases where he has tied the men in bed, then led the women to other parts of the home for sexual assaults.

The East Area Rapist last struck October 29 north of Whitney Avenue. After this morning's attack was reported at 5:00 a.m. sheriff's deputies took into custody a possible suspect in an El Camino Avenue restaurant. The man was questioned, taken to the scene of the rape and held in custody about two hours before he was released. City police simultaneously broadcast a description of a suspicious car that had been spotted in the area at the time of the rape. The car was described as a 1966 blue Chevrolet with Arizona license plates.

The rapist has struck 25 times in the East and North Area of Sacramento County, once in the South Area and once in Stockton since his first rape was reported June 18, 1976. He has been the subject of the most intensive manhunt in the County's history police have said.

Detectives have checked out in one fashion or another more than 5000 men reported as possible suspects. Still they have no idea of whom they are looking for or what kind of man he really is, detectives say.

The rapist was described in the spring as a man in a "homosexual panic" caused by feelings of sexual inadequacy attributed to his having a small penis. After talking to several more victims however, sheriff's deputies Tuesday revised the sexual description of the rapist to say he has an average size penis neither abnormally small nor large.

His strikes are punctuated by silence in what sheriff's Detective Carol Daly has described as mental torture on the victims, not just physical attacks. His big thing is being master over their minds once he gets them tied up she said. "That's his big trip." **END OF ARTICLE**

Masked Bike Rider Eludes Police

A bicycle-riding man wearing a ski mask eluded police in the East Area early Sunday.

First spotted by sheriff's deputies on the Watt Avenue bridge at 2:30 a.m., the bike rider was wearing a ski hood which covered his head and had an opening for his face. Deputies lost sight of the man but he reportedly was spotted again two hours later by city patrolmen near an apartment complex on La Riviera Drive near Watt.

He left the bicycle there. Officers said it was listed as stolen in Redding.

The East Area rapist, who reportedly wears a mask during his attacks, has struck three times in the area of La Riviera Drive and Watt. However, officers said later Sunday that the bike rider probably was not the rapist.

December 12, 1977 – then there is this small article – sounded like it was him, looked like it was him – why were the sheriff's deputies not able to stop this guy and at least question him? The last line of the article makes me just shake my head because this could have been the end of the East Area Rapists reign of terror.

In Brief – Masked Bike Rider Eludes Police ARTICLE

A bicycle riding man wearing a ski mask eluded police in the East area early Sunday.

First spotted by sheriff's deputies on the Watt Avenue Bridge at 2:30 a.m. the bike rider was wearing a ski hood which covered his head and had an opening for his face. Deputies lost sight of the man but he reportedly was spotted again two hours later by city patrolmen near an apartment complex on La Riviera Drive near Watt.

He left the bicycle there. Officers said it was listed as stolen in Redding.

The East Area rapist, who reportedly wears a mask during his attacks, has struck three times in the area of La Riviera Drive and Watt. However, officers said later Sunday that the bike rider **probably was not the rapist. END OF ARTICLE**

My opinion and possibly many others would think that it PROBABLY WAS the rapist.

Chapter Ten
Murders in Rancho Cordova, California
February 2, 1978

Maggiore Murders Rancho Cordova – article with composites

2 Suspected In Slayings

The slayings of an Air Force sergeant and his wife, who were gunned down in the back yard of a Rancho Cordova home Feb. 2, may have been committed by two young men, a spokesman for the sheriff's department said today.

Along with the announcement, composite sketches of the two suspects, made from neighbors' descriptions, were released.

Sgt. Brian Maggiore, 21, and his wife, Katie, 20, were accosted while walking their dog and shot to death at the rear of a home on La Gloria Drive in Rancho Cordova.

William Miller, assistant to the sheriff, said two young men were seen on La Gloria minutes

before the shooting. One was wearing a brown leather-type jacket, gathered at the waist with a zippered front, small collar and dark stain on the back. He was also wearing brown pointed boots. The other man was wearing a dark jacket, zippered in front with slash pockets, dark pants and black shoes or boots. He was also wearing brown leather gloves, Miller said.

Slaying suspects

The composite on the left looks like the young man who chased me in 1971

I have mentioned previously – is it possible that two people are responsible for all of the crimes of EAR and ONS? Could it be possible an older brother brought his younger brother along in the beginning prior to the Southern California attacks? There has been plenty of speculation to go around. The article on the previous page states the following:

284

The slayings of an Air Force Sergeant and his wife, who were gunned down in the backyard of a Rancho Cordova home February 2, may have been committed by two young men, a spokesman for the sheriff's department said today.

Along with the announcement composite sketches of the two suspects, made from a neighbor's description, were released.

Sgt. Brian Maggiore, 21, and his wife Katie, 20 were accosted while walking their dog and shot to death at the rear of a home on La Gloria Drive in Rancho Cordova.

William Miller, assistant to the sheriff, said two young men were seen on La Gloria minutes before the shooting. One was wearing a brown leather type jacket gathered at the waist with a zippered front, small collar and dark stain on the back. He was also wearing brown pointed boots. The other man was wearing a dark jacket, zippered in front with slash pockets, dark pants and black shoes or boots. He was also wearing brown leather gloves, Miller said. **END OF ARTICLE**

Officers Return To Murder Scene Hunting For Clues

In an effort to find the killers of a young Rancho Cordova couple, the Sacramento Sheriff's department returned to the scene of the crime

Reno Train Trip Rescheduled

The local Mental Health Association's weekend train excursion to Reno, postponed last month, has been rescheduled for March 31, the group announced.

The $35 "Fun Trip to Reno" includes round trip train fare, lodgings and some meals. An association spokesman said the fare is tax deductible as a contribution.

Thursday night, hoping to develop new leads:

Sgt. Brian Maggiore, 21, and his wife Katie, 20, were shot to death six weeks ago as they walked their dog in Rancho Cordova. A dozen investigators went door to door Thursday night, talking to residents on La Gloria and La Alegria Drives about what they might have seen the night of the murders.

Maggiore was found shot in the chest in the backyard at 10165 La Alegria Drive. His wife was found a short distance away with a head wound.

The Bee's Secret Witness program is offering a $2,500 reward for information leading to the arrest and conviction of the killers.

March 17, 1978 **ARTICLE**

In an effort to find the killers of a young Rancho Cordova couple, the Sacramento Sheriff's Department returned to the scene of the crime Thursday night, hoping to develop new leads:

Sgt. Brian Maggiore, 21 and his wife Katie, 20 were shot to death six weeks ago as they walked their dog in Rancho Cordova. A dozen investigators went door to door Thursday night, talking to residents on La Gloria and La Algeria Drives about what they might have seen the night of the murders.

Maggiore was found shot in the chest in the backyard at 10165 La Alegria Drive. His wife was found a short distance away with a head wound.

The Bee's Secret Witness program is offering a $2,500.00 reward for information leading to the arrest and conviction of the killers. **END OF ARTICLE**

(Because this is a very old article of course Secret Witness is no longer offering the money shown in the article) The **article does say killers. Plural.**

Deputies Report No Leads In Rancho Cordova Killings

Sacramento County homicide investigators Friday said they had no leads or suspects in the gunshot deaths of a young Rancho Cordova Air Force sergeant and his wife.

Brian K. Maggiore, 21, and Katie Maggiore, 20, were gunned down Thursday night by a man who apparently confronted them as they walked their dog along a quiet residential street.

Authorities said Maggiore and his wife of less than two years then fled into the backyard of a home on La Alegria Drive where the killer followed and shot them.

The suspect, spotted by area residents as he fled the scene of the shooting, was described as white, in his mid 20s, 6-feet to 6-feet-2-inches tall, slight of build, with dark hair and wearing a brown leather coat with a large stain on the back and dark pants and shoes.

The Maggiores were married in July 1976.

Maggiore was a 1974 graduate of Fresno High School. He joined the Air Force after graduation and served in Texas, Mississippi and Alaska before his assignment to Mather Air Force Base.

Mrs. Maggiore was graduated from McLane High School in 1976.

Maggiore is survived by his parents, Mr. and Mrs. James Maggiore of Fresno; brothers Michael of San Jose and Steven of Fresno; a sister, Cynthia of Fresno; and his grandparents, Mr. and Mrs. Alex Sommers, of Fresno.

Mrs. Maggiore is survived by her parents, Mr. and Mrs. Kenneth L. Smith, of Clovis; brothers Kenneth and Keith, both of Clovis; and her grandparents, Mr. and Mrs. Herman Klomp of Pinedale and Mrs. Pearl Smith of Clovis.

Funeral arrangements were pending.

ARTICLE February 1978

Sacramento County homicide investigators Friday said they had no leads or suspects in the gunshot deaths of a young Rancho Cordova Air Force sergeant and his wife.

Brian K. Maggiore, 21, and Katie Maggiore, 20, were gunned down Thursday night by a man who apparently confronted them as they walked their dog along a quiet residential street.

288

Authorities said Maggiore and his wife of less than two years then fled into the backyard of a home on La Alegria Drive where the killer followed and shot them.

The suspect, spotted by area residents as he fled the scene of the shooting, was described as white, in his mid-20's, 6 feet 2 inches tall, slight of build with dark hair and wearing a brown leather coat with a large stain on the back and dark pants and shoes.

The Maggiores were married in July 1976.

Maggiore was a 1974 graduate of Fresno High School. He joined the Air Force after graduation and served in Texas, Mississippi, and Alaska before his assignment to Mather Airforce Base.

Mrs. Maggiore was graduated from McLane High School in 1976.

Maggiore is survived by his parents, Mr. and Mrs. James Maggiore of Fresno; brothers Michael of San Jose, and Steven of Fresno; a sister Cynthia, of Fresno; his grandparents, Mr. and Mrs. Alex Summers of Fresno.

Mrs. Maggiore is survived by her parents, Mr. and Mrs. Kenneth L. Smith of Clovis; brothers Kenneth and Keith, both of Clovis; and her grandparents, Mr. and Mrs. Herman Klomp of Pinedale and Mrs. Pearl Smith of Clovis.

Funeral arrangements were pending.

END OF ARTICLE

February 19, 1978 Incident in South Sacramento – Is this the same guy who after murdering the Maggiore's decided to rob someone a couple of weeks later? Same physical description as EAR. Hard to imagine because it is not his MO, but the frantic escape at all costs is. I had to include this as a possibility. There is much speculation to this story. I felt it necessary to consider this crime as a possibility that this was EAR.

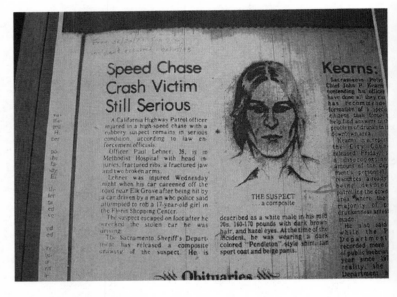

Article February 20, 1978

Speed Chase Crash Victim Still Serious

A California Highway Patrol officer injured in a high speed chase with a robbery suspect remains in serious condition, according to law enforcement officials.

Office Paul Lehner, 39, is in Methodist Hospital with head injuries, fractured ribs, a fractured jaw and two broken arms.

Lehner was injured Wednesday night when his car careened off the road near Elk Grove after being hit by a car driven by a man who police said attempted to rob a 17-year-old girl in the Florin Shopping Center.

The suspect escaped on foot after he wrecked the stolen car he was driving.

The Sacramento Sheriff's Department has released a composite drawing of the suspect. He is described as a white male in his mid-20's. 160-170 pounds with dark brown hair and hazel eyes. At the time of the incident, he was wearing a dark colored "Pendleton" style shirt, tan sport coat and beige pants. **END OF ARTICLE**

I have one question about this report. Was this criminal really attempting to rob this 17-year-old girl or was he actually attempting to abduct her? It would be interesting to find out what the actual crime report says from Officer Lehner.

The description of what the suspect was wearing in this article – the dark colored Pendleton shirt sounds very much like the description given of the man seen running from attack number 32 at Seamas and Piedmont in April 1978. It was stated he was wearing a "blue plaid flannel shirt and a windbreaker. It also stated he had a mustache.

Rapist
Continued From Page A1

room, the rapist awakened them, threatening them with a weapon. As in earlier attacks, he carried a knife and a gun.

According to Sgt. Bob Grude, the rapist tied the husband before sexually assaulting the wife.

The intruder spent about two hours in the house, ransacking it before leaving. Grude said that the rapist took items belonging to the couple but declined to specify what was taken.

Investigators said they are positive this is the same man who struck last Sept. 26, sexually assaulting a 27-year-old North Stockton housewife,

and who, on Jan. 28 in Sacramento, raped two teen-age girls in their home near American River College.

Grude said the rapist's method of operation was a "carbon copy" of earlier attacks. The assailant wore a ski mask and gloves and carried a knife, gun and flashlight.

No children or pets were in the home when the rapist struck.

The Stockton assault marked the 11th time the east area rapist has attacked married couples, each time tying the husband in bed before sexually assaulting the wife.

3/19/78

ARTICLE East Rapist in Stockton – March 1978 (Victim #31)

The east area rapist has struck for a second time in Stockton, attacking a woman in her early 20's after awakening her and her husband in bed, the Stockton Police Department reported Saturday.

In the last 22 months, the rapist has victimized 29 women and girls in Sacramento County in addition to the two in Stockton.

Stockton Police Investigators said the man entered the single-family residence in the Parkwood's neighborhood at about 11 p.m. Friday through a back door with a broken lock.

After entering the couple's bedroom, the rapist awakened them, threatening them with a weapon. As in earlier attacks, he carried a knife and gun.

According to Sgt. Bob Grude, the rapist tied the husband before sexually assaulting the wife.

The intruder spent about two hours in the house, ransacking it before leaving. Grude said that the rapist took items belonging to the couple but declined to specify what was taken.

Investigators said they are positive this is the same man who struck last Sept. 26, sexually assaulting a 27-year-old North Stockton housewife, and who, on Jan. 28 in Sacramento raped two teen age girls in their home near American River College.

Grude said the rapist's method of operation was a "carbon copy" of earlier attacks. The assailant wore a ski mask and gloves and carried a knife, gun and flashlight.

No children or pets were in the home when the rapist struck.

The Stockton assault marked the 11th time the east area rapist has attacked married couples, each time tying the husband in bed before sexually assaulting the wife. **END OF ARTICLE**

Chapter Eleven

Composites, Profiles, Descriptions, Possible Evidence

Witness Aids Police Artists With Description Of Killer

A new witness has provided Sacramento Sheriff's Department artists with a better description of one of two suspects in the Feb. 22 killing of a young Rancho Cordova couple.

The witness worked with the artist to improve on a sketch of one of the men detectives believe shot Sgt. Brian Maggiore, 21, and his wife, Katie, 20, while they walked their dog in the vicinity of La Gloria and La Alegria drives.

The witness said the man wore a brown, waist-length jacket with an orange dragon embroidered on the left front pocket.

The suspect is described as white, in his early twenties, six feet tall, with a slender build and brown hair.

Another white man, 21 to 23 years old, 5 feet 10 inches tall with a neatly trimmed mustache was observed running away from the crime scene and is also wanted by detectives in the murder.

NEW DESCRIPTION from a witness   FIRST SUSPECT search still on

April 16, 1978 Sacramento Bee ARTICLE – Witness Aids Police Artists With Description of Killer – this article is about the two suspects

A new witness has provided Sacramento Sheriff's Department with a better description of one of the two suspects in the February 2nd, killing of a young Rancho Cordova couple.

The witness worked with the artist to improve on a sketch of one of the men detectives believe shot Sgt. Brian Maggiore, 21, and his wife Katie, 20, while they walked their dog in the vicinity of La Gloria and La Alegria drives.

The witness said the man wore a brown, waist length jacket with an orange dragon embroidered on the left front pocket.

The suspect is described as white, in his early twenties, six feet tall with a slender build and brown hair.

294

Another white man, 21 to 22 years old, 5 feet 10 inches tall with a neatly trimmed mustache was observed running away from the crime scene and is also wanted by detectives in the murder.

END OF ARTICLE

After this article came out EAR left Sacramento to commit attacks elsewhere – the new composites must have been unnerving to him. They must have looked enough like him to make him leave the area because he did go and did not return to Sacramento to commit his attacks.

The masked rapist composite

Possible evidence from papers found near the scene
of an attack

Trails, Buildings, a Lake. This looks like a rough map of a planned community. These notebook pages were collected at the scene of a rape in Danville, in Contra Costa County in December 1978.

Shoe prints and two independent bloodhounds established his exit route, a trail that led from a victim's house to some nearby railroad tracks. Where the trail stopped abruptly was where investigators believe the rapist got into a vehicle. It is believed he dropped the papers unintentionally when opening a car door. The papers found were on college rule paper with three-hole punch from a notebook. Were there any fingerprints on any of these pages? I am certain they must have been tested for that.

Essay supposedly written by EAR – this could be a false piece of evidence left to misdirect police. But, on the other hand maybe it is authentic and EAR made a mistake in leaving this behind. The next pages tell you what this says clearly:

Mad is the word, the word that reminds me of 6th grade. I hated that year.

I wish I had known what was going to be going to be during my 6th grade year, the last and worst year of elementary school. Mad is the word that happens in my head about to my 6th grade year as a 6th grader. My madness was one that was caused by disappointments that hurt me very much. Disappointment from my teacher, such as field trips that were planned, then canceled. My 6th grade teacher gave me a lot of disappointment which made me very mad and made me be at a state of hatel in my heart, no one ever let me down that hard befor and I never hated anyone as much as I did him. Disappointment wasn't the only reason that made me mad in my 6th grade class, another was getting in trouble at school especially talking that's what really bugged me was writing sentences, those awful sentence that my teacher made me write, hours and hours I'd sit and write 50 - 100 - 150 sentance day and night I write those dreadful paragraphs which embarrased me and more important it made me ashamed of myself which in turn, deepdown in side made me realye that writing sentance wasn't fair it wasn't fair to make me suffer like that, it just wasn't fair to make me sit and write until my bones ached, until my hand felt every horrid pain if ever had and as I wrote, I got madder and madder, until I cried, I cried because I was ashamed I cried because I was discoted, I cried because I was mad, and I cried for myself, kid who kept on having to write those dreadful sentances. My angyness from sixth grade will soar my memory for life and I will be ashamed for my sixth grade year forever

It is thought the East Area Rapist dropped this out of the car he was driving away from the scene. The essay talks about how angry he was when his sixth grade teacher made him write the same thing over and over again until his hand hurt. He talks about how disappointed he was in the sixth grade by this particular teacher.

Misspelled words are from the original author and were copied as written.

"Mad is the word. The word that reminds me of 6th grade. I hated that year. I wish I had known what was going to be going on during my 6th grade year, the last and worst year of elementary school. Mad is the word that remains in my head about my dreadful year as a 6th grader. My madness was one that was caused by disappointments that hurt me very much. Dissapointments from my teacher, such as field trips that were planed, then canceled. My 6th grade My 6th grade teacher gave me a lot of disappointments which made me very mad and made me built a state of hated in my heart, no one ever let me down that hard befor and I never hated anyone as much as I did him. Disappointment"

"Wasn't the only reason that made me mad in my 6th grade class, another was getting in trouble at school especially talking that's what really bugged me was writing sentences. Those awful sentences that my teacher made me write, hours and hours Id sit and write 50-100-150 sentence day and night. I write those dreadful paragraphs which embarrassed me and more important it made me ashamed of myself which in turn, deep down inside made me realize that writing sentence wasn't fair it wasn't fair to make me suffer like that, it wasn't fair to make me sit and wright until my bones ached, until my hand felt every horrid pain it ever had and as I wrote, I got mader and mader until I cried, I cried because I was ashamed I cried because I was discosted, I cried because I was mad, and I cried for myself, kid who kept on having to write those blane (Damn?) sentences.

My angriness from sixth grade will scar my memory
for life and I will be ashamed for my sixth grade year
forever."

Chapter Twelve

Jesse James, Excitements Crave

Does the Original Night Stalker look like Jesse James with his blue eyes and European good looks? I compared the composites from newspapers and old photographs of Jesse James. The distinctive nose shown on composites bears some resemblance to a possible Scandinavian ancestry.

Jesse James

Yet another composite from the series of attacks

WANTED

DEAD OR ALIVE

$5,000.00
FOR THE CAPTURE
OF THE MEN WHO
ROBBED THE BANK
AT NORTHFIELD
MINN.

BELIEVED TO BE
JESSE JAMES AND
HIS BAND OR THE
YOUNGERS.
THESE MEN ARE
DESPERATE.

JESSE OR FRANK JAMES

NOTORIOUS ROBBER OF
TRAINS AND BANKS

$5,000.00

Contact: Pinkerton's
Detective Agency
and
Union Pacific Railroad
Agency

REWARD

THIS NOTICE TAKES the PLACE of ALL PREVIOUS
REWARD NOTICES.
CONTACT SHERIFF, DAVIESS COUNTY, MISSOURI

JULY 26, 1881

James Brother

This poem is said to have been written by The East Area Rapist December 1977 and was sent to a KVIE 6 television station as well as the Sacramento Bee and the Sacramento Mayor's office

Excitements Crave

All those mortal's surviving birth
Upon facing maturity,
Take inventory of their worth
To prevailing society.

Choosing values becomes a task;
Oneself must seek satisfaction.
The selected route will unmask
Character when plans take action
Accepting some work to perform
At fixed pay, but promise for more,
Is a recognized social norm,
As is decorum, seeking lore.

Achieving while others lifting
Should be cause for deserving fame.
Leisure tempts excitement seeking,
What's right and expected seems tame.

"Jessie James" has been seen by all,
And "Son of Sam" has an author.
Others now feel temptations call.
Sacramento should make an offer.

To make a movie of my life
That will pay for my planned exile.
Just now I'd like to add the wife
Of a Mafia lord to my file.
Your East Area Rapist
And deserving pest
See you in the press or on T.V.

After reviewing the poem on the previous page I have to say that my immediate feeling is that this was not a joke. His comments in the poem about see you in the press or on TV reflect how very little he cared about his victims. It truly was all about him. He had modeled himself after outlaws and serial killers thinking that this way of living would be outside the boring mundane way of living within society and within society's rules. This would be his claim to fame and infamy. Just look at Jesse James. He was not a good guy. To a young boy growing up this must have seemed an exciting way to live. A folk hero, a bad guy. An outlaw may have been his original goal, but as he grew and indulged in peeping activities his path changed into burglary, raping and then killing.

Truly I believe that this man, as a child did not feel that he fit into normal society. He did not fit and was an outsider in his classes at school, in his neighborhood. He would show everyone and so channeled his rage at not understanding connections, people, rules and social norms. He would become stronger, smarter and more important than anyone he knew, anyone he had met.

He would become important and become a legend. He knew that people would find it fascinating to contemplate and theorize about who he is, who he was. He knows that if he is to become known that he can take credit for what he has done. He also knows that if he does not come forward or if the detectives and volunteers that still try to solve the mystery can't or don't figure it out before he dies that he will still be talked about, that stories will still be written and long after he and we have died.

What all of the families of the victims want is for this man to be identified and caught so that even if he only lives another 10 years or so that he will have to face the consequences of his actions. Like BTK was when arrested this man is now in his 60's and so was able to live his life having never paid for his crimes. That in itself is the most offensive of all of the parts to this story.

The people he murdered, the people he took their lives from missed everything that was to come. They missed growing up as in Janelle Cruz's case, having families' or if they did have a family they did not get to share in their lives, see them graduate from high school, college, get married, have families of their own. Lyman and Charlene Smith, Keith and Patrice Harrington, Cheri Domingo, and Gregory Sanchez, Manuela Witthuhn, Dr. Debra Manning and Dr. Robert Offerman, Katie and Sgt. Brian Maggiore, Janelle Cruz, as well as possibly Professor Snelling from Visalia did not get to finish what they had started, did not get to fulfill their own dreams or at the very least be with their families, share in their lives. This man took absolutely everything from them and yet he remains free and unfettered. He can watch a ball game, walk down the street, and feel the sun on his face.

Chapter Thirteen

Moving South – The Murders

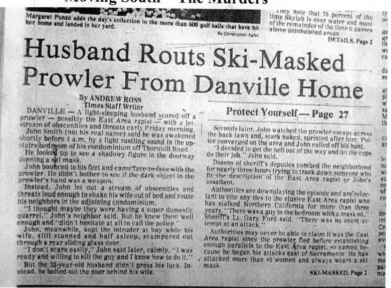

Margaret Punzo adds the day's collection to the more than 600 golf balls that have hit her home and landed in her yard.

By Christopher Aglor

They note that 75 percent of the time Skylab is over water and most of the remainder of the time it passes above uninhabited areas.

DETAILS, Page 2

Husband Routs Ski-Masked Prowler From Danville Home

By ANDREW ROSS
Times Staff Writer

DANVILLE — A light-sleeping husband scared off a prowler — possibly the East Area rapist — with a jet stream of obscenities and threats early Friday morning.

John Smith (not his real name) said he was awakened shortly before 4 a.m. by a light rustling sound in the upstairs bedroom of his condominium off Thornhill Road.

He looked up to see a shadowy figure in the doorway donning a ski mask.

John bounced to his feet and came face-to-face with the prowler. He didn't bother to see if the dark object in the prowler's hand was a weapon.

Instead, John let out a stream of obscenities and threats loud enough to shake his wife out of bed and rouse his neighbors in the adjoining condominium.

"I thought maybe they were having a super domestic quarrel," John's neighbor said. But he knew them well enough and "didn't hesitate at all to call the police."

John, meanwhile, kept the intruder at bay while his wife, still stunned and half asleep, scampered out through a rear sliding glass door.

"I don't scare easily," John said later, calmly. "I was ready and willing to kill the guy and I know how to do it."

But the 32-year-old husband didn't press his luck. Instead, he bolted out the door behind his wife.

Protect Yourself — Page 27

Seconds later, John watched the prowler escape across the back lawn and, stark naked, sprinted after him. Police converged on the area and John called off his hunt.

"I decided to get the hell out of the way and let the cops do their job," John said.

Dozens of sheriff's deputies combed the neighborhood for nearly three hours trying to track down someone who fit the description of the East Area rapist or John's assailant.

Authorities are downplaying the episode and are reluctant to cite any ties to the elusive East Area rapist who has stalked Northern California for more than three years. "There was a guy in the bedroom with a mask on," Sheriff's Lt. Gary Ford said. "There was no overt attempt at an attack."

Authorities may never be able to claim it was the East Area rapist since the prowler fled before establishing enough parallels to the East Area rapist, so named because he began his attacks east of Sacramento. He has attacked more than 40 women and always wears a ski mask.

SKI-MASKED, Page 2

Husband Routs Ski-Masked Prowler from Danville Home

By Andrew Ross -Times Staff Writer July 5, 1979
(Partial article)

Danville – A light sleeping husband scared off a prowler – possibly the East Area Rapist with a jet stream of obscenities and threats early Friday morning.

John Smith (not his real name) said he was awakened shortly before 4 a.m. by a light rustling sound in the upstairs bedroom of his condominium off Thornhill Road.

He looked up to see a shadowy figure in the doorway donning a ski mask.

John bounced to his feet and came face to face with the prowler. He didn't bother to see if the dark object in the prowler's hand was a weapon.

Instead, John let out a stream of obscenities and threats loud enough to shake his wife out of bed and rouse his neighbors in the adjoining condominium.

"I thought maybe they were having a super domestic quarrel," John's neighbor said. But he knew them well enough and "didn't hesitate at all to call the police."

John, meanwhile, kept the intruder at bay while his wife still stunned and half asleep, scampered out through a rear sliding glass door.

"I don't scare easily, "John said later, calmly. "I was ready and willing to kill the guy and I know how to do it."

But the 32-year-old husband didn't press his luck; instead, he bolted out the door behind his wife.

Seconds later, John watched the prowler escape across the back lawn and, stark naked, sprinted after him. Police converged on the area and John called off his hunt.

"I decided to get the hell out of the way and let the cops do their job." John said.

Dozens of sheriff's deputies combed the neighborhood for nearly three hours trying to track down someone who fit the description of the East Area Rapist or John's assailant.

Authorities are downplaying the episode and are reluctant to cite any ties to the elusive East Area Rapist who has stalked Northern California for more than three years. "There was a guy in the bedroom with a mask on," Sheriff's Lt. Gary Ford said. "There was no overt attempt at an attack."

Authorities may never be able to claim it was the East Area Rapist since the prowler fled before establishing enough parallels to the East Area Rapist, so named because he began his attacks east of Sacramento. He has attacked more than 40 women and always wears a ski mask.

End of article

The article lacked the second page in the archives that I was able to find. This incident certainly seems like an aborted attack by EAR and was the predecessor to the first murders in Goleta.

For all intents and purposes this is the last known possible attempted attack by EAR prior to moving to Goleta in the fall of 1979.

Goleta is approximately 321 miles from Danville on highway 101 south and takes approximately 4 hours and 45 minutes to arrive.

Following are news articles about the murders that began to occur in Southern California starting in 1979 until 1981. Then five years would go by until the last one that we know of in 1986.

SHERIFF'S DETECTIVES examine photos taken at the scene of a double murder discovered yesterday in Goleta.

Goleta Valley doctor, woman found slain

A Goleta Valley orthopedic surgeon and a Santa Maria clinical psychologist believed to be his girlfriend were found murdered yesterday in his condominium on Avenida Pequena, sheriff's deputies reported.

Dr. Robert J. Offerman, 44, and Debra (Dee) Alexandria Manning, 35, were found dead at 11:19 a.m. in the bedroom of Offerman's residence at 767 Avenida Pequena, detectives said.

Detective William Baker said that both victims had been shot to death. Time of death was tentatively set at about 3 a.m. Sunday. Neighbors had heard shots, Baker said, but didn't report them, thinking they were holiday firecrackers.

No motive has yet been established, but murder-suicide has been ruled out, Baker said.

The murders were discovered by a friend who came to Offerman's residence to keep a tennis date, Baker said.

Offerman, who had been in practice here since 1968, had medical offices at 211 W. Pueblo St. and 5333 Hollister Ave. He was in the process of a divorce, officers said.

Ms. Manning was granted a final divorce Friday from her husband, Dr. Brian J. Kinry, also an orthopedic surgeon, of Santa Maria. She had moved to Santa Maria four years ago, and had practiced clinical psychology at 504 E. Plaza Drive for .... years, ... in Santa Maria said today.

Detectives declined to release any information on the type of gun used in the murders, or the number of gunshot wounds.

A special recorded telephone hot line has been set up, Baker said. Persons with information on the killings were asked to call either the detective office at the Sheriff's Department, or the hot line, 964-5988, and leave a message.

Goleta Valley doctor, woman found slain
(Unknown which paper this came from)

A Goleta Valley orthopedic surgeon and a Santa Maria clinical psychologist believed to be his girlfriend were found murdered yesterday in his

315

condominium on Avenida Pequena, sheriff's deputies reported.

Dr. Robert J. Offerman, 41, and Dr. Debra (Dee) Alexandria Manning, 35, were found dead at 11:33 a.m. in the bedroom of Offerman's residence at 767 Avenida Pequena, detectives said.

Detective William Baker said that both victims had been shot to death. Time of death was tentatively set at about 3:00 a.m. Sunday. Neighbors had heard shots, Baker said, but didn't report them thinking they were holiday firecrackers.

No motive has yet been established, but murder-suicide has been ruled out, Baker said.

The murders were discovered by a friend who came to Offerman's residence to keep a tennis date, Baker said.

Offerman, who had been in practice here since 1968, had medical offices at 231 W. Pueblo St. and 5333 Hollister Ave. He was in the process of a divorce, officers said.

Ms. Manning was granted a final divorce Friday from her husband, Dr. Brian J. Kinlry, also an orthopedic surgeon, of Santa Maria. She had moved to Santa Maria four years ago, and had practiced clinical psychology at 504 East Plaza Drive for the last three years XXXXX in Santa Maria said today. (Not clear in the article so I have put X's here)

Detectives declined to release any information on the type of gun used in the murders or the number of gunshot wounds. A special recorded telephone hot line has been set up Baker said. Persons with information on the killings were asked to call either the detective office at the Sheriff's Department, or the hotline XXX-XXXX, and leave a message.

END OF ARTICLE

The phone number of course is 37 years old so I have not repeated it here.

March 17, 1980 Article

Santa Barbara News Press

Lawyer, wife found beaten to death

S.B. News-Press 3-17-1980 p.g. A-3

VENTURA (AP) — Police are investigating the murder of attorney Lyman R. Smith, 43, said to have been under consideration for a judgeship, and his wife Charlene, 33, who were apparently beaten to death in their bedroom.

The bodies were found about 2:13 p.m. yesterday by Smith's 12-year-old son, Gary, according to police Lt. Randy Adams. The boy lives with his mother, Smith's ex-wife, and had come over for a Sunday visit, Adams said.

"A preliminary investigation indicates the Smiths received bludgeoning injuries about the head with club-type weapons," Adams said. "An autopsy is scheduled to determine the exact cause of death."

Police have established no motive and Adams said he preferred not to comment on whether the house showed signs of forcible entry or burglary.

"Smith was under consideration for appointment to be a Superior Court judge," Adams said.

Ventura (AP) – Police are investigating the murder of attorney Lyman R. Smith, 43 said to have been under consideration for a judgeship, and his wife Charlene, 33 who were apparently beaten to death in their bedroom.

The bodies were found about 2:13 p.m. yesterday by Smith's 12-year-old son, Gary, according to police Lt. Randy Adams. The boy lives with his mother, Smith's ex-wife, and had come over for a Sunday visit, Adams said.

"A preliminary investigation indicates the Smiths received bludgeoning injuries about the head with club type weapons," Adams said. "An autopsy is scheduled to determine the exact cause of death"

Police have established no motive and Adams said he preferred not to comment on whether the house showed signs of forcible entry or burglary.

"Smith was under consideration for appointment to be a Superior Court Judge," Adams said.

(I corrected the age posted for Charlene in this article) **End of article**

Lawyer, wife found slain in Ventura home
Son finds beaten pair in Clearpoint bedroom

Ventura County Star 3-17-1980

By Skip Rimer
and Ritz Beamish

A prominent attorney and his wife were found slain Sunday in the bedroom of their expensive Ventura hillside home, where they had apparently been bludgeoned to death more than two days earlier.

Lyman R. Smith, 43, believed to be a leading candidate for appointment to one of two vacancies on the Superior Court, and his wife, Charlene, 33, were found just after 2 p.m. Sunday by Smith's 13-year-old son, Gary, who had come over to the house to mow his father's lawn, according to Smith's ex-wife, Marjorie.

The boy, who lives with his mother about one-half mile from Smith's Clearpoint home, went into the bedroom and found his father lying face down in bed, she said. The boy's stepmother was lying face up next to Smith, though she was covered with a sheet or blanket, sources said. Both had been beaten about the head with a club-type instrument, police said.

A log, possibly used to kill the couple, was found lying on the bed, sources said. Investigators, however, would confirm only that a log was found in the bedroom, and said they did not know if it is the murder weapon.

Smith, whose legal practice was headquartered in Santa Paula, where he was active in civic affairs, was long a prominent figure in the county's Democratic Party leadership.

Marjorie Smith told the Star-Free Press that her ex-husband's house had been ransacked and a bedroom alarm clock, set for early morning, was still ringing when Gary entered the unlocked house.

Ventura police Sgt. Gary Adkinson however, said the house had been ransacked and said there apparently was no burglary. He said there were no signs that either a struggle had taken place or that someone had broken into the home.

Adkinson said investigators do not believe the home was burglarized. He said they are investigating the deaths as a double slaying.

The scene was apparently bloody and Gary tried to call his mother. When she did not answer, he called police, who arrived at the home, 573 High Point Drive, about 2:15 p.m.

The area was quickly sealed off by police until a search warrant could be obtained from Superior Court Judge Marvin H. Lewis, a friend of the Smiths, who lives just up the street from the couple.

There were no suspects in custody as of this morning, and police would not speculate on a possible motive for the slayings.

Two gardeners, who were working at the house when Gary arrived, were questioned by police, but are not considered suspects, investigators said.

According to neighbors and friends, Mrs. Smith was last seen alive Thursday night in front of her house. Smith, a member of the Santa Paula firm of Romney, Smith & Drescher, was at work Thursday, but did not call in the next day, Phil Drescher, one of his law partners, said.

Smith missed an appointment Friday, but others in the office covered for him, Drescher said. They figured he had taken on another assignment

(Continued on A-2, Col. 2)

Cont'd To Next Page

Cont'd From Previous Page

Attorney, wife found murdered

Continued from A-1

without telling them.

"We didn't think that much of it because it was just one appointment Friday," he said. "He was out of the office a lot recently."

Smith's former wife, who also has custody of their other two children, Jenny, 11, and Jay, 13, said Smith usually talked to the boys and his daughter at least once a week.

"He didn't call on the weekend and we figured maybe he was on a trip or something," Ms. Smith said.

Neighbors said they thought it was strange that both of the Smiths' cars were in front of their home Friday, but said they did not hear or see anything unusual late Thursday or early Friday, when the couple is believed to have been killed.

Lewis said he went over to Smith's house Friday evening to talk to him about the pending Superior Court appointments, but got no answer when he knocked on the door. He said he called on the phone when he got home, but again got no answer.

An autopsy was scheduled for today to determine the cause and probable time of death.

Ms. Smith learned of the slayings when she drove to Smith's house to see if Gary was mowing the lawn and saw dozens of police cars outside the residence.

"I kind of feared the worst, and, of

course, it was pretty true," she said.

While police were waiting for the search warrant, Smith's daughter rode up to the home on a Moped. She was crying and had to be comforted by officers.

Police went into the home about 9:25 p.m. after receiving the warrant. District Attorney Michael D. Bradbury was at the home when officers went inside, but he did not enter the house.

Friends and colleagues expressed shock when told of the killings. They praised Smith as one of the county's outstanding attorneys.

"He was a highly competent attorney," said Drescher. "He was uniformly respected by his peers, and he was understanding kind. He was a terrific and capable guy."

Smith, a former deputy district attorney, was one of four attorneys whose names have been submitted by the governor to the State Bar for evaluation in connection with a possible appointment to one of two vacancies on the Superior Court.

The other three attorneys whose names have been submitted are Assistant Public Defender Ken Cleaver, Bill Peck of Ventura and Ventura City Councilman Ronald Harrington.

Drescher, who knew Smith for 17 years, said his partner had an excellent chance at being appointed to the bench.

"Any way you cut it, Lyman had to get one of them," Drescher said.

Lewis, who learned of the killings when he and his wife, Claire, drove by the Smith house on a shopping trip shortly after police arrived, said he was stunned.

"He was an excellent attorney," Lewis said of Smith. "He was someone who never lost his temper. He had good judgment and an ability to get along with people."

Mrs. Lewis, who used to work with Mrs. Smith when both of them were legal secretaries in the Municipal Court, said she had lunch Thursday with Mrs. Smith, who was in good spirits.

"She was really enjoying her new job," Mrs. Lewis said. "She was really up and everything was going (well) for her."

Mrs. Smith had just begun a new job in home decorating, Mrs. Lewis said.

Superior Court Judge Steven Stone, a former law partner and one of Smith's closest friends, could not believe Smith was dead.

"I am really stunned and shocked," Stone said. "Although I've seen a

number of horrible crimes in my courtroom, it hits you harder when you're close to the victim, and I was very close to him."

Stone said he last talked with Smith about Wednesday or last week. He said the pending judicial appointment was discussed.

"He was very pleased and happy that his name had been submitted by the governor," Stone said.

"Lyman was highly thought of by the bench, Bar and clients," he added. "He was a genuine credit to his profession. He was a remarkably able lawyer. It's a real loss to the legal community."

Edwin F. Beach, a former law partner of Smith's and now an appellate court justice, said today he was shocked by news of Smith's death.

"I'm stunned," Beach said. "It's a tragic loss to the profession. He was an excellent attorney who could handle many different kinds of things."

Smith was born in Pocatelo, Idaho, on April 7, 1936. He received his law degree from Boalt Hall, University of California, and joined the Ventura County District Attorney's Office as a law clerk in October 1961.

After passing the State Bar exam, Smith became a deputy district attorney in January 1962. He stayed with the office until October 1963, when he joined Stone and Beach to form the Santa Paula law firm of Beach, Stone & Smith. Drescher joined them about two years later.

Eventually, Beach and Stone left to go on the bench and Elaine Romney joined the firm, forming what is today known as Romndy, Smith & Drescher.

He was a past secretary of the Ventura County Bar Association.

Smith was married to Marjorie for 17 years before they separated in 1972. He and Charlene celebrated their fourth wedding anniversary in December.

They lived alone in their Clearpoint home. Charlene Smith had no children.

Smith was a former chairman of the Ventura County Democratic Central Committee and former trustee of the Santa Paula High School District. He was president of the Santa Paula Boys' Club and the Santa Paula Rotary Club.

He was also a former owner of Maverick International Airlines, which was formed to fly cattle to Iran. The company went out of business during the recent crisis in that country.

He had been a member of the Saticoy Country Club since 1971.

Services for the couple are pending.

The second page of this article talks about Lyman as a person, as an attorney and what a great reputation he had. "He was a genuine credit to his profession" said Edwin F. Beach, a former law partner, and now an appellate court justice. "It's a tragic loss to the profession."

"He was a highly competent attorney" said Drescher, (also a partner). "He was uniformly respected by his peers and he was uniformly liked" "He was a terrific and capable guy."

Lewis (a neighbor) said "He was an excellent attorney." "He was someone who never lost his temper." "He had good judgment and an ability to get along with people."

Superior Court Judge Steven Stone, a former law partner and one of Smith's closest friends said "Lyman was highly thought of by the bench, bar and clients." "He was a genuine credit to his profession." "He was a remarkably able lawyer it's a real loss to the legal community."

The personal and professional connections Lyman Robert made show how well thought of he was. He was his father's son when it came to how much people liked and respected him.

Smiths were slain as they slept

Ventura County Star — 3-19-1980

By Gregg Zoroya
and Skip Rimer

Lyman R. Smith, 43, and his wife Charlene, 33, Ventura, were evidently attacked while they slept, killed quickly in their beds and then tied up, according to information from police, investigators and other sources. (Obituary C4).

Sources close to the case quoted police as saying the violent deaths of the prominent attorney and his attractive wife were so sudden—"they didn't know what hit them."

Ventura Police Capt. Paul Lydick said a fire log found in the bedroom appears to have been the murder weapon. This log was reportedly found on the bed.

Twelve-year-old Gary Smith found his father and stepmother dead Sunday in the bedroom of their Ventura hillside home.

"The victims had retired for the night," Lydick said, "and died as a result of a single blunt force injury to the head of each of them."

The captain said he wouldn't characterize the slayings as execution style. Other sources close to the case supported that by quoting officers as saying that though the couple were tied up when found, they had been bound after they died.

"It's too early to tell if it's a random act of violence," Lydick said. But, he said, "homicide is very rarely a random act."

Ending a three-day silence, in which little or no information about the investigation was released, Lydick said, "There's a lot of rumors going around from sources that are inaccurate, and that generates a lot of problems."

He said both bodies were bound and covered with bed sheets.

"Neither of the victims appeared to be sexually molested and their bodies were not mutilated," said Lydick.

"There was no evidence found of forced entry to the residence or any indication of a robbery or burglary."

Smith and his wife were believed to have been killed sometime Thursday night or Friday morning.

shaken and puzzled by the deaths Tuesday.

"Just the not knowing is dreadful," said one close friend of the family, who asked not to be named. "You have this overwhelming feeling that somebody ought to be in jail and you wonder how close they (police) are to an arrest."

Emotional shock waves that have yet to dissipate were generated by the news of the killings.

Many of those contacted reflected on the fact that Smith was a leading candidate for appointment by the governor to one of two vacancies on the Superior Court. A partner in the Romney, Smith & Drescher law firm—headquartered in Santa Paula, Smith was also a prominent figure in the county's Democratic Party leadership and was involved in a wide range of civic affairs.

Little has been said, however, about his wife, whom friends have

(Continued on A-2, Col. 4).

Lawyer

Continued from A-1

described as a bubbly and popular person.

"She was a fantastic person. There wasn't anybody who didn't fall in love with Charlene immediately," said longtime friend Claire Lewis, wife of Superior Court Judge Marvin Lewis. The Lewises live near the Smith home in the Clearpoint area.

"She could walk into a room and everyone would know she was there because of her presence, her personality," said Mrs. Lewis.

One person who has suffered a particularly severe loss is Jill Kazen Morrill of Thousand Oaks, a longtime friend of Mrs. Smith.

"We were (like) sisters, to one another for the last 20 years and our names were synonymous," said Mrs. Morrill. "No one thought of me without thinking of her and no one thought of her without thinking of me."

The Smiths — both in second marriages — had no children together and Mrs. Morrill said that Charlene Smith had "incredible fondness and deepest love for my two children. They were the children she never had, Tiffany-Ann, 9½, and Brett Adam, 4½," she said. "They were just like Lyman and Charlene's own kids."

Born Charlene Herzenberg on April 17, 1946, the future Mrs. Lyman Smith was a Ventura County native.

She was also an only child. Her parents died when she was an infant, so she was raised by her grandmother, Gladys Bertenberg.

Mrs. Smith grew up in Camarillo, attending elementary schools and graduating from Adolfo Camarillo High School with a major in business in 1964.

After one year at Ventura College, she went to work as a legal secretary for the Camarillo law firm of Taylor, Stone and Storch.

In the next several years she would work as a legal secretary for at least three firms, working finally at Smith's firm in Santa Paula in 1967.

She was married in late 1965 to Michael Doyle, a young automobile club employee who later entered the sheriff's academy and became a deputy.

That marriage ended in May of 1972.

She and Smith were married in 1975.

Mrs. Smith left employment with Smith's firm to work in the Municipal Court offices in Camarillo, Oxnard and Simi Valley. She quit that job in August 1979.

During the remaining five months of her life, Mrs. Smith was self-employed. For a time, she ran "The Gold Cellar," a gold business in which she sold gold jewelry.

Most recently she looked forward to decorating the interior of some condominiums her husband had helped finance.

Mrs. Smith's grandmother, her only known surviving relative, died in 1977.

Article from previous page typed for clarity:

Smiths were slain as they slept

Ventura County Star by Gregg Zoroya and Skip Rimer

March 19, 1980

Lyman R. Smith, 43, and his wife Charlene, 33, Ventura, were evidently attacked while they slept, killed quickly in their beds and then tied up according to information from police investigators and other sources.

Sources close to the case quoted police as saying the violent deaths of the prominent attorney and his attractive wife were so sudden "they didn't know what hit them."

Ventura police Capt. Paul Lydick said a fire log found in the bedroom appears to have been the murder weapon. The log was reportedly found on the bed.

Twelve-year-old Gary Smith found his father and step mother dead Sunday in the bedroom of their Ventura hillside home.

The victims had retired for the night." Lydick said, and died as a result of a single blunt force injury to the head of each of them."

The captain said he wouldn't characterize the slayings as execution style. Other sources close to the case supported that by quoting officers as saying that though the couple were tied up when found, they had been bound after they died.

"It's too early to tell if it's a random act of violence." Lydick said. But, he said, "homicide is very rarely a random act."

Ending a three-day silence in which little or no information about the investigation was released, Lydick said, "There's a lot of rumors going around from sources that are inaccurate, and that generates a lot of problems."

He said both bodies were bound and covered with bed sheets."

"Neither of the victims appeared to be sexually molested and their bodies were not mutilated," said Lydick.

"There was no evidence found of forced entry to the residence or any indication of a robbery or burglary."

Smith and his wife were believed to have been killed sometime Thursday night or Friday morning.

It appears part of the article was cut off and then archived here

The article continues as follows next page:

"Just the not knowing is dreadful." Said one close friend of the family, who asked not to be named. "You have this overwhelming feeling that somebody ought to be in jail and you wonder how close they (police) are to an arrest."

Emotional shock waves that have yet to dissipate were generated by the news of the killings.

Many of those contacted reflected on the fact that Smith was a leading candidate for appointment by the governor to one of two vacancies on the Superior Court. A partner in the Romney, Smith and Drescher law firm headquartered in Santa Paula, Smith was also a prominent figure in the county's Democratic Party leadership and was involved in a wide range of civic affairs.

Little has been said, however, about his wife, whom friends have described as a bubbly and popular person.

"She was a fantastic person. There wasn't anybody who didn't fall in love with Charlene immediately", said longtime friend Claire Lewis, wife of Superior Court Judge Marvin Lewis." The Lewis's live near the Smith home in the Clearpoint area.

"She could walk into a room and everyone would know she was there because of her presence, her personality," said Mrs. Lewis.

One person who has suffered a particularly severe loss is Jill-Karen Morrill of Thousand Oaks, a longtime friend of Mrs. Smith.

"We were (like) sisters to one another for the last 20 years and our names were synonymous." said Mrs. Merrill. "No one thought of one without thinking of her without thinking of me."

The Smiths – both in second marriages – had no children together and Mrs. Merrill said that Charlene Smith had "incredible fondness and deepest love for my two children. They were the children she never had. Tiffany Ann, 9-1/2", and Brett Adam, 4-1/2 she said." They were just like Lyman and Charlene's own kids."

Born Charlene Herzenberg on April 17, 1946, the future Mrs. Lyman Smith was a Ventura County native.

She was also an only child. Her parents died when she was an infant, so she was raised by her grandmother, Gladys Herzenberg.

Mrs. Smith grew up Camarilla, attending elementary schools and graduating from Adolfo Camarillo High School with a major in business in 1964.

After one year at Ventura College she went to work as a legal secretary for the Camarillo law firm of Taylor, Stone and Storch.

In the next several years she would work as a legal secretary for at least three firms, working finally at Smith's firm in Santa Paula in 1967.

She was married in late 1969 to Michael Doyle a young automobile club employee who later entered the Sheriff's Academy and became a deputy. That marriage ended in 1972.

She and Smith were married in 1975. Mrs. Smith left employment with Smith's firm to work in the Municipal Court offices in Camarillo, Oxnard and Simi Valley. She quit that job in August 1979.

During the remaining five months of her life Mrs. Smith was self-employed. For a time, she ran "The Gold Cellar." A gold business in which she sold gold jewelry.

Most recently she looked forward to decorating the interior of some condominiums her husband helped finance.

Mrs. Smith's grandmother, her only known surviving relative, died in 1977.

END OF ARTICLE (A correction to this article is the Smiths' were married in 1975).

The victims were not asleep when murdered. This is not ONS' MO. He needed the foreplay of binding them scaring them, terrorizing them, raping Charlene, and then killing them. ONS never came in and just killed them as they slept. Charlene was raped when she was alive. Whoever gave this information to reporters for the purpose of this article at the time it was written was misinformed or giving misinformation purposefully. Later reports corrected these ideas.

Police mum about leads in slaying of lawyer, wife

Ventura County Star 3-18-1980

By Gregg Zoroya

Ventura police detectives continued probing the deaths of attorney Lyman R. Smith, 43, and his wife Charlene, 33, today, but were offering no new information about what had happened or why.

The two were found, bludgeoned to death, in the bedroom of their hillside home in the Clearpoint area of Ventura Sunday.

Investigators were especially close-mouthed about how the killings occurred.

A 7-hour autopsy conducted Monday at County General Hospital, Ventura, confirmed that both had died as the result of blows to the head by a blunt object. Ventura County Medical Examiner-Coroner Dr. Ronald Kornblum estimated the time of death for the prominent attorney and his attractive wife at sometime Thursday night or Friday morning.

"I'm very optimistic that we may solve the case. We have no suspects. We have no motive in the case yet. It's just under active investigation," said Capt. Paul Lydick.

Twelve-year-old Gary Smith, who first found the bloody bodies of his father and stepmother in their bedroom Sunday afternoon, and then calmly notified authorities, seemed to be handling the crisis well Monday evening.

"We talked about it and he gets it all out and I think he's going to do very well," said his mother, Marjorie Smith.

Gary missed school Monday, but will probably attend class today, his mother said.

Predicting that things may get worse as a memorial service for the boy's father draws closer — it's tentatively set for 2 p.m. Friday at Santa Paula Episcopal Church — Ms. Smith remained confident her son would be fine.

"He's really a level-headed kid," she said. "He doesn't keep anything inside. That's important. But he doesn't dwell on it, either."

Neighbors around the Smiths' expensive Clearpoint home were a bit skittish Monday night as they considered how close violence had come to their own lives.

"I'm sure it's not going to make sleeping too easy," one man said, after asking that he not be identified. "What really unnerves me is that I figure in this neighborhood there's enough homes (with people) observing other homes, it surprises me that this kind of thing could have occurred."

"I guess it doesn't matter where you live," said Susan Petresco, whose home overlooks the Smith residence. "If somebody's going to come and get you, they're going to come and get you."

Although she said she is not really frightened that the slaying occurred so close by, Mrs. Petresco said, "We probably will be keeping the door locked anyway, just to keep it safe."

Some neighbors speculated, as others have, that Smith's death may be related to his widespread activity in civic affairs. A leading candidate for appointment to one of two vacancies on the Superior Court, Smith was also a prominent figure in the county's Democratic Party leadership.

He was a member of the Santa Paula law firm of Romney, Smith & Drescher.

"He was very quiet," said Joan Taylor, who with her husband Don lives just below the Smith residence on High Point Drive.

They, like other residents, noticed nothing unusual between Thursday, when the Smiths were last seen alive, and Sunday, when their bodies were

(Continued on A-2, Col. 1)

Slaying

Continued from A-1

found, although Mrs. Taylor can remember an eerie feeling when her huge dog Saxon woke her at 2 a.m. Friday and led her out the back door.

"He went around to the side gate (facing the Smith home) and just looked around. He didn't bark, and there wasn't a sound around," said Mrs. Taylor.

"It was kind of scary, really," she said of the whole affair.

"It's comforting to have Saxon around, isn't it?" Taylor asked his wife at one point.

The executor of Smith's will is his law partner, Phil Drescher. Drescher said the memorial service will be under the direction of the Robert A. Steller Funeral Home.

The mood at many businesses and government offices turned toward the brutal slayings Monday. At the noon meeting of the Santa Paula Rotary, of which Smith was a member and past president, the mood was particularly somber.

In a short address, acknowledging Smith's untimely death, president Elbert "Eb" Tate said nothing prepared him, as chief Rotarian, for the sudden shock of losing a fellow member.

"I do not know what Lyman would wish us to do in this situation," Tate said to the dozens of other members present. "I can only rely on my own belief that our tasks and functions must continue. Although our rage and grief may be concealed, the resumption of our ways is evidence of deep regard and no disrespect."

Ventura County Star by Greg Zoroya March 18, 1980 **ARTICLE**

328

Police Mum about leads in slaying of lawyer, wife

Ventura police detectives continued probing the deaths of attorney Lyman R. Smith, 43, and his wife Charlene, 33, today, but were offering no new information about what had happened or why.

The two were found, bludgeoned to death, in the bedroom of their hillside home in the Clearpoint area of Ventura Sunday.

Investigators were especially close mouthed about how the killings occurred.

A 7-hour autopsy conducted Monday at County General Hospital, Ventura, confirmed that both had died as the result of blows to the head by a blunt object. Ventura County Medical Examiner-Coroner Dr. Ronald Kornblum estimated the time of death for the prominent attorney and his attractive wife at some time Thursday night or Friday morning.

"I'm very optimistic that we may solve the case, We have no suspects. We have no motive in the case yet. "It's just under active investigation," said Capt. Paul Lydick.

Twelve year old Gary Smith, who first found the bloody bodies of his father and stepmother in their bedroom Sunday afternoon and then calmly notified authorities, seemed to be handling the crisis well Monday evening.

"We talked about it and he gets it all out and I think he's going to do very well." Said his mother Marjorie Smith.

Gary missed school Monday, but will probably attend class today, his mother said.

Predicting that things may get worse as a memorial service for the boy's father draws closer – it's tentatively set for 2 p.m. Friday at Santa Paula Episcopal Church – Ms. Smith remained confident her son would be fine.

"He's really a level headed kid." She said. "He doesn't keep anything inside. That's important. But he doesn't dwell on it either."

Neighbors around the Smith's expensive Clearpoint home were a bit skittish Monday night as they considered how close violence had come to their own lives.

"I'm sure it's not going to make sleeping too easy," one man said, after asking that he not be identified. "What really unnerves me is that I figure in this neighborhood there's enough homes (with people) observing other homes, it surprises me that this kind of thing could have occurred."

"I guess it doesn't matter where you live," said Susan Petresco, whose home overlooks the Smith residence. "If somebody's going to come and get you."

Although she said she is not really frightened that the slaying occurred so close by, Mrs. Petresco said, "We probably will be keeping the door locked anyway, just to keep it safe."

Some neighbors speculated as others have, that Smith's death may be related to his widespread activity in civic affairs. A leading candidate for appointment to one of two vacancies on the Superior Court, Smith was also a prominent figure in the county's Democratic Party leadership.

He was a member of the Santa Paula law firm of Romney, Smith & Drescher.

"He was very quiet," said Joan Taylor, who with her husband Don lives just below the Smith residence on High Point Drive.

They like other residents, noticed nothing unusual between Thursday, when the Smiths were last seen alive, and Sunday when their bodies were found, although Mrs. Taylor can remember an eerie feeling when her huge dog Saxon woke her at 2:00 a.m. Friday and led her out the back door.

"He went around to the side gate (facing the Smith house) and just looked around. He didn't bark and there wasn't a sound around." Said Mrs. Taylor.

"It was kind of scary, really," she said of the whole affair.

"It's comforting to have Saxon around, isn't it?" Taylor asked his wife at one point.

331

The executor of Smith's will is his law partner, Phil Drescher. Drescher said "the memorial service will be under the direction of Robert A. Stetler Funeral Home.

The mood at many businesses and government offices turned toward the brutal slayings Monday. At noon the meeting of the Santa Paula Rotary of which Smith was a member and past president, the mood was particularly somber.

In a short address, acknowledging Smith's untimely death, president Elbert "Eb" Tate said nothing prepared him, as chief Rotarian for the sudden shock of losing a fellow member.

"I do not know what Lyman would wish us to do in this situation." Tate said to the dozens of other members present. "I can only rely on my own belief that our tasks and functions must continue. Although our rage and grief may be concealed, the resumption of our ways is evidence of deep regard and no disrespect."

END OF ARTICLE

Photo by Bob Sammell

Smiths eulogized

350 attend services for slain couple

Ventura County Star
By Gregg Zoroya
3-22-1980

"Certainly there is nothing in life that prepares us for violent, senseless deaths."

Nothing, that is, except the resources of the family, the consolation of friends and the solace of religious beliefs, the Rev. Leonard Dixon (retired) told a crowded Santa Paula church Friday.

Dixon was speaking before 350 persons at the memorial service for Lyman R. Smith and his wife, Charlene. He had performed the couple's wedding ceremony in 1975.

The memorial service was held approximately a week after Mr. and Mrs. Smith were beaten to death while they slept in the bedroom of their Ventura home. Their bodies were not discovered until Sunday.

The bodies were cremated before the services.

"For the survivors," said Dixon, "death is never an easy experience. But the sting of such cruelty as this fills us with different emotions. It fills us with loneliness, sorrow, anger..."

Judges, state and local government officials, attorneys and a host of other friends and acquaintances filled the chapel of St. Paul's Episcopal Church. All the pews were filled, and people sat in the choir seats, the aisle

and in the balcony, and stood in the back and in the foyer.

"It is a testimony to the abiding nature of their lives that so many have gathered for this service of love and memorial," Dixon said.

Six Ventura police investigators and a sergeant continue to investigate the slayings. Both Smiths were killed by a single blow to the head. Police believe the weapon might have been a log which was found lying on their bed.

The case has a variety of bizarre twists. There was no forced entry into the house, although it is believed the two were attacked after they went to bed, and evidence shows their hands were bound after they were killed.

"I will make no attempt to explain why they were taken so brutally from us," Dixon continued.

He eulogized Smith, who had been a leading candidate for a Superior Court vacancy at the time of his death, as part of a family circle, as a counselor, friend, benefactor ("particularly to the youth") and a co-worker in many walks of life.

Of Smith's 33-year-old wife, Charlene, Dixon said she was "always active," interested, energetic and creative.

"They were not church-going people," said Dixon. "But that is not to

say they weren't religious."

He said their personal yearning was for the eternal values of life, "those things that abideth long after other things have withered and decayed."

As the service drew to a close and people stood to leave, these first down the aisle were watched solemnly by the hundreds present. They were the family members and closest friends. Among them were Smith's parents and his children.

Most notable was 12-year-old Gary Smith, whose calm, young face reflected an endurance and composure far beyond his years.

Sunday, he was the person who found the bodies of his father and step-mother.

Dixon, quoting an English cleric, said, "the death of a good person is like the putting out of a perfumed candle."

"The light is extinguished, but the fragrance remains."

March 22, 1980 Ventura County Star by Gregg Zoroya - Smiths eulogized ARTICLE

350 attend services for slain couple

"Certainly there is nothing in life that prepares us for violent, senseless deaths."

Nothing, that is except the resources of the family, the consolation of friends and the solace of religious beliefs, the Rev. Leonard Dixon (retired) told a crowded Santa Paula church Friday.

Dixon was speaking before 350 persons at the memorial service for Lyman R. Smith and his wife, Charlene. He had performed the couple's wedding ceremony in 1975.

The memorial service was held approximately a week after Mr. and Mrs. Smith were beaten to death while they slept in the bedroom of their Ventura home. Their bodies were not discovered until Sunday. The bodies were cremated before the services.

For the survivors, said Dixon, "death is never an easy experience." But the sting of such cruelty as this fills us with different emotions. It fills us with loneliness, sorrow, anger...."

Judges, state and local government officials, attorneys and a host of other friends and acquaintances filled the chapel of St. Paul's Episcopal Church. All the pews were filled, and people sat in the chair seats, the aisle and in the balcony, and stood in the back and in the foyer.

"It is a testimony for the abiding nature of their lives that so many have gathered for this service of love and memorial." Dixon said.

Six Ventura police investigators and a sergeant continue to investigate the slayings. Both Smiths were killed by a single blow to the head. Police believe the weapon might have been a log which was found lying on their bed.

The case has a variety of bizarre twists. There was no forced entry into the house, although it is believed the two were attacked after they went to bed, and evidence shows their hands were bound after they were killed.

"I will make no attempt to explain why they were taken so brutally from us." Dixon continued.

He eulogized Smith who had been a leading candidate for a Superior Court vacancy at the time of his death, as part of a family circle, as a counselor, friend, benefactor" (particularly to the youth") and a co-worker in many walks of life.

Of Smith's 33-year-old wife, Charlene, Dixon said she was "always active," interested, energetic and creative.

"They were not church going people." Said Dixon. "But that is not to say they weren't religious."

He said their personal yearning was for the eternal values of life. "Those things that abideth long after other things have withered and decayed."

As the service drew to a close and people stood to leave, those first down the aisle were watched solemnly by the hundreds present. They were the family members and closest friends. Among them were Smith's parents and his children.

Most notable was 12-year-old Gary Smith, whose calm, young face reflected an endurance and composure far beyond his years.

Sunday, he was the person who found the bodies of his father and step-mother.

Dixon, quoting an English cleric, said "the death of a good person is like the putting out of a perfumed candle." The light is extinguished, but the fragrance remains. **END OF ARTICLE**

Smith murder case:
No leads, no suspects, nothing

By Gregg Zoroya

Police have no suspects, no clear-cut leads and no motives in the case.

Three weeks and two days have gone by since young Gary Smith visited his father's Ventura home on a Sunday afternoon to help mow the lawn.

The 12-year-old boy was the first to discover the bodies of his father, prominent attorney Lyman R. Smith, 43, and stepmother Charlene, 33, who had both been beaten to death in the bedroom of their expensive hillside home.

That first week, four police investigators and a sergeant spent nearly 80 hours each over seven days trying to crack the case.

But since then, investigators have been working closer to an eight-hour-a-day, five-day-a-week work week.

One of the detectives, Dick Haas, regarded by many police officials as one of the best detectives, if not the best, in the Ventura Police Department, has left for an investigative position with the District Attorney's Office. It is still not clear whether he will be able to continue to investigate the Smith case from that department. But three investigators and a sergeant remain on the case full time, which has meant placing a heavier load on other detectives in the investigative bureau.

Detectives on the Smith case have put in more than 200 hours of overtime interviewing more than 100 people.

"Any kind of a complicated crime investigation can be frustrating. However, we're still optimistic that we'll solve the case," said Capt. Paul Lydick, head of investigation.

"Usually, if you have a clear-cut motive in the case, that will lead to a suspect or suspects. But in the absence of that, it just makes it that much more difficult," Lydick said.

Police believe the couple died approximately three or four days before they were found. When Smith and his wife went to bed, Thursday night, March 13, they set the alarm for an early hour, because Friday Smith had an appointment at his law firm of Rohney, Smith & Drescher in Santa Paula.

Sometime during the night someone got into the house without force, took a log from near the fireplace, and in the darkness slipped into the bedroom where the couple were sleeping.

It took only one blow to the head of each from the large piece of wood to kill Smith and his wife, police said.

Nothing was taken from the house, there was no mutilation of the bodies and no sexual molestation.

But the hands of the victims were bound.

According to sources, the autopsy indicated initially that the couple's hands were bound after they died. However, it is no longer clear whether the binding occurred before or after death.

But there is evidence that Smith and his wife probably died instantly.

Authorities say that in nearly every autopsy of a homicide, the medical-examiner coroner searches for one small human organ that can give some indication of the emotional state of the victim at the time of death — the adrenal gland.

According to Dr. Peter Speth, assistant county medical-examiner coroner, this case was no exception.

A small, fleshy gland, about the size of a half-dollar when it is heal-

(Continued on A-2, Col. 8)

Smith case
Continued from A-1

thy, the adrenal gland secretes adrenalin and adrenal cortical hormones into the bloodstream — the fight or flight hormones — at times of stress.

"In that sort of situation, hormones would be secreted in large quantities into the bloodstream," said Dr. Ronald Kornblum, Ventura County Medical-Examiner Coroner, explaining the process. "These (reactions) are part of the autonomic nervous system. It happens whether you want it to or not.

"Presumably (when someone has died under stress) the gland has shrunk, because it has excreted all of its contents into the bloodstream," said Kornblum.

The Smiths' adrenal glands indicated Smith and his wife were not terrified, that they did not suffer, but died instantly, authorities said.

Kornblum stresses that such evidence is not conclusive. The gland is too small and varies too much in size from one person to another for precision.

But examining it is helpful, he said. "It goes along with your subjective opinion. But it would have to remain that, suggestive, speculative."

To summarize this article, it is a repeat of others already in the book. The reason it is important is what the medical examiner said about the autopsy and what he had to say about the victims. Here are the last few paragraphs of the article:

"According to sources, "the autopsy indicated initially that the couple's hands were bound after they died. However, it is no longer clear whether the binding occurred before or after death. But there is evidence that Smith and his wife probably died instantly. Authorities say that in nearly every autopsy of a homicide, the medical examiner coroner searches for the one small human organ that can give some indication of the emotional state of the victim at the time of death – the adrenal gland.

According to Dr. Peter Speth, assistant county medical examiner, coroner, this case was no exception. A small fleshy gland, about the size of a half dollar, when it is healthy, the adrenal gland secretes adrenalin and adrenal cortical hormones into the bloodstream – the fight or flight hormones – at times of stress."

"In that sort of situation, hormones would be secreted in large quantities into the bloodstream." Said Dr. Ronald Kornblum, Ventura County Medical Examiner Coroner, explaining the process. "These (reactions) are part of the autonomic nervous system. It happens whether you want it to or not. Presumably (when someone has died under stress) the gland has shrunk, because it has excreted all of its contents into the bloodstream," said Kornblum.

The Smith's adrenal glands indicated Smith and his wife were not terrified, that they did not suffer, but died instantly, authorities said. Kornblum stresses that such evidence is not conclusive. The gland is too small and varies too much in size from one person to another for precision. But examining it is helpful, he said. "It goes along with your subjective opinion. But it would have to remain that, suggestive, speculative." **END OF ARTICLE**

Speculation – I would love to compare what a medical examiner would think after reviewing the files almost 40 years later. I would love to see a report from 1980 compared with one written today. The field has expanded and changed due to technological advances and Forensic Science advances. It would be interesting to read an updated version. As I mentioned, I am hoping that each jurisdiction has had their medical examiner take a fresh look at all of these homicides with new knowledge and fresh eyes. If they have not, it is my hope that they will and soon. There could be some other piece of information that not only connects all of these murders but gives us one more piece to the puzzle.

Leads Run Down

Double Slaying Motive Sought

A motive in the bludgeon deaths of attorney Lyman Robert Smith and his wife, Charlene, remained a mystery today as detectives continued to search for leads into the double homicide, Ventura Police Capt. Paul Lydick said

"We haven't been able to establish a reason for the slayings or find any suspect," said Lydick, who is heading the investigation into the deaths.

The bodies of Smith, 43, and his 33-year-old wife were found Sunday, bound and beaten inside their fashionable hillside home in Ventura, by Smith's son, Gary, 12, when he went to the residence to mow the lawn

The couple appeared to have been bludgeoned with a firewood log that was found in the bedroom near the bodies, according to Lydick

Lydick said the log, which appeared to be covered with blood, is believed to be the weapon used to kill the Smiths. The log is being examined at the Ventura County Sheriff's Department Crime Laboratory.

The captain said investigators concluded their investigation at the crime scene Wednesday. He said the house was thoroughly examined for possible evidence that could lead to the Smiths' assailant.

The Smiths were slain sometime late last Thursday or early Friday, possibly by someone they knew, according to Lydick.

He said investigators could find no sign of a forced entry into the house and Mrs. Smith reportedly always made sure the doors of the house were locked before she and her husband retired for the night.

Investigators also could find no evidence that the lawyer and his wife had been robbed or their home burglarized, Lydick said.

"The Smiths seemingly had no enemies. Both were well liked, and Smith had a good chance of being appointed to a Superior Court judgeship," he added.

Smith was a partner in the Santa Paula law firm of Romney, Smith and Drescher

340

A motive in the bludgeon deaths of attorney Lyman Robert Smith and his wife Charlene, remained a mystery today as detectives continued to search for leads into the double homicide, Ventura Police Capt. Paul Lydick said.

"We haven't been able to establish a reason for the slayings or find any suspect." Said Lydick, who is heading the investigation into the deaths.

The bodies of Smith, 43, and his 33-year-old wife were found Sunday, bound and beaten inside their fashionable hillside home in Ventura, by Smith's son, Gary, 12, when he went to the residence to mow the lawn.

The couple appeared to have been bludgeoned with a fireplace log that was found in the bedroom near the bodies, according to Lydick. Lydick said the log, which appeared to be covered with blood, is believed to be the weapon used to kill the Smiths. The log is being examined at the Ventura County Sheriff's Department Crime Laboratory.

The captain said investigators concluded their investigation at the crime scene Wednesday. He said the house was thoroughly examined for possible evidence that could lead to the Smiths' assailant.

The Smiths were slain sometime late last Thursday or early Friday, possibly by someone they knew, according to Lydick. He said investigators could find no evidence of a forced entry into the house and Mrs. Smith reportedly always made sure the doors of the house were locked before she and her husband retired for the night.

Investigators also could find no evidence that the lawyer and his wife had been robbed or their home burglarized, Lydick said. "The Smiths seemingly had no enemies. Both were well liked and Smith had a good chance of being appointed to a Superior Court judgeship, he added."

Smith was a partner in the Santa Paula law firm of Romney, Smith and Drescher.

END OF ARTICLE

I am repeating the following statement to make sure a note is made in your minds about the fact that within a couple of days of the Smith murders one of the investigators said he thought it may be murder committed by someone they knew. This was the path taken for the next two plus years enabling the case in Ventura County, CA to go cold. It seems they had already made up their minds in retrospect.

"The Smiths were slain sometime late last Thursday or early Friday, possibly by someone they knew, according to Lydick." It is unfortunate that LE thought this from the beginning of the investigation never considering any other possibility.

In looking at topographic maps of the area surrounding the High Point Drive address and contemplating why ONS chose this house and these people and since it is more unlike other places geographically that ONS attacked this is what I think. ONS could have easily picked just about any house in this neighborhood and have escaped easily. I do believe he picked Charlene and in this case the geography did not matter as much as in other attacks. I have included topographic maps to show the terrain in this particular case.

This picture shows High Point Road in front of Smith House X is on the roof. The black trail I have marked is open and easy to enter and leave out the back yard of the Smith residence to El Malabar where a car was parked waiting for ONS to leave the neighborhood.

This next picture again shows High Point marked by X on far right of photo. Turn left to El Malabar X is where ONS may have parked and continued a short distance and then turned left again on La Fonda. La Fonda takes you to Foothill which takes you all the way down to Ventura Highway and other highways. I have arrows pointing to his route in my map. It literally takes you out of the area that fast to a highway.

This last picture shows High Point Drive and the X shows you the Smith house from the front of the house driveway. I have marked in black the path from the side of the house where the woodpile was that takes you out and onto the street where the car was waiting for ONS which is El Malabar. Did he really pick Charlene or was the house and the ease of his ability to get in and out an overriding factor? You decide.

I found that in this neighborhood the way the streets aligned it was such an easy escape down to main thoroughfares and the highway. This made this house an easier choice once he had picked Charlene as his victim. From Marina Park where it is speculated ONS could have seen Charlene it was only a 15-minute drive to High Point Drive. After stalking her and checking out the neighborhood and when planning his escape route, he found it suited his plan perfectly. It was reported that an unknown vehicle had been seen and had been parked on El Malabar prior to the murders. It makes sense geographically. This is where I would have parked. It truly was not far from there to the 101 Highway (Ventura Highway)

As a side note Ventura California is only a 2 hour and 49-minute drive to Laguna Niguel.

The murders of Keith and Patrice Harrington took place five months after the Smith Murders. It proved more difficult to obtain news articles written at the time. I gathered information reported about the crimes from miscellaneous reports accumulated from the internet, and from reading Richard Shelby's book as well as Larry Crompton's book on the subject of ONS and EAR.

On August 19, 1980, 5 months after the Smith murders in a gated community in Niguel Shores another senseless murder of a couple occurred. The Harrington murders were no less brutal than all of the others that took place before them and after them.

Keith Harrington was a third year medical student and his new wife of four months was a registered nurse. Apparently ONS would watch through windows and was just outside their bedroom. Both Keith and Patrice were found with markings on their bodies indicating they had been bound. Patrice had been raped. The cord had been cut and removed. Some of it was on Keith's lower back. This was odd. Both had been bound with their hands behind their back. Both had been bludgeoned with the bedspread over their heads. The murder weapon was never found. After their assailant murdered them he must have taken down the spread, cut their bindings and just let some fall where they would. He then covered them again. Again, there was no forced entry into the house. There was another bruise on Patrice Harrington. It was "a circular contusion" on her shoulder and could be said to be consistent with a bite mark."

Did ONS leave a bite mark on Patrice and then Manuela as he learned about the crimes of Ted Bundy? The bite marks left on one of Ted's victims were highly publicized with many forensic experts of the day trying to make the point that they could definitively say that these bite marks had come from Ted Bundy. There appeared to be reasonable doubt however. The forensics of the time period were in their comparative infancy in the late 1970's and early 1980's.

On February 6, 1981 in Irvine California 28-year-old Manuela Witthuhn was murdered while lying on her bed. The cause of death was a skull fracture. A ball of fibers was noted on her skin at the base of her spine. This was also noted on Lyman Smith at the scene of his murder. The weapon was removed from the scene. A rear sliding glass door had pry marks and damage to the frame.

I have modified some descriptions of reports and have not gone into as much of the gruesome details. The reality as a person reads through these gruesome descriptions of the victims last moments they are all difficult to wrap your head around. All of the murders were very brutal, very terrifying. These couples and other people did not escape with their lives. One of the reasons I did not go into greater detail and also why I did not include all of the attacks from the very beginning of this man's crimes until his last known victim in 1986 is because the sheer number of attacks and the sheer brutality he used even in the beginning is too much to take in its entirety.

Two found slain in Goleta; case similar to one in '79

By Dave Hardy
News-Press Staff Writer
S.B. News-Press 7-28-81

Sheriff's detectives are today investigating similarities between the brutal murder of a man and a woman found yesterday at 449 Toltec Way in Goleta and the nearby fatal shootings of a couple 1½ years ago.

The Toltec Way victims were identified today as Cheri Domingo, 35, a divorcee who was house-sitting at the residence, and her former boyfriend, Greg Sanchez, 28.

Mrs. Domingo was staying at the residence with her 15-year-old daughter, Debbie, who was with friends in Santa Barbara the night of the slay-ings, said Russ Birchim, sheriff's public information officer.

Sanchez, of 7240 Davenport Road, Goleta, had broken up with Mrs. Domingo about six months ago, close friends of Mrs. Domingo said, adding that the two had remained good friends.

The cause of the deaths was still undetermined this afternoon, said Birchim. An autopsy was to be performed today.

Deputies said the bodies were found about 11:30 a.m. yesterday by a real estate agent who came to look at the house. The property was put on the market three months ago after the death of the owner, who was a relative of Mrs. Domingo.

After discovering the murders yesterday, the agent then reportedly called the listing agent and told her, "I don't know what to say, but there's a body of a man face down in the bedroom." Detectives were then called.

A neighbor, who said she couldn't sleep Sunday night, said she heard a gunshot and dogs barking about 3:20 a.m.

See Page A-3, Col. 1

Two found slain in Goleta; case similar to one in '79 By Dave Hardy News-Press Staff Writer S.B. News Press 7-28-81 **ARTICLE**

Sheriff's detectives are today investigating similarities between the brutal murder of a man and a woman found yesterday at 449 Toltec Way in Goleta and the nearby fatal shootings of a couple 1-1/2 years ago.

The Toltec Way victims were identified today as Cheri Domingo, 35 a divorcee who was house-sitting at the residence, and her former boyfriend, Greg Sanchez, 28.

Mrs. Domingo was staying at the residence with her 15-year-old daughter Debbie, who was with friends in Santa Barbara the night of the slayings, said Russ Birchim, sheriff's public information officer.

Sanchez, of 7240 Davenport Road, Goleta, had broken up with Mrs. Domingo about six months ago, close friends of Mrs. Domingo said, adding that the two had remained good friends.

The cause of the deaths was still undetermined this afternoon, said Birchim. An autopsy was to be performed today.

Deputies said the bodies were found about 11:30 a.m. yesterday by a real estate agent who came to look at the house. The property was put on the market three months ago after the death of the owner who was a relative of Mrs. Domingo.

After discovering the murders yesterday, the agent then reportedly called the listing agent and told her, "I don't know what to say but there's a body of a man face down in the bedroom." Detectives were then called.

A neighbor who said she couldn't sleep Sunday night said she heard a gunshot and dogs barking about 3:20 a.m.

Second Page of the same article next page:

Two are found slain in Goleta residence

Continued from Page A-1

Virginia Wood told the News-Press, "I heard that gunshot just as plain as anything in the world, and I heard a woman scream."

Sgt. Bill Baker, head of the sheriff's major crimes unit, would tell the News-Press only that the most recent killings could be described as "brutal."

Birchim said that investigators are "looking into the possibility" that the same person who murdered the couple on Toltec Way may have also killed Goleta surgeon Robert Offerman and Santa Maria psychologist Debra Manning in Offerman's condominium at 767 Avenida Pequena on Dec. 30, 1979. But Birchim declined to comment on any similarities between the two killings.

A number of coincidences mark the two sets of slayings:

— Both couples were killed in the bedroom and found about the same time of day.

— Manning and Offerman were believed to have been shot at about 3 a.m.

— Neighbors in both slayings said they heard what could have been gunshots, but didn't report them because they thought they were holiday firecrackers.

To aid the investigation, detectives called in a 3-year-old bloodhound named Duchess from the San Luis Obispo County Sheriff's Department.

Mrs. Domingo was laid off two weeks ago from her job as corporate administrator of Trimm Industries, a Santa Barbara-based company that manufactures computer furniture, said Maurna De Vane, a neighbor and friend who was laid off from Trimm at the same time.

She described Mrs. Domingo as a very sociable, tidy and intelligent woman who was considering going into business for herself as a business consultant.

"She liked reading, swimming and dancing. She was really into people", and fitness. She was very thin, very fit," said Mrs. De Vane.

An electronic engineering technician at Burroughs, Sanchez was planning to move to Florida soon, Mrs. De Vane said.

A neighbor of Sanchez described him as "very good looking" and "always in good spirits."

"He was real nice, real easygoing. Just the other day I said hello to him I used to borrow his vacuum cleaner," said the young woman.

A memorial service for Mrs. Domingo has been scheduled for 8:30 p.m. tomorrow at El Montecito Presbyterian Church, said Martha Spoon, Mrs. Domingo's mother. Burial is to follow in San Diego, where the woman grew up and met her former husband, Roger Domingo.

The couple married and moved to Goleta. He was a substitute teacher with the Goleta Union School District. When they divorced, she stayed in this area and he moved back to San Diego. Their son, David, 14, moved back to San Diego with his father last year, said Mrs. Spoon.

Mrs. Domingo's survivors also include her father, Wayland Cliff Smith Jr. of San Diego; a sister, Linda Moreno of Anaheim; a brother, Steven W. Smith of San Diego; and her grandparents Mr. and Mrs. Wayland Smith Sr. of San Diego.

Virginia Wood told the News-Press, "I heard that gunshot just as plain as anything in the world, and I heard a woman scream."

Sgt. Bill Baker, head of the sheriff's major crimes unit, would tell the News-Press only that the most recent killings could be described as "brutal". Birchim said that investigators are "looking into the possibility" that the same person who murdered the couple on Toltec Way may have also killed Goleta surgeon Robert Offerman and Santa Maria psychologist Debra Manning Offerman's condominium at 767 Avenida Pequena on Dec. 30, 1978. But Birchim declined to comment on any similarities between the two killings. A number of coincidences mark the two sets of slayings.

Both couples were killed in the bedroom and found about the same time of day

Manning and Offerman were believed to have been shot at about 3 a.m.

Neighbors in both slayings said they heard what could have been gunshots, but didn't report them because they were holiday firecrackers.

To aid the investigation, detectives called in a 3-year-old blood hound named Duchess from the San Luis Obispo County Sheriff's Department.

Mrs. Domingo was laid off two weeks ago from her job as corporate administrator of Trimm Industries, a Santa Barbara based company that manufacturers computer furniture, said Maurna De

Vane a neighbor and friend who was laid off from Trimm at the same time. She described Mrs. Domingo as a very sociable, tidy and intelligent woman who was considering going into business for herself as a business consultant.

She liked reading, swimming and dancing. She was really into people and fitness. "She was very thin, very fit" said Mrs. DeVane. An electronic engineering technician at Burroughs, "Sanchez was planning to move to Florida soon," Mrs. DeVane said. A neighbor of Sanchez described him as "very good looking" and "always in good spirits." "He was real nice, real easygoing." "Just the other day I said hello to him. I used to borrow his vacuum cleaner said the young woman."

"A memorial service for Mrs. Domingo has been scheduled for 8:30 p.m. tomorrow at El Montecito Presbyterian Church" said Martha Spoon. Mrs. Domingo's mother. Burial is to follow in San Diego, where the woman grew up and met her former husband Roger Domingo.

The couple married and moved to Goleta. He was a substitute teacher with the Goleta Union School District. When they divorced she stayed in the area and he moved back to San Diego. "Their son, David, 14, moved back to San Diego with his father last year" said Mrs. Spoon.

Mrs. Domingo's survivors also include her father, Wayland Cliff Smith, Jr. of San Diego, a sister, Linda Moreno of Anaheim, a brother, Steven W. Smith of San Diego and her grandparents, Mr. and Mrs.

Wayland Smith Sr. of San Diego. **END OF ARTICLE**

Double Murder in Goleta May Be Linked to '79 Killings

7-30-81 Santa Maria Times & Goleta Voice

THERE IS "A good possibility" Monday's double homicide in Goleta is linked to a similar dual murder that happened just a few blocks away in December 1979, according to sheriff's deputies.

Shot and bludgeoned to death were Greg Sanchez, 28, and his friend Cheri Domingo, 35, found dead in the front bedroom of a home at 449 Toltec Way, Goleta, by a realtor who was inspecting the house.

According to sheriff's deputy Russ Birchim, detectives feel it is possible the deaths may be linked to a similar, unsolved homicide of Goleta orthopedic surgeon Robert Offerman and Debra Manning, a Santa Maria psychologist, who were found shot at Offerman's home at 767 Avenida Pequena in 1979, just a few blocks from Monday's murder.

Domingo, a divorced mother, was house-sitting with her 16-year-old daughter Debbie who happened to be spending the night with friends. The owner of the house, Bernard Maas, died earlier this year and his heirs — to whom Domingo is related — had the house up for sale.

Partial results of an autopsy showed a number of severe head wounds to both Sanchez and Domingo, and at least Sanchez was shot also.

"There doesn't appear to be anything taken from the house," said Birchim, who described the murders as "brutal." The bodies were found about noon on Monday by the realtor. A neighbor told police that about 3:30 a.m. on Monday morning she heard shots and a woman scream and when she woke and told her husband, he passed it off as firecrackers, Birchim reported.

Although the Sheriff's department is not releasing many details until the full autopsy is finished, the detectives feel there are similarities with the Offerman/Manning murders due to the close proximity of the crimes, the theory that there is one man involved, forced entry into the houses, the similar times (3 a.m.) of the crimes and, no robbery.

A psychological profile of a possible killer was made after the Offerman/Manning murders and one will be developed for this case also, Birchim said.

Sanchez was described by friends as the boyfriend of Domingo, although they had split up recently but remained good friends. Sanchez worked as a technician at Burroughs in Goleta and Domingo was unemployed at the time of her death, having been laid off from an administration job at Trimm Industries recently.

—John Hankins

July 30, 1981 Santa Maria Times & Goleta Voice article by John Hankins

There is a good possibility Monday's double homicide in Goleta is linked to a similar dual murder that happened just a few blocks away in December 1979, according to sheriff's deputies.

Shot and bludgeoned to death were Greg Sanchez, 28, and his friend Cheri Domingo, 35, found dead in the front bedroom of a home at 449 Toltec Way, Goleta, by a realtor who was inspecting the house.

According to sheriff's deputy Russ Birchim, detectives feel it is possible the deaths may be linked

353

to a similar, unsolved homicide of Goleta surgeon Robert Offerman and Debra Manning, a Santa Maria psychologist, who were found shot at Offerman's home at 767 Avenida Pequera in 1979, just a few blocks from Monday's murder.

Domingo, a divorced mother, was house sitting with her 16 year old daughter Debbie who happened to be spending the night with friends. The owner of the house, Bernard Mass, died earlier this year and his heirs – to whom Domingo is related – had the home up for sale.

Partial results of an autopsy showed a number of severe head wounds to both Sanchez and Domingo, and at least Sanchez was shot also.

"There doesn't appear to be anything taken from the house," said Birchim, who described the murders as brutal." The bodies were found about noon on Monday by the realtor. A neighbor told police that about 3:30 a.m. on Monday morning she heard shots and a woman scream and when she woke she told her husband, he passed it off as firecrackers, Birchim reported.

Although the Sheriff's department is not releasing many details until the full autopsy is finished, the detectives feel there are similarities with the Offerman/Manning murders due to the close proximity of the crimes, the theory that there is one man involved, forced entry into the houses, the similar times (3:00 a.m.) of the crimes and no robbery.

A psychological profile of a possible killer was made after the Offerman/Manning murders and one will be developed for this case also, Birchim said.

Sanchez was described by friends as the boyfriend of Domingo, although they had split up recently but remained good friends. Sanchez worked as a technician at Burrough's in Goleta and Domingo was unemployed at the time of her death having been laid off from an administration job at Trimm Industries recently. **End of article**

Following is a news article about the possible link between the murders from 1981.

This article appears as it was formatted from the original article as copied from the internet. I felt this article was important to show the thinking at the time of the investigations. Note the date of July 1981.

Tie Hinted in Pair of Goleta Murders
By Eric Malnic
Los Angeles Times, 29 July 1981
Goleta- There may be a connection between the murders of a couple here this week and the 1979 murder of a couple in the same neighborhood, Santa Barbara County sheriff's deputies said Tuesday.
Investigators of the 1979 murder developed a psychological profile of the killer that they said indicated he might strike again.
In the latest case, the bodies of Cheri Domingo, 35, and her boyfriend, Greg Sanchez, 28, were found about noon Monday in the front bedroom of a home.

355

Both had been beaten severely on the head and Sanchez had also been shot at least once.

Deputies said the woman had been house-sitting at the residence since the death several months ago of a relative who owned the property. Neighbors said they heard loud reports and a scream about 3 a.m. Monday but ignored the sounds, thinking they resulted from someone setting off fireworks.
The bodies were discovered about eight hours later by a real estate agent who came to look at the house.

About three blocks away, on Dec. 30, 1979, orthopedic surgeon Robert Offerman and Santa Maria psychologist Debra Manning were found shot to death in Offerman's condominium.

Profile Developed
Deputies revealed few details about the 1979 crime, but officers indicated that a profile developed from evidence indicated that the murderer was a psychopath who might kill again.

There were a number of similarities in the murders. They occurred in the same neighborhood, they occurred at about the same time of day and the victims in both cases were unmarried couples whose bodies were found together in a bedroom.
Officers investigating the latest case said Sanchez was an electronics technician who lived in the Santa Barbara area. Mrs. Domingo, a divorcee, was laid off two weeks ago from her job at a computer hardware firm.

The woman had two children—a 15-year-old daughter who was staying with friends the night of the attack, and a 14-year-old son who lives with his father in the San Diego area. **END OF ARTICLE**

This article also appeared in 1981.

'Night Stalker' Theory Connecting Eight Southland Slayings Disputed. ARTICLE
By John Hurst
Los Angeles Times, 2 August 1981, pg. A3, A24.
SANTA BARBARA - Is a psychopathic "Night Stalker" murdering Southern California couples in their beds? Or has the Santa Barbara County Sheriff's Department been overeager—as two other police agencies claim—in linking eight southern California murders and a knife attack to one killer still on the loose?

The controversy and confusion began last week when the Santa Barbara County Sheriff's Department said it believed there is a link between the murders of a couple found bludgeoned to death in a Goleta home Monday and the shooting death of another couple in a home a few blocks away 19 months ago.

Psychologist Draws Profile
Authorities also said they believe the same killer committed a nonfatal knife attack on another couple in the same neighborhood 22 months ago and went

357

on to say they suspect a link to the bludgeon murders of a Ventura couple in March, 1980, and an Orange County couple in August, 1980.

Santa Barbara County sheriff's spokesman Russ Birchim said deputies have dubbed the killer the "Night Stalker," and authorities said a "profile" developed by a local psychologist had indicated "a high probability" that the murderer would strike again even before the latest homicide.

"There is a person out there killing people," said Sgt. William Baker, head of the sheriff's major crime division. "We believe there is a strong possibility that the three (Santa Barbara cases) are connected."

Regarding the Orange County and Ventura murders, Baker said:

"I would say there is a strong suspicion (That they are linked to the Santa Barbara cases) but to a lesser degree because I'm not as familiar with those jurisdictions cases."

But authorities in Ventura and Orange County are skeptical that the murders in those jurisdictions are linked to the Santa Barbara cases.
"We see no connection between the killings," said Ventura Police Sgt. Larry White, in charge of the Ventura homicide investigation. "We don't know what if any link there might be."

He contended that Santa Barbara County authorities "jumped the gun" with their announcement of a suspected link and said there had been no communication between the two departments immediately prior to that statement that a link is suspected.

Similarly, Orange County authorities are unconvinced.

"I think they (Santa Barbara County authorities) are very premature at this point," said Darryl Coder, Orange County sheriff's investigator. "They're still coordinating their investigation. . .

"We had a double homicide in August of last year, he continued, "and we put out a bulletin (to other law enforcement agencies) that anybody with a double homicide contact us. . . We were contacted by just about everybody in the state. . . The fact that you have a male and a female killed on a bed does not make the cases the same. . .

"Shortly after our homicide," Coder continued, "San Diego had a homicide, male and female in bed together. We ran down there and it turned out it was a dope rip-off."

"It is not uncommon," he went on, "to have a male and female (killed) in their house. Most people do go to bed at night, and because they are killed in bed does not make those cases that similar."

The Santa Barbara crimes aside, Coder was similarly skeptical of any connection between the Orange County and Ventura murders. "We don't feel that (there is a connection)," he said. "We never felt that."

The eight homicides and the knife attack, committed between Oct. 1, 1979 and July 27, 1981, share several striking similarities, but there are notable differences.

In every crime the victims were a man and a woman in their bedroom, probably in bed. In each case, the scene of the crime was a comfortable to fashionable home. In most cases the weapon was a bludgeon. But in another it was a gun. In one it was a knife with the threat of a gun. In the latest, it was a gun and a bludgeon.

No Sexual Molestation. This was part of this article – the words ("No Sexual Molestation") I do not know how this statement could have been made as it is known that Charlene Smith was raped.

In none of the cases has sexual molestation of the victims been reported.
In at least one case, the victims were tied up, but in some cases authorities deny that binds were used and in others they refuse to say. In four cases, nothing is believed to have been stolen from the victims' homes. But in one case, a small amount of cash was taken, according to police.

In the Santa Barbara County murders, the male victims were found on the floor and the females in bed, according to police. But in the Ventura and Orange County cases, all the victims were reportedly found in bed.

In all the Santa Barbara cases, the victims were unmarried couples, leading to speculation that the killer might be a demented moralist. But in the Ventura and Orange County murders, the couples were married.

In Santa Barbara County, all three crimes occurred within a square mile. All were near a creek bed that meanders through Goleta, an area adjacent to Santa Barbara that is made up largely of newish tract homes.

In two of the Santa Barbara crimes, the same caliber gun was used, according to police, but ballistics tests on recovered bullets have not yet determined whether or not the same weapon was used in the two cases.

These are the crimes under investigation:

—Early on Oct 1, 1979, a Goleta couple, who asked not to be identified, were accosted in their bed by a man armed with a kitchen knife. According to a source, the intruder shined a flashlight on them and, threatening to "blow your head off," forced the woman to tie up the man with cord. If the intruder had a gun, according to sources, the couple never saw it in the darkness.

The intruder put a pair of shorts over the head of the woman, according to a source, and forced her into another room and tied her up, continually threatening murder.

In the meantime, the man, still bound, was able to get out of the house and yell for help. The intruder ran from the home, jumped on a bicycle and, with a neighbor chasing him, made his getaway, according to sources.

Police recovered the bicycle, which was stolen, and the kitchen knife, but refused to say whether they obtained fingerprints. Police say a small amount of cash was taken from the couples' home, the only known robbery in the cases.

Because of the darkness, the couple was able to give only the sketchiest description of their assailant: A man, probably white, medium height, medium to slender build, late teens or early twenties, wearing dark clothing.
—During the early morning of Dec. 30, 1979, a few blocks from the home of the unidentified Goleta couple, Dr. Robert Offerman, 44, an orthopedist, and Debra Manning, 35, a psychologist, were shot to death in the bedroom of Offerman's condominium.

Offerman was found on the floor and Manning on the bed. Police won't say whether either victim had been tied up.

—On March 16, 1980, attorney Lyman Smith, 43, and his wife Charlene Smith, 33, were found bludgeoned to death in a bedroom of their expensive home in a quiet residential neighborhood of Ventura, about 35 miles from Goleta. Police said at the time of the murder that both bodies were found in bed and early reports indicated that a fireplace log found on the bed was believed to be the murder weapon. Police now are tighter-lipped and won't comment on the weapon or whether the
victims were tied up.

—On Aug 21, 1980, Keith Harrington, 24, a medical student, and his wife of four months, **Anne** Harrington, 27, a nurse, were found bludgeoned to death in the bedroom of their home in fashionable Niguel Shores in South Orange County, more
than 100 miles from Ventura where the previous victims were killed. Both victims were found in bed. They reportedly were not tied up. **(They got the victims' name wrong above) Her name was Patrice.**
—Last Monday, 11 months after the Harrington's were murdered, Cheri Domingo, 35, and her boyfriend, Greg Sanchez, 28, were found bludgeoned to death in a bedroom of the spacious Goleta home that Domingo had been housesitting while it was up for sale.

The house is probably 150 miles from the Harrington home, but it is only a few blocks from the condominium in which Offerman and Manning were killed.

As in the Offerman-Manning killing, Sanchez was found on the floor and Domingo on the bed, according to authorities. And, in addition to being bludgeoned, Sanchez was shot once with a bullet of the same caliber that killed Offerman and Manning, police say.

"You've got people being shot to death," said Santa Barbara county sheriff's Sgt. Baker. "You've got people being bludgeoned to death. So now you've got something that brings them together. Because now you've got some elements you have bludgeoning and shooting. But Santa Barbara County sheriff's officers refused to give details of why they suspect a link to murders in Ventura and Orange County.
END OF ARTICLE

Goleta murders
Sheriff's department seeks link

Goleta Valley News
By LORI SCHWEITZER   8-6-1981

In the wake of the double slaying of a Goleta couple last week by a man county sheriff's are calling "not altogether sane," Goleta residents are urged to take extra precautions against a possible recurrence of the crime.

"We stress the value of locks" said sheriff's department Public Information Officer Ross Birchim.

"We would also be glad to come to your house and do a security check," he added. As a service to the community the department will send an officer to inspect a home and assure that it is as safe as possible from intruders.

Residents of the neighborhood around 449 Toltec Way, the scene of last week's brutal bludgeoning murder, are enthusiastically heeding the sheriff's warnings. Birchim said at least seven have responded to the department's offer to run security checks and sheriff's deputy Brent Morris reportedly has been contacted to help set up two neighborhood watch groups in the area.

These residents have cause to be especially cautious. The victims of last week's murder were the third in a series of Goleta crimes sheriff's deputies believe are connected. The sheriff's department also believes the victims of these crimes were chosen at random.

The attacks first drew the attention of the sheriff's department on October 1, 1979, when an unnamed Goleta couple were reportedly terrorized in their home on Queen Anne Lane, less than a mile north of Toltec Way, by a man brandishing a kitchen knife.

The attacker found the couple in their bedroom. He forced the woman to tie up the other victim and then took her into another room where he tied her up. Both victims reported the attacker threatened to kill them.

The first victim, however, managed to escape from the house screaming for help and scared the intruder away. The incident occurred at approximately 2 a.m.

Two months later, on December 30, 1979, a Goleta couple was found shot to death in this bedroom of their Avenida Pequena condominium, a few blocks from the Queen Anne Lane incident. It was estimated at the time that the victims, Dr. Robert Offerman, a 44-year-old orthopedist, and his girlfriend Debra Manning, a 35-year-old psychologist, were murdered at 3 a.m. in the morning.

As a result of the investigation of the Offerman-Manning murder sheriff's deputies made the connection to the Queen Anne Lane incident and federal investigators were called in to prepare a psychological profile. Later the department released a description of a possible suspect based on the information given by the Queen Anne couple and the FBI profile.

The killer was described as a white male in his early 20's with light brown hair. Furthermore, on the basis of the psychological profile sheriff's believed the killer was a psychopath and that he might strike again. On July 27, 1981, the brutal murder of another unmarried Goleta couple possibly fulfilled that prophesy.

The almost unrecognizable bodies of Cheri Domingo, aged 35, and her 24-year-old boyfriend Greg Sanchez were also found in the bedroom. A real estate agent discovered the victims who were housesitting while the Toltec Way home was for sale. The agent had gone by to check the place before showing it.

Police have described the scene of the Domingo-Sanchez murder as "gruesome." In fact, it took several days for the coroner's report which revealed both victims died from head beatings. Sanchez, however, was also shot. The bullet which went through Sanchez body was recovered from the scene but no ballistics report has been released. Birchim

reports that no actual weapons were recovered.

Several aspects of the Domingo-Sanchez murder led the police to connect it to the other two incidents. Although there is a tight lid on information about the investigation now underway, Birchim listed some of the similarities among the three incidents.

— All three incidents involved unmarried couples.

— All three occurred in the early morning hours, thus the name "Night Stalker" which some investigators are calling the attacker.

— The incidents occurred within a mile radius of each other in similar type homes, priced in the $200,000 range.

— There was no sign of struggle, in the two murder incidents. None of the incidents involved sexual assaults or burglary.

— The crime scenes in the two murders were in bedrooms and the toilet attack was initiated in the bedroom.

— All three incidents involved forced entry. But there are also dissimilarities. None of the crimes involved the same weapons or combination of weapons, for instance. Investigators are not releasing information
Please turn to page 11

Murder...

Continued from page one regarding the bullets or fingerprints recovered from both murder scenes.

Following the Offerman-Manning murder, the sheriff's department contacted other counties in an attempt to connect the attacks to other similar crimes. Two homicides, one in Orange County and one in Ventura County, fit the pattern.

The Orange County incident involved the bludgeoning death on August 19, 1980, of Keith Harrington, a 24-year-old medical student, and his wife of four months, Patty Harrington, a 27-year-old nurse. As in the Goleta attacks the victims were found in the bedroom, nothing was taken from the home, ruling out burglary as a motive, and there were no signs of resistance. The home was an exclusive one in a posh area south of Laguna Beach.

ment to a judgeship.

Similarities were discussed among the three jurisdictions after the Offerman-Manning murders. Following the Domingo-Sanchez incident, sheriffs released information that they believed the "Night Stalker" was responsible and reportedly sighted the Orange and Ventura murders as possible acts of the same man.

According to a recent article in the Los Angeles Times, however, both Orange and Ventura County officials thought Santa Barbara sheriffs "jumped the gun" in connecting the latest murders with the cases in their jurisdictions.

In defense of the department, Birchim points out that those connections were made a year ago and added that regardless of any connections, Santa Barbara sheriffs were concentrating only on the Goleta crimes.

That concentration, according to Birchim in-

As early as 1981 detectives and many others debated about whether the murders that were occurring in Southern California in Orange County, Ventura County and Santa Barbara County were

365

linked. Unfortunately, it appears that this discussion and this train of thought were dismissed. As it turned out they were all linked to the same man as we now know.

As a side note it has been speculated that Santa Barbara County did not want the publicity that would surround a serial rapist/killer in their area at the time. President Ronald Reagan had a ranch in Santa Barbara County during the ONS murders. Santa Barbara was reluctant to acknowledge any real connection to the other counties early on. It wasn't until a couple of years ago that Santa Barbara County really got involved allowing DNA testing to at last connect their murder cases with all of the other counties. When this much time goes by there are periods of time that cases are cold cases in every county. It is unfortunate that resources or a lack thereof make it so. These murders sat on the back burner or in archived boxes for many years. New detectives came and went in all the counties over the course of the last 30 to 40 years. That's life. It is time to solve these cases.

From Larry Crompton's book Sudden Terror comes this:

"On January 23, 1999, Forensic Scientist Mary Hong matched DNA evidence from Ventura Police Department's Lyman and Charlene Smith murders to the suspect's DNA from Harrington, Witthuhn and Cruz homicides. Twelve years after the Janelle Cruz murder, DNA evidence had proven what CLUE investigators had believed; the murders were committed by the same person."

"The suspects M.O. and the type of crimes appeared similar to the Domingo/Sanchez and Offerman/Manning homicides and the Duffy/Playa attempt, all in Santa Barbara County. Santa Barbara Sheriff's Department, however, concluded that their homicides were not related to the serial/murderer and refused to participate in a coordinated investigation."

CLUE was the name of the Countrywide Law Enforcement Unsolved Element, (CLUE) formed by the Orange County Sheriff's Department.

The similarity between this picture of the creek bed in Goleta (San Jose Creek) and Morrison Creek where I grew up is striking. It is speculated that the Original Night Stalker used San Jose Creek as one of his means of escape in the Goleta area.

Running through the center of Goleta, San Jose
Creek

**San Jose Creek and its relationship
geographically to the attempted attack in Goleta
and the two murders in Goleta area.**

To put the geography in perspective over the course
of all of the murders from 1979 until 1986 from
Goleta to Laguna Niguel (Dana Point) it takes 2
hours and 32 minutes to go from one place to
another. From Goleta to Ventura, California takes 37
minutes. From Goleta to Irvine it takes 2 hours and
18 minutes. From Irvine to Laguna Niguel (Dana
Point) it is 28 minutes. None of these locations were
really all that far from each other.

RAPIST'S TRAIL OF TERROR

The East Area Rapist is suspected of committing 30 attacks, including one murder of a couple in Sacramento County, from 1976-1978. Locations are approximate.

SACRAMENTO COUNTY

KEY

	RAPE	MURDER
1976	○	
1977	○	
1978	●	■
1979	●	■
1980-86		■

1978 murder of the Maggiores in Rancho Cordova

5 miles

VALLEY AND EAST BAY

The East Area Rapist is suspected of committing an additional 16 crimes in the region between 1976 and 1979.

San Joaquin Co. ○●
Stanislaus Co. ●●
Yolo Co. ●●●
Contra Costa Co. ●●●●●●
Santa Clara Co. ●●
Alameda Co. ●

SOUTHERN CALIFORNIA

10 murders and one attack in Southern California between 1979 and 1986 now are believed to have been committed by the same person.

Santa Barbara Co. ●■■■■
Ventura Co. ■■
Orange Co. ■■■■

Source: ear-ons.com   **SHARON OKADA** sokada@sacbee.com

369

I think this is an important connection

Check out the date of article in Sacramento and that night March 13, 1980 Murders in Ventura County, CA

Updates on the investigation

March 13, 1980 – this article was in the Sacramento Bee on the same day that in Ventura County ONS murdered Lyman and Charlene Smith in the middle of the night

Police Debate Tie Between East Area Rapist, Killings

By Wayne Wilson
Bee Staff Writer

There is a difference of opinion among detectives investigating the possibility that a double homicide in Santa Barbara County was committed by Sacramento's East Area rapist.

Santa Barbara Sheriff's Sgt. William Baker said Wednesday he does not believe the Dec. 30 killings of a Goleta Valley orthopedic surgeon and his psychologist girlfriend were committed by the same man believed to be responsible for 44 sexual assaults in Northern California.

Baker's opinion is shared by Sacramento Sheriff's Lt. Ray Root, but Root said Wednesday that the detective assigned to the case in Sacramento, Sgt. James D. Bevins, feels fairly strongly that there's a very strong possibility it is the same man.

Root said the Sacramento Sheriff's Department will maintain contact with authorities in Santa Barbara as the investigation continues.

Baker said more dissimilarities seem to be developing since the two agencies began investigating the possibility of a connection between the crimes.

The more we go into it, the less and less there seems to be a possibility of a connection," Baker said.

Root said the factor that convinced him there was no connection was the apparent ineptitude exhibited by the killer in Santa Barbara. In the double homicide and in another crime, a residential robbery, tied to the killings.

"In both of the incidents—down there, it is obvious the guy lost control of the situation, lost control of the people, and eventually had to kill somebody," Root said.

The homicide victims, Drs. Robert J. Offerman, 44, and Debra A. Manning, 35, were found shot to death in the bedroom of Offerman's Goleta Valley condominium.

"It appears the male victim had actually gotten his hands untied and was attacking whomever killed him," Root said.

"In the residential robbery, the female victim actually got out of the house screaming and he had to run out and grab her and drag her back in. Then the male got out of the house and was hiding in the backyard shrubbery when the robber split."

Root said that scenario does not fit the East Area rapist, who never lost control of a situation.

"It just doesn't seem reasonable to me that the guy could go through 40 or so rapes and maintain absolute control and then go to Santa Barbara and suddenly lose control of three different people in two different situations, back to back."

Root conceded there were similarities that bear investigating: the method of entry into the residences; the method of tying the victims; the conversations reported.

But he indicated there were not enough points of similarity to make a positive determination one way or another and said it was his gut feeling that the Sacramento and Santa Barbara incidents are not related.

Bevins, who could not be reached for comment, is still working on the possibility that a relationship exists, however. The Bee has learned that Bevins has been circulating in Sacramento the photo of a sole-print, identified as a size 9½ Adidas running shoe, apparently found at the scene of the Offerman-Manning homicides.

Article typed for clarity:

Police Debate Tie Between East Area Rapist,
Killings By Wayne Wilson – Bee staff writer

There is a difference of opinion among detectives investigating the possibility that a double homicide in Santa Barbara County was committed by Sacramento's East Area rapist.

Santa Barbara Sheriff's Sgt. William Baker said Wednesday he does not believe the Dec. 30 killings of a "Goleta Valley orthopedic surgeon and his psychologist girlfriend were committed by the same man believed to be responsible for 44 sexual assaults in Northern California.

Baker's opinion is shared by Sacramento Sheriff's Lt. Ray Root, but Root said Wednesday that the detective assigned to the case in Sacramento. Sgt. James D. Bevins feels fairly strongly that there's a very strong possibility it is the same man.

Root said the Sacramento Sheriff's Department will maintain contact with authorities in Santa Barbara as the investigation continues. Baker said more dissimilarities seem to be developing since the two agencies began investigating the possibility of a connection between the crimes.

"The more we get into it, the less and less there seems to be a possibility of a connection." Baker said.

Root said the factor that convinced him there was no connection was the apparent ineptitude exhibited by the killer in Santa Barbara in the double homicide and in another crime a residential robbery, tied to the killings.

"In both of the incidents down there, it is obvious the guy lost control of the situation, lost control of the people, and eventually to have to kill somebody." Root said.

The homicide victims, Drs. Robert J. Offerman, 44, and Debra A. Manning, 35 were found shot to death in the bedroom of Offerman's Goleta Valley condominium.

It appears the male victim had actually gotten his hands untied and was attacking whomever killed him." Root said. "In the residential robbery, the female victim actually got out of the house screaming and he had to run out and grab her and drag her back in. Then the male got out of the house and was hiding to the backyard shrubbery when the robber split.

Root said that the scenario does not fit the East Area rapist, who never lost control of a situation.

"It just doesn't seem reasonable to me that this guy could go through 40 or so rapes and maintain absolute control and then go to Santa Barbara and suddenly lose control of three different people in two different situations, back to back."

Root conceded there were similarities that bear investigating: the method of entry into the residences; the method of tying the victim; the conversations reported.

But he indicated there were not enough points of similarity to make a positive determination one way or another and said it was his gut feeling that the Sacramento and Santa Barbara incidents are not related.

Bevin's, who could not be reached for comment, is still working on the possibility that a relationship exists, however. The Bee has learned that Bevin's has been circulating in Sacramento the photo of a sole print, identified as a size 9-1/2 Adidas running shoe, apparently found at the scene of the Offerman-Manning homicides.

END OF ARTICLE

The debate went on for some time about whether there was a connection. Many were incorrect in their belief that there was no connection. **The day this article was published March 13, 1980 in Sacramento which stated this criminal was inept because he lost control of some of his victims was probably enough to spur him on. Unfortunately, this was to be Lyman and Charlene's last day alive. I believe there is a direct connection between this article being published in Sacramento on this date and the murders of Charlene and Lyman Smith in the middle of the night in Ventura, CA.**

In the beginning Ventura County looked in all of the wrong places for the culprit of the Smith murders.

Unfortunately, it was to take a very long time to connect these murders with the Goleta murders and others. This criminal kept changing some of what he did to try and confuse some of the detectives in some of the counties he would run through. It must have been extremely funny to him as the news reports came in speculating over and over. Sometimes ONS would use a gun and sometimes he bludgeoned and used a gun. He changed some of what he did on purpose. Because of the focus on one of Lyman Smith's former business associates, the trail or case went cold in Ventura County. When it was suggested that the cases in Goleta or Santa Barbara were connected the different jurisdictions and counties denied that they really believed there was any connection. If the detectives believed there was a connection it was usually denied in news articles and stories at the time which was very soon after the initial murders took place even until the late 1980's.

Manuela Witthuhn – February 1981

Autopsy shows housewife died of blow

IRVINE — An autopsy performed Saturday revealed that a 28-year-old housewife whose body was found Friday died Thursday about midnight from a blow to the head with a blunt instrument, police reported.

Police said the slaying of Manuela E. Witthuhn does not appear to be connected to other crimes in the area and said they have no suspects.

Source of articles above and below unknown.
Taken from internet images

Manuela Witthuhn

Very rapidly it appears the investigations hit a dead end (within a year) dead end ... an inactive investigation???

While the debate continued the perpetrator disappeared until 1986

Janelle Cruz was murdered May 4, 1986 as reported in the Register in Irvine California

Bludgeoned body identified as Irvine teen

The Register

Irvine police Thursday tentatively identified the body of a woman who was found bludgeoned to death this week as 18-year-old Janelle Lisa Cruz.

The teen-ager was found dead Monday afternoon inside her home when a real estate agent showed the house to a prospective buyer, police Lt. Al Muir said.

An autopsy Tuesday showed Cruz died of multiple blows to the head. Muir said police were "99 percent sure" that the body is that of Cruz, but a positive identification was still being sought by the county Coroner's Office through dental records.

No suspects have been arrested, and police have yet to find the weapon used to kill the young woman, he said. No motive for the slaying has been established.

Cruz's mother, Diane Stein, and her stepfather, Alan Stein, were on vacation in Cancún, Mexico, when the discovery was made, Muir said. Both returned to Irvine late Wednesday.

Muir said Cruz lived in the single-story house on Encina in Irvine's Northwood Village with her mother and stepfather.

Muir said this was Irvine's first homicide case for 1986.

The Register (Irvine, California) May 1986

Irvine police Thursday tentatively identified the body of a woman who was found bludgeoned to death this week as 18-year-old Janelle Lisa Cruz.

The teenager was found dead Monday afternoon inside her home when a real estate agent showed the house to a prospective buyer, police Lt. Al Muir said.

An autopsy Tuesday showed Cruz died of multiple blows to the head. Muir said police were "99 percent sure" that the body is that of Cruz, but a positive identification was still being sought by the county Coroner's Office through dental records.

No suspects have been arrested, and police have yet to find the weapon used to kill the young woman, he said. No motive for the slaying has been established.

Cruz's mother Diane Stein, and her stepfather Alan Stein were on vacation in Cancun Mexico, when the discovery was made, Muir said. Both returned to Irvine late Wednesday.

Muir said Cruz lived in the single story house on Encina in Irvine's Northwood Village with her mother and stepfather.

Muir said this was Irvine's first homicide case for 1986.

END OF ARTICLE

Back to trying to solve the case

So, was the murder of Janelle Cruz really the last known attack and murder in 1986? Or is this last attack in October 1987 something that can be attributed to ONS? In Larry Crompton's book,

Sudden Terror, he reports the following happened in Oakdale California.

"On Monday, October 12, 1987, a thirty-one-year-old Oakdale woman was attacked by an unknown assailant. The woman was sleeping when a subject entered the rear yard of the residence, retrieved an oak log from a woodpile and entered the house through a laundry room window. The intruder struck her in the head several times with the log fracturing her skull multiple times.

The woman woke up screaming, thinking she had a nightmare. Noting blood, she thought she had cut herself while sleeping. Approximately one hour later she called the police. Her ten-year-old daughter sleeping in a separate room was unharmed.

Investigator Pool was contacted by Stanislaus County probation officer on Friday, February 19, 1999 after a request for assistance teletype sent by Pool to California's four parole regions. Pool responded to Oakdale, however after talking to investigators he could not establish the attack was related to the southern California murders." **END OF ARTICLE-END OF QUOTE**

Here are a couple of articles about whether or not these crimes could be linked:

ARTICLE:
RAPIST MOVES TO CONTRA COSTA
By 1978, the rapist started hitting Contra Costa County, attacking women in Concord, Danville and San Ramon.

"He would go into nice homes, usually occupied by a man and a woman," said Karen Sheldon, director of the Contra Costa Sheriff's Department crime lab. "He would tie up the male. He then put dishes or something on his back so there would be noise if the guy moved while the suspect was committing the rape. I think he liked to have a man present. He enjoyed the risk."

The rapist frequently threatened to kill both the man and woman if the dishes fell off and broke.
A task force was formed to try to solve the crimes, said District Attorney Gary Yancey, but leads fizzled out, and, although some suspects were investigated, no one was charged.

For years, women throughout the Bay Area were fearful of his return, keeping their windows locked and worrying about break-ins, but the criminal never struck again.

Last year, the crime lab, which was reviewing old cases, prepared a genetic profile of the rapist. Investigators remembered an old rumor that the suspect might have moved to Southern California; so on little more than a hunch, they began contacting police in Santa Barbara and Irvine and ended up at Orange County's crime lab.

In January, the DNA profile of the East Area Rapist was matched to the unidentified killer.

MURDERS SHARED CHARACTERISTICS
The murders in Laguna Niguel, Ventura, Goleta and Irvine shared characteristics. Police believe the assailant picked his targets carefully and, after breaking in, committed a "blitz" attack. Police have definitively linked six murders to the same suspect as the East Area Rapist, but they believe he may have killed four others in similar attacks.

In several cases, the murderer broke in at night while a couple were sleeping and tied them up before bludgeoning them to death. In at least one case, he raped the woman while the husband lay helplessly bound nearby.

The behavioral profile that police had already assigned to the Orange County slayings suggested the killer chose victims in upper-middle-class to affluent communities, that he was a skilled burglar and that his previous sexual relationships involved bondage and sadism.

Orange County officials are still seeking a suspect who matches the killer's genetic profile. Fitzpatrick said the DNA work had been sent to the state Department of Justice's DNA Lab in Berkeley, where a genetic databank of known felons is being compiled. No match has been made yet, but Fitzpatrick is hopeful that as more criminals are entered into the system, a suspect will be identified.

If a match is made, the man could not be charged with the Northern California rapes, because the statute of limitations has expired. But Sheldon said it was worth it to go through old cases to try to identify the perpetrator.

"It was good detective work," Sheldon said. "It's not common. It was a challenge just getting people interested in a case that had passed a statute of limitations."

And Yancey, who was on the task force 20 years ago as a deputy prosecutor, said knowing that a suspect had been identified could bring closure to the victims. "I think it's very important for the peace of mind for those individuals," Yancey said.

Last week, Attorney General Bill Lockyear encouraged police and prosecutors throughout California to review unsolved sexual assault cases without suspects and unsolved rape-murders to determine whether DNA testing of biological evidence could allow them to target a suspect.

Even if the statute of limitations in old cases has expired, preventing the suspect from being prosecuted, there's still a benefit to doing the DNA work, said Contra Costa Deputy District Attorney

Paul Sequeira, who heads the sexual assaults division.

"I like the idea of knowing who the guy is," Sequeira said. "I think it's better that (the victims) know who he is. It's scary to know there's this Mr. X out there. At least if they knew who it was, they could keep tabs on him." **END OF ARTICLE**

Interesting.... Keep tabs on him? If we knew who he was wouldn't we arrest him? I found that particular statement rather odd. Everyone makes mistakes.

Here is just one article about linking the DNA of the murderer to the East Area Rapist from 2001. It is now 15 years later and no arrests have been made. At last, proof that the East Area Rapist and The Original Night Stalker are the same man.

Lieutenant Larry Crompton had a gut feel all along that The East Area Rapist and the man responsible for 10 murders in Southern California were and are the same man. He is correct.

San Francisco Chronicle

DNA Links '70s 'East Area Rapist' to Serial Killings Evidence suggests suspect moved to Southern California - Erin Hallissy and Charlie Goodyear, Chronicle Staff Writers Wednesday, April 4, 2001

The East Area Rapist forged a trail of terror from Sacramento to San Ramon in the late 1970s, randomly breaking into women's homes and raping them while their husbands were kept silent.
Just as suddenly as he began his spree of 40 rapes, the attacker disappeared at the end of the decade without ever being identified.

Now, through recently analyzed DNA evidence, the Contra Costa County crime lab has linked the notorious East Area Rapist with an elusive serial killer who slew 10 people in Southern California coastal communities between 1979 and 1986.

The rapist-killer's identity is still unknown, but police say it is clear that the same man described in police records as methodical, sexually deviant and with above-average intelligence, committed all the crimes. It is a finding that has relieved investigators, who thought they would never solve the cases, and also has worried them, because the man remains unidentified. "This guy is about as bad as you can get," said Frank Fitzpatrick, director of the Orange County crime lab, which analyzed the genetic profile on the serial killings. "The speculation is that he was either arrested (for a different crime) or died or moved out of state."

Retired Sacramento County sheriff's detective Richard Shelby, who investigated the East Area Rapist cases, said yesterday he thought the suspect was still alive and might have a family.

"He called one of the victims," Shelby said. "It was 1990 or 1991. She talked to him for a minute. She could hear kids in the background and a woman."

Shelby believes the East Area Rapist first struck in 1974 with a burglary in which he violently beat a dog to death. Two years later, a couple of sexual assaults in the Sacramento area convinced police a serial rapist was at work.

"In all the cases, he tied them so tight their hands would turn black," Shelby said. "He always used a new pair of shoelaces to bind them." In most cases, he was armed and wore a mask -- a welder's mask in one case.
END OF ARTICLE

The following article was written in October 2000. At long last Ventura County had an answer. The murders were certainly not committed by someone the Smith's knew and they were not committed by any so called enemies.

Lyman & Charlene Smith murder revealed to be work of serial killer
October 13, 2000
By Peggy Kelly
Santa Paula News

This article has been condensed and quoted

"There was no doubt that attorney Lyman Smith was an intense, ambitious man who was on the brink of being appointed a Ventura County Superior Court judge, an announcement expected within days of his murder. When Lyman and his wife, Charlene, were battered to death in their bed over 20 years ago, the mystery of just who killed them included several suspects; one man, who had lost a small fortune in a failed business deal with Smith, was released after prosecutors started their case against him. Police investigators were convinced the murders were committed by someone known to Lyman Smith, but the murder did not bear the marks of a grudge crime: after all, a known enemy isn't prone to kill the spouse, in this case Charlene Smith. Furthermore, if an enemy had indeed committed the brutal crime, they would have brought a weapon, say a gun, to murder the couple at their ocean view Ventura home."

"Tying Charlene and Lyman together - they were found trussed with drapery cords - also smacked of something much more than a grudge killing, as well as her rape. The Smiths were beaten to death with a log from their own fireplace, a murder that now has been linked by advanced DNA testing to an elusive serial killer, a man believed to be white, fair haired. A serial killer who might still be out there."

"It wasn't until the mid-1990s that the Orange County Sheriff's Department started investigating a string of murders that DNA samples from the crimes were tied to the Smiths: now, they are believed to be the only Ventura County victims of the killer, who first struck in Goleta and then worked his way south and is responsible for six killings, perhaps half a dozen more." **END OF ARTICLE**

It never crossed the minds of many that the brutal murders occurring in Southern California were or could be the work of a serial killer. At least it sure seemed that way according to what LE stated to the media.

There are inaccurate statements in the article previous page. For example, the comments about Charlene and Lyman being bound together are not true. The log used to kill them was not from the fireplace, it was from the stack on the side of the house outside the bedroom that the killer grabbed on the way in.

Criminal Investigative Analysis

Sometime after 1986 after all of the murders ceased that we know of Leslie D'Ambrosia, Florida Department of Law Enforcement, Miami Regional Operations Center in consultation with and review by Detective Sergeant John Yarbrough, Los Angeles County Sheriff's Department Homicide Bureau provided an analysis on the series of homicides of six of the victims that had been connected to the same man.

The dates of occurrence were from March 13, 1980 starting with the Smith murders and ending on May 5, 1986 with the murder of Janelle Cruz. I have highlighted a few particular areas of this fifteen-page report in order that you might see the professional analysis by Special Agent D'Ambrosia and others. It is important to enlighten and to give greater understanding of the man responsible for the crimes. If you are interested to read this entire report it can be found online listed here:

http://www.ear-ons.com/nightstalkerprofile.pdf

As D' Ambrosia states, "The final analysis is based on probabilities."

VICTIMS

"All six victims died as a result of excessive beatings to the head with a blunt force instrument. The first two victims, the SMITHS, had ligatures tied around their wrists and ankles. The HARRINGTONS and MANUELA WITTHUHN had ligature marks on their wrists and ankles.

JANELLE CRUZ had a bruise abrasion on her right wrist and evidence of a soft ligature used on her wrists.

All four female victims were sexually assaulted. Analysis of the semen revealed that unknown DNA profiles in all four cases were from one donor, and therefore one individual was responsible for these attacks.

Two of the female victims had circular contusions. One was located on the shoulder of PATRICE HARRINGTON and the other was located on the buttocks of MANUELA WITTHUHN. The shoulder injury was described as a possible bite mark, the other as being consistent with a punch."

SUMMARY:

"Evidence reveals that the male victims were likely eliminated prior to the sexual assault and murder of the female victims. The offender used a great deal of physical force when he bludgeoned the female victims. The women suffered crushing blows to their heads resulting from beatings with blunt force instruments. The amount of force used by the offender was extreme especially considering that they were bound and compliant and, therefore, unable to resist their attacker. The behavior of the victims during the assaults did not cause the offender to increase the amount of force used because they were not resistant. More force was used than was necessary to kill the victims. The female victims were all sexually assaulted.

The fact that the killer attacked his victims inside their homes is significant. The few serial killers that have been known to attack inside the victims' residences proved to have histories of committing burglaries. In these four cases, the offender also was able to enter in a stealth manner without alerting his victims. Based on these facts we would surmise that your offender would likely be an accomplished cat burglar.

Research has provided information on the likely characteristics and traits of this type of offender. He would likely have been described by those who knew him as being neat, articulate, intelligent and organized. He also would likely have been described as rigid, arrogant, domineering and possessing an attitude of superiority. He would be further described as manipulative, a chronic liar, and unremorseful. He may have an interest in survivalist groups or racial prejudicial groups. This type of offender does not suffer from delusions where there is no sense of reality. He would know the difference between right and wrong. The offender was very methodical. After the first crime, he took care not to get blood spatter on himself when striking his victims by covering the bodies.

His behavior was repetitive with respect to his performing the same acts during each crime. He arrived at the crime scenes prepared with a "kit". He selected his victims through peeping. He approached the victims in the same manner. He bludgeoned all the victims to death and sexually assaulted all the women in the same manner.

He planned his attacks very carefully, with great attention to detail, and likely would have rehearsed his attacks, either literally or in his fantasy many times. Virtually every phase. Weapons, transportation, travel routes, instruments of torture, and bindings-would have been pre-planned, with the exception of the victim. This type of offender used a method of killing that reflected his desire for complete mastery and control over his victims. In those scenes where two victims were killed; the offender was not discouraged by the fact that two people were present. In fact, it is more likely that the offender was gratified with his ability to have complete mastery over two people. Since this offender enjoyed the infliction of pain, whether physical or psychological, the elimination of the targeted victims' spouses served two purposes: one, the increased pleasure of controlling more than one person; and two, to have complete mastery over the targeted victims through the fear and pain inflicted by the killing of their spouses. This would cause the female victims to suffer enormously while being restrained and unable to defend themselves. All this was at the core of the offender's desires and was reflected in his methods of killing.

Your offender made the conscious decision to bludgeon his victims to death rather than to use some other simpler form of murder. This is apparent because he brought blunt force instruments into the victims' homes. It is likely that he chose this violent form of death due to his enormous hate for the female victims. In doing so, they would suffer greatly.

To kill them easily or quickly would not have been satisfying for him. This offender was angry with women and used sex and physical force as weapons to punish and degrade them. He exhibited extreme anger and rage toward his female victims when he bludgeoned them to death. This behavior revealed his intense rage for the female victims and what they represented. He used excessive levels of force as the result of his rage, which was exhibited in the form of frenzied attacks on his victims. It is possible that in the mind of the killer these victims were a symbolic representation of a conflict involving a female. He blamed these women for his problems and believed he was superior to all women. He was getting even with women for their real or imagined wrongs. The victims were bound when they were killed and, therefore, were not able to resist their attacker. The amount of force used by the offender was extreme especially considering that they were bound and compliant.

We believe the offender disguised his motivation for the crimes because he did not want the murders linked together. Manipulating law enforcement into investigating the crimes separately would decrease the total information collected and therefore would decrease the likelihood of the cases being solved.

This is the most likely of all offenders to record his crimes. This can be done in many forms such as photographs, audio recordings, sketches, writings or newspaper clippings. In the first homicide of LYMAN and CHARLENE SMITH, newspaper accounts listed many details of the crime and the investigation. We believe the offender read the newspaper articles because he altered his behavior following their publication. We believe therefore the offender likely saved the newspaper articles concerning the homicides. The recording of these events is so that the offender, again, can fantasize and relive his crimes. Such fantasy provides sexual gratification for the offender."

End of report

Again, this report was condensed down to just a few pages to highlight and summarize things that might be helpful to the public in thinking about who they might know that may fit descriptions included. There is quite a bit of information and analysis on the original fifteen-page document. This partial report and analysis is published for educational and informational purposes only in the interest of this book and I am using them as set forth under Section 107 (the Fair Use doctrine) of the U.S. Copyright Act of 1976.

I have used this information to educate the public about what has been reported about this perpetrator. In the interest of furthering the story and in the hopes that any information will be used to help solve the crimes.

Chapter Fourteen
Visalia Ransacker Prior to becoming EAR/ONS

I could not ignore the activities of the Visalia Ransacker and the at length discussion Richard Shelby has written about in his book. I have a hard time thinking of VR as a separate individual from EAR and ONS. I truly believe the prowling's and ransacking in Visalia could have been committed by the same individual known as the East Area Rapist. In 1974 this guy had to be between 19 and 25. My belief is that he was more likely 19. I think he could have relatives in the area of Visalia as he graduated from high school in approximately 1972 or 1973. This gave him the freedom to go stay wherever he pleased. Once again I am speculating as I believe this is how the story went. I am entitled to my opinion.

The reason I want to discuss this chapter of the criminals' wanderings is because there are similarities to point out and also because I believe if VR and EAR are the same guy he was in training for what was to come. He was developing his prowling patterns, he was discovering what he liked, what excited him and he was deciding how he could be successful in this line of work as it were. He certainly did not receive any great pay out monetarily or from things he would randomly take. His payoff came in learning his craft and in the excitement and satisfaction he got from figuring out how he would be successful as a burglar. I could be wrong. If he always had murder on his mind I think this could be how he began and how he worked to become EAR and then ONS. I think he thought it was fun to see what he could get away with. He knew he was fast on his feet. He knew he could jump fences and run away into the night. He knew how not to call attention to himself. He was organized and methodical about what he did minimizing the risk to himself. He realized early on that it worked best if he were to enter residences ahead of time looking for weapons and anything that could take him by surprise, harm him or kill him. He also decided that attacking women alone would also minimize his risk.

I am thinking he was practicing breaking and entering in a community that was smaller than a city and that had easy escapes. This guy as I have stated before was studying and schooling himself on how to be the ultimate outlaw. I truly believe that he wanted to be extremely prepared for what he was about to do next. Breaking in and raping women.

This guy was logical practiced, and ready when he raped in Sacramento for the first time. It must have been a most exhilarating high for him to do it and get away with it. It was an adrenaline rush never before experienced. So, I tend to lean towards the Visalia Ransacker being the same guy as EAR. The timeline fits, and there are several similarities in his MO. I think the guy graduated from high school in 1973 or 72. I think he set about learning his trade as an outlaw soon after his graduation. I also think that these types of crimes could possibly have been what he tried to do as a teenager in his own neighborhood and then thought better of it. He moved out of the range of his home.

On September 11, 1975, Claude Snelling, a journalism professor at the College of the Sequoias in Visalia was shot while trying to stop an intruder from kidnapping his daughter in the middle of the night. Professor Snelling was killed. In December of the same year a detective on stakeout where traces of a prowler had been found attempted to arrest a masked man. The suspect got away because he feigned surrender and then shot at the officer. The prowler escaped before a cordon was established in the area. After this incident with the detective the burglary spree stopped in Visalia. A few months later the soon to be East Area Rapist began attacks in Sacramento.

By the time the perpetrator started the rapes in Sacramento he was very well practiced. There were over 125 crimes in Visalia over the time span of April 6, 1974 until December 10, 1975. VR loved the rush he got from breaking and entering. Six months would go by before the first reported rape in Sacramento June 18, 1976.

The LA Times and Sacramento UPI picked up this story on July 23, 1978

Headlines were Sacramento's 'East Area Rapist' May Be Visalia Killer

Sacramento (UPI) – Authorities are investigating whether the notorious East Area Rapist in Sacramento is a man known to Visalia police as The Ransacker and a murderer, the Sacramento Union reported Saturday.

The East Area Rapist, named for his attacks primarily in the eastern suburbs of Sacramento, has assaulted nearly 40 women and teenagers since October, 1975. Some of his attacks have occurred outside the city, in Davis and Stockton areas.

The Ransacker committed more than 125 ransacking burglaries in Visalia during the early 1970's and is believed to have shot and killed a journalism instructor who tried to stop the Ransacker from abducting his teen age daughter, the paper said.

Composite Visalia Ransacker

Police Seeking To Link Rapist, Snelling Slayer
Visalia Times-Delta, 18 May 1977, By Miles
Shuper - **ARTICLE**

Two Visalia police detectives are in Sacramento
today probing the possibility that a man being sought
as a suspect in the raping of 23 women could be the

Visalia Ransacker and possibly the killer of Claude
Snelling.

A number of similarities in physical description and
actions of the Sacramento rapist and the Visalia
ransacker have swung the Visalia investigation, the
most intensive in the city's history, to the state's
capital city. Although it has never been proved,
investigators have been working on the premise that
the ransacker is the same person who killed the
College of Sequoias journalism instructor Sept. 11,
1975.

Lt. Roy Springmeyer said today, "Because of the
degree of the similarity in the physical descriptions
and the methods used, we just can't afford to
overlook the possibility that the same person could
be responsible for the rapes and the Visalia
crimes."

Detectives Bill McGowen and Duane Shipley left
Visalia early today to meet in Sacramento with
investigators probing the rapes in which the attacker
now has threatened to kill two persons. The
increasing violent behavior of the Sacramento
attacker matches the psychological profile compiled
during investigation of the Visalia Ransacker case
and the murder of Snelling, investigators said.

In the Sacramento case, psychologists believe the
rapist is trying to prove himself sexually because he
"has difficulty establishing a normal sexual
relationship."

When psychologists compiled a profile of the man responsible for the Visalia crimes, they said he probably would become more violent and dangerous.

Officers also are convinced that the man who shot Snelling is the man who shot at Detective McGowen during a Dec. 10 stakeout of a neighborhood in which a prowler, believed to be the Ransacker, had been working. McGowen was not hurt, but a bullet pierced the veteran officer's flashlight. It was between the time of the Snelling murder and the shot fired at the officer that the string of Sacramento rapes began, generally in October, 1975.

Visalia investigators said the first Sacramento rapes during late 1975 could have been committed by the man sought in the Visalia cases. In Sacramento the frequency of the rapes has been increasing along with the degree of violence. In recent weeks the rapist has become increasing bold and on six occasions the sexual attacks were committed after the victims' husbands were tied up by the attacker. In most of the earlier attacks, however, the victim was alone in the home. The rapist typically wears a mask, ties up people and ransacks the house.

The Sacramento attacks have occurred in middle-income and upper-income residential areas and a local group calling itself the east Area Rapist Surveillance Patrol is offering a $10,000 reward for the arrest and conviction of the rapist.
In Visalia $4,000 is being offered for the arrest and conviction of Snelling's killer. Visalia police Sgt.

John Vaughan who has been heading the Snelling murder investigation said today he has copies of many of the Sacramento rape investigation reports and the profiles of the crime patterns.

They are being closely studied and compared to the information gathered by Visalia officers during the 20-month investigation of the Visalia slaying and the nearly four-year probe of the ransacking burglaries, Vaughan said. There also are similarities of the composite pictures of the Snelling-ransacker suspect and the Sacramento rapist.

The Visalia subject is described as between 25 and 30 years of age, 5-foot, 10 inches in height and 180 to 200 pounds in weight. He was described as having short, straight blond hair, a pale smooth round face and stubby feet and hands. The subject is believed to be left handed, and often wore a dark ski mask.

The subject in the Sacramento cases is described as between 19 and 30 years of age with blue or hazel eyes, five-foot eight to 10 inches in height, with a "good build" and dirty blond or medium brown hair. The Sacramento rapist also wears a ski mask.

In Sacramento during a news conference, Fred Reese, chief deputy sheriff said "This individual is probably in a homosexual panic caused by his inadequate endowment." Reese said the rapist, who typically carries a gun or and a knife but has never disfigured or wounded any victim, probably had a "domineering" mother and an "absent" father or a weak father. Reese based his comments of reports of psychologists and psychiatrists who have studied all known facts about the rapist.

END OF ARTICLE

Article from the Visalia Times Delta from 2015

Is it possible that Visalia was the training ground, back in the 1970s, for one of California's most prolific serial-rapist/murderers? In a book that was recently published, "Hunting a Psychopath," author Richard Shelby states: "There are some who strongly believe he actually began his crime spree in 1974, in Visalia, California, where he was called the Visalia Ransacker." Shelby, who retired from the Sacramento Sheriff Department, was the original investigator of the East Area Rapist.

If you lived in Tulare County during the '70s, you may have the one piece of information that will solve Visalia's 100-plus home burglaries (along with the murder of a College of the Sequoias professor, Claude Snelling); Northern California's 50-plus rapes; and Goleta, Ventura, Irvine and Huntington Beach's 12 known murders. The rapes in Northern California and the murders in Southern California have been linked by DNA. The questions remain: Did the suspect start in Visalia? Did he then commute or move to the Northern and Southern California locations? Did the Visalia Ransacker morph into the person known as the East Area Rapist/Original Night Stalker?

The Visalia Ransacker was described as approximately 5-foot, 9-inches, light-colored skin, short hair, size $9^1/_2$ shoe. On Dec. 10, 1975, during a neighborhood stakeout, the Ransacker pulled off a knit cap with his right hand, while pulling a revolver from his pocket with the other hand, at the same time saying, "Don't hurt me." He shot at Officer McGowen, hitting his flashlight. A composite drawing resulted from McGowen's description.

The East Area Rapist was described as approximately 5-foot, 9-inches, athletic build, late teen to 25, possibly ambidextrous with a tendency towards left hand, size $9-9^1/_2$ shoe, light-brown, shoulder-length hair worn in a semi-shag. A composite drawing of the EAR can be seen at *www.ear-ons.com*

The Visalia Ransacker ended his Visalia crime spree prior to the first known attack in Northern California, which happened in Ranch Cordova on June 18, 1976. However, the suspect may have been in the Sacramento area prior to this attack. Additional pictures, information, and timelines can once again be found: *www.ear-ons.com*

Please, if you have any ideas or information that may help, contact the Sacramento Sheriff's Department at 916-874-5057 or EARInfo@sacsheriff.com; Visalia's anonymous crime line at 559-734-5302, or the Santa Barbara Sheriff's Criminal Investigations Bureau at 805-681-4150.

A copy of "Hunting a Psychopath" recently was donated to the Tulare County Public Library or can be ordered online.

M.J. Smith lives in Visalia

http://www.visaliatimesdelta.com/story/opinion/2015/03/25/visalia-training-ground/70406130/

As of 2017 all of the above phone numbers and contact information are correct and can be used to speak with Law Enforcement.

Whether or not there truly is a connection between the Visalia Ransacker and the man known as the East Area Rapist remains to be seen. He either is the same guy or he's not. The speculation has gone on for more than 40 years. We just don't know the answer apparently. No evidence, no proof, no DNA no connection? We may never know.

Note: Joseph James DeAngelo is believed to also be the Visalia Ransacker.

Chapter Fifteen

Descriptions given by various victims
Summary of ONS, EAR and VR
Someone knows him

The suspect walked funny, appeared to have a genuine stutter, 5'9" white, blonde, blue eyes. Natural voice may have been high pitched. In his phone call recordings, he sounds like he has a high pitched voice even through a whisper. It is possible that he intentionally tried to make us think his voice was higher pitched in an attempt to confuse investigators.

In Larry Crompton's book, Sudden Terror, the description of the criminal as told by the victim during the Fourth Parkway attack said that when he spoke he stuttered. He asked the victim "are you llllistening?" She also said he spoke in a high pitched whisper. Detective Shelby described a possible suspect as pencil necked and he has been described as thin to medium build much like a swimmer. I am thinking he would have been a good candidate for track team. Possibly left handed, various descriptions said he had short stubby fingers. It was also mentioned this man held a gun in his right hand. There are conflicting reports about whether or not it is thought that he is right or left handed. I think he is right handed because he held a gun in his right hand and used it on more than one occasion with his right hand. It was also mentioned he had a stiff or odd gait it was also stated he had a funny gait as if he were bowlegged.

EAR muttered to himself, sometimes cried, mentioned his mother sometimes when out of the room from a victim. This may have been to try and throw off investigators. Sometimes wore what were thought to be corduroy pants because of the sound they made as well as victims' descriptions of corduroy. He had wooden matches or left matches at the locations of at least two crime scenes. He appeared to be a smoker but no one smelled it on him. He also appeared to drink beer that he brought with him. No one smelled it on him. Could he have stashed it outside of homes he was going to hit? Hard to imagine a stalker, prowler, and rapist bringing beers to his own break in. He may have put it outside prior to the break-ins when he removed screens and did his reconnaissance. It is possible he did not drink the beer but poured it out somewhere.

It is also my opinion that all of these things were variable and changeable in order to throw investigators off. He either smoked or he didn't – he either drank or he didn't – that about sums that up. Unless somewhere in any one of the counties there is or was a beer can tested for his DNA. If so and if his DNA was on the can then we could say he actually drank the beer.

During the murders he used bludgeon with fireplace logs, wrench and other items readily available at the scene. He covered victims before or after bludgeon. In the case of Janelle Cruz, he placed her body diagonally across the bed and covered her. He learned that he did not want blood spatter after the murders of Lyman and Charlene Smith and then covered victims prior to bludgeoning them.

Questions I Have

A glove was found not far from the crime scene of the Harrington murders. It was a motor cross glove found in August 1980. Apparently there was blood found on this glove. Did the blood evidence from the glove definitively connect the glove to the Harrington murders? I have since heard a report that semen may also have been on the glove. Is this true? If the glove was connected to the murders it would seem that if this glove is still in evidence in Orange County that it could be tested for fingerprints on the inside of the glove in each finger.

I am certain the glove was tested extensively back in 1980 and possibly again as forensics evolved. I am hoping it could be done again currently since forensic science has evolved to the point where the techniques and processes could likely be used to find the perpetrator via possible fingerprint evidence.

The processes they now use could actually possibly lift a print from the inside. Since DNA is unknown and ONS is not in the system I would think that his fingerprints are in the system. Has this been done? I am told that the gloves have been tested over time however, I am not aware of the last time they were tested in relation to the latest techniques in forensic science that have evolved even in the last three years. If these gloves have not been tested recently and if there is any evidence remaining inside them after 37 years I would love to know when were they last tested, is there any remaining evidence inside them and what were the results if this has been done within the last five years? It has been 37 years since the Smith and Harrington murders. These are the things that LE does not share and these are all of the unanswered questions family members and victims would like to know the answers to.

It would seem that this criminal must have had to give fingerprints for a passport, a job or some other normal activity. Because forensics has evolved and improved this is the very first thing I would do at this late date. If this is a possibility and if it was successful in telling us this man's identity, I would not have to ask the rest of my questions.

DNA legislation in California Proposition 69 - Bruce Harrington (Keith Harrington's older brother) was instrumental in moving this legislation forward

California Proposition 69, the DNA Initiative, was a successful 2004 California ballot proposition that allows for the collection of DNA samples from all felons and from people who have been arrested for certain crimes. As of 2009, all adults arrested for or charged with any felony in California must provide a sample for inclusion in the database.

California currently maintains the third largest DNA database in the world.

https://en.wikipedia.org/wiki/California_Proposi tion_69_(2004)

The Original Night Stalker/East Area Rapist case was the motivating factor in the passage of legislation leading to the establishment of California's DNA database, which authorizes the collection of the DNA of all the accused and convicted felons in California. California's DNA data retrieval and storage program is considered by researchers to be second only to Virginia's in size and effectiveness in solving cold cases. While the California DNA database motivated by this case has solved numerous previously unsolved cold cases across the country, the original case remains unsolved.

https://en.wikipedia.org/wiki/Original_Night_Stalker

DNA and fingerprints –

Many of us watch CSI Crime shows, Forensic Science shows and digest the advances in techniques used in forensic science to solve crimes. The following information derived from sources credited tells us some basics in the fingerprinting area of forensic science. Scientists have worked tirelessly over time to learn and to advance their methods to help in solving crimes. The ever famous gloves from OJ Simpson's alleged crimes must have been tested. Certainly they had to have been tested for DNA. Did any forensic scientist test the inside of the gloves using advanced methods of the day (1995) to try and lift prints from the inside of the gloves? It seems that evidence would have or could have been destroyed when they had OJ try on the gloves during his trial.

The phrase, if they don't fit you must acquit we have all heard.

They had OJ try on the gloves on top of latex gloves which of course made them very tight. I have also learned from reports that OJ normally took medication to reduce swelling in his hands and joints. He was advised to stop taking it so that when he was instructed to try on the gloves in this case that his fingers would be swollen making the gloves too tight in all of the fingers. But, did they try to lift fingerprints from each finger and the palm of these famous gloves on the inside? Surely OJ's epithelial cells had to have been found inside these gloves when originally examined? Or wasn't it done? (Well that is another discussion altogether) If these gloves were tested today as I am sure they must have been in great detail? Would we find OJ's fingerprint or palm print on the inside of these gloves or possibly someone else's?

"According to *Forensic Science*, there are three types of fingerprints. D.P. Lyle, *Forensic Science (ABA Fundamentals)*, p. 255 (2012):

- **Patent prints** are easy to locate since they are visible to the naked eye. Patent prints occur when someone has a substance on their fingers such as grease, paint, blood, or ink that leaves a visible print on a surface.
- **Plastic prints** are also easy to locate but are less common than patent prints since they occur when someone

408

touches an object such as wax, butter, or soap and leaves a three-dimensional impression of the finger on the object.

- **Latent prints** are the most common type of print and take the most effort to locate since they are invisible. Latent prints occur when someone touches any porous or nonporous surface. The natural oils and residue on fingers leave a deposit on surfaces which mirror the ridges and furrows that are present on the individual's finger."

Acknowledging the information above I move on to the advances in forensics when it comes to testing the inside of gloves over time. Also, of note is the gloves found near the crime scene of the Harrington murders in 1980 is that the gloves were just gloves and were not latex. What follows with permission is some of what I had heard and read about in trying to get a good fingerprint from difficult surfaces.

"IAI Educational Conference St. Louis, Missouri; August, 2004

Author: M.J.M. (Theo) Velders, Politie Brabant Zuid-Oost, Eindhoven, the Netherlands
Presenter: J.N. (Jan) Zonjee, BVDA, Haarlem, the Netherlands / website: http://www.bvda.com email: info@bvda.nl

Up until 2001, I succeeded only once in my 30 years as a crime scene officer to visualize a fingerprint in a latex glove. I had tried many times to treat disposable latex and vinyl gloves with chemical means, but virtually all these attempts failed to produce a result.

Then in the middle of 2001, a colleague handed me four latex gloves which had been thrown away by burglars when leaving a crime scene. As so often before, I started working on the gloves, treating two of them with ninhydrin and the others with cyanoacrylate fuming. Unfortunately, both methods failed to visualize any prints.

Idea

- After this disappointment, I wondered if it might be possible to get any fingerprints off of these gloves using a black gelatin lifter.

- With a piece of PVC tubing, stuck in the fingers of each glove, every finger was rolled ten 360¡ revolutions over a length of black Gellifter.

To my amazement, a number of excellent prints were lifted from these chemically treated gloves. I had a strong suspicion that this could be a real breakthrough.

Looking for a solution
- Were these results with the four latex gloves a coincidence, or could it be that lifting prints with a Gellifter was the solution to a big problem?

To get more certainty, I started a comparative examination, looking at all the methods that have been mentioned to visualize prints in gloves and at the lifting with the Gellifter.

Researching the internet, I found that colleagues around the world have used the following methods:

1. Ninhydrin and DFO
2. Iodine
3. Cyanoacrylate (CA) fuming, usually followed by treatment with fluorescent staining solutions
4. Sticky-side powder
5. Gentian violet

6. Physical developer"

END OF PAPER

The author of this paper Mr. Theo Velders is a very nice gentleman and I want to say it was a pleasure speaking with you. Thank you for your help.

Lined leather gloves may leave a print that is as unique as a human fingerprint. When discovered by authorities, **latent fingerprints may also be recovered from the inside of these gloves.**
Picture and comment from:
https://en.wikipedia.org/wiki/Glove_prints

Evidence of diamond knot left behind in the Smith murders – ONS did not use this knot again after it was talked about in news articles

Photographs of ligatures taken from images on the
internet from an unknown source

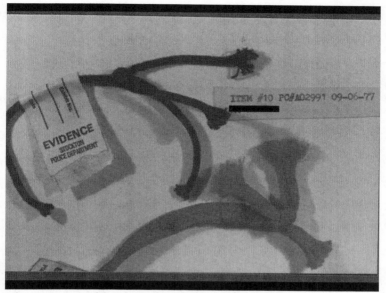

Ligatures used in the 1970's East Area Rapist
crimes Stockton

Footprint of EAR

It would seem that if one were curious about the origins and the ancestry of the culprit (and we are) that if enough DNA exists from samples taken at crime scenes and from victims that we could determine whether or not the person we are seeking is German, Swedish, Dutch, English, Irish or whatever he is. It would seem we could narrow our field at it and so inch by inch we can discover who the person might look like under his mask. Maybe the powers that be have already done this and have not shared it with the public. Update: This has been done and the public is waiting for information

If I were a detective or criminalist another step I would have taken as soon as it was available would have been to contact Tony Frudakis Ph.D. who developed the latest technique called Biogeographic testing. His technique is to take 1/10 of 1% of a person's DNA, in this case the killer, to determine the physical characteristics of our perpetrator. There is also a marker in our genetics that can tell us with 92% accuracy whether the criminal has blue or green eyes. These new DNA tests show the limitations of behavioral profiles and eyewitnesses. Back in 2005 Dr. Frudakis used this new DNA test for the first time in a criminal case. Dr. Frudakis is a molecular biologist. The DNA witness test was used to identify a serial killer in Baton Rouge Louisiana. This was more than a decade ago. This test ascertains the exact ancestry of an individual based on information in their DNA. Since all humans are descended from a common genepool he could make an indirect inference through a very precise knowledge of the subject's ancestral background. In this case of serial killer Derek Todd Lee eyewitnesses and profilers at first thought the criminal they were searching for was white. 92.3% of US serial killers (94.4% internationally) are male, but only 52.1% are white. From 1990 to 2010, data tells us that 52.1% of US serial killers were white, while 40.3% were black and only 27% are in their mid- to late-20s.

In the Louisiana case the test identified the killer as 85% African and 15% Native American. They were looking for a white man and had to change gears in order to find the perpetrator. All of the pieces of the puzzle began to fit together once investigators knew for a fact that they were looking for a black man in this case. The biogeographic technology has a 99% accuracy rate.

Dr. Frudakis said "I don't think it is too far out there to say in the future there will probably be a lot less crime than there is today because people are going to realize that when they commit that rape or they commit that murder they might as well take their driver's license out of their wallet and toss it on the ground cuz they are going to get that information anyway."

As a side note about the Lee case, the serial killer was married and had two children. He was a laborer who burglarized and then also stalked women, and was a peeper as well. He would follow women home and knew when they were alone. He received the death penalty. Mr. Lee died from heart disease on January 21, 2016 after being held in the Louisiana State Penitentiary at Angola from October 14, 2004 until his death. He was credited with murdering at least 7 women.

In the beginning of the East Area Rapist's crimes in Sacramento a town hall meeting was held. Tapes exist that show the people in the audience as the person with the camera panned around the room. There is a gentleman sitting in one of the rows (and who is rather blurry). Many had suspected this might be EAR. Since the first edition of this book it appears this man has been identified and cleared. The man I am speaking of is sitting there on the right as we look at the film but in reality is sitting on the left side of the room. He was wearing a puffy jacket and was actually called puffy jacket guy for a while. He looks somewhat like a composite of EAR. He is listening intently to the discussion by Detective Carol Daly. Detective Daley has stated she is certain the perpetrator had to have been at this meeting that night. It was stated that if EAR was in attendance he had heard a man suggest that it was impossible to attack a woman with her husband there – that he, the husband would be able to protect his wife. Within a few months this man and his wife were attacked. The perpetrator had to have followed this man home or found him from seeing him at this meeting.

There were unidentified fibers found on Lyman Smith as well as on Cheri Domingo's body. What were they? Where had they come from? Did the killer place them on the bodies to try and throw off the investigators? Or were they simply a byproduct of torn towels used as gags and blindfolds? I would say most likely fragments of towels.

The wrench that allegedly was used to kill Janelle Cruz, was the autopsy report consistent with the wrench as the weapon? It certainly could do the damage that was found to have been done to Janelle.

There were matches found at Manuela Witthuhn's crime scene. Burnt wooden matches. Matches were also found at the scene of the Harrington murders. Were others found at other scenes? The beer cans or bottles found at some of the rapes in Sacramento, were there fingerprints on anything? It seems apparently not. We know that when EAR heard that a victim's body was checked for fingerprints he did not remove his gloves again as he touched anyone.

In Larry Crompton's book he states that a latent palm print was found on the front side of the envelope EAR sent with his poem Excitement's Crave in 1977. Does anyone still have the envelope in their evidence? Was it thrown away because supposedly the rape cases were too old to prosecute? What happened to the envelope?

Apparently there was also a fingerprint from a rape crime scene that had been taken off of a lamp. Larry stated in his book that "the copy he had made of the fingerprint from the lamp was still in his possession, but not the original." As I understand it the person thought to belong to this fingerprint did not match it. Was this print ever matched to anyone? Is this copy still in anyone's possession so that it can be tested using today's techniques and advances? The fingerprint or palm print evidence could finally tell us who this person is since the DNA is not matched to someone in the data base. This criminal must have had to give a fingerprint in the last 37 years in some capacity. Does anyone know where the envelope is? I have asked. No one that I have spoken to seems to know. There are files in Sacramento.

My opinions and summary about things this person may have said, things he may have in his possession, possible ways to recognize this person who may be someone you know:

This person was interested in or obsessed with crime or true crime magazines or television shows of the time (1970's) and maybe late 1960's. In particular, he read and most likely collected newspaper articles relating to anything Ted Bundy did that was reported in the Sacramento Bee or Sacramento Union in the mid to late 1970's. He was possibly obsessed with Ted Bundy and anything related to this criminal or serial killers in general. EAR will have articles about his own crimes including the murders of at least 10 people in his collection. He also will have copies of articles about his own escapades from Sacramento and all of the other counties he hit.

He also (or they also) were very interested in the history of outlaws in particular Jesse James and his brother. He may have read The Most Dangerous Game by Richard Connell. He may own a copy of this classic story. He likely has a collection of newspaper articles of crimes of Ted Bundy and or other serial killers. His secret hiding place will contain all of his mementos from things he took from victims of the rapes and prior to that from prowling's in Visalia. His collection is really rather extensive because of the sheer numbers of people he attacked or prowled. The collection will definitely include items taken from the murder scenes. I cannot imagine he could give up his most prized remembrances' of these events. He will have a very secret place that he hides these items.

It is certainly possible he absolutely loved the Clint Eastwood movies of the day which were titled Outlaw Josey Wales, The Good, The Bad and the Ugly, Hang em High, and others. In the 1970's my boyfriend and I would go to the triple showing of Clint Eastwood movies at the Southgate drive-in right off highway 99 in South Sacramento. Was the

East Area Rapist also there prior to his beginning the rapes? Does anyone out there know a person who they could describe as I have above? The Butch Cassidy and the Sundance Kidd movie with Paul Newman and Robert Redford was playing at the State Theater off Florin Road in 1973-74. Does this jog anyone's memory of a person they knew who saw this movie over and over? The theater is right down the street from my South Sacramento neighborhood off Sky Parkway and Florin Road. He could have walked there from his home in these neighborhoods. He could have seen these films over and over. Probably liked the part where Butch Cassidy and the Sundance Kidd escaped to Bolivia. (You may read this with amusement but these are things that could trigger a memory of someone you know)

This person attacked the most in October of each year he was active. What was his trigger? His attacks in October far outnumbered those of other months. It also is stated that this individual relocated or it is speculated he relocated. For example, from July 5, 1979 until October 1979 it was said he relocated (or popped up in different counties). I don't believe this is what happened. If you are familiar with the area, it is not a very long drive from Sacramento to Stockton. It is also not really a very long drive from Sacramento to Concord. If this person is from Sacramento and this is his home base it is not unrealistic to believe he has relatives not far from Sacramento that he could stay with – even for just a couple of days. I do not believe he ever really relocated anywhere. I believe he is still in

Sacramento to this day. He could be dead, but the statistics are so far in his favor.

He wore corduroy pants frequently and especially on Friday and Saturday nights in the commission of his crimes. He brought a kit of his own with him that included a ski mask, gloves and a gun as well as a flashlight and some other tool. Shoe laces or ties cut in lengths. Pry bar or screwdriver or ice pick type tool. If someone you know or knew then had these types of items in their vehicle or in a sport bag with a zipper in their possession and who might have explained it away with some other explanation. Look at the kit Ted Bundy carried on page 246. Did you know someone who may have had items like these in a duffle bag?

Reread my other descriptions of this criminal's physical characteristics. Also carefully read more on other's descriptions following:

Descriptions from Sacramento attacks of suspect from various victims:

He had a body tan in the late summer months. Faded by late fall with his tan line the length of boxer shorts (which was the standard length of shorts in the 1970's).

Suspect's eyes were seen frequently – one victim was shown a number of high school photos from various local Sacramento schools. She repeatedly came to a student who had sleepy looking eyes with heavy overlaying lids. The most consistent description of color was hazel or blue.

423

EAR acquired a tattoo on his left or right forearm sometime in 1977. The tattoo may have resembled a bull, similar to the Schlitz Malt Liquor Bull. When comparing whether or not a tattoo was seen previous to September 1977 – none was seen by victims in 1976 – it seems to have appeared sometimes during the summer of 1977. (We do not know if the tattoo's existence is really true) There seems to be doubt among people I have spoken with.

The individual was lean and muscular more like a swimmer. EAR was naturally athletic and agile. Does this mean he ran track in high school or was on the swim team? It was also said his thighs were muscular (he rode a bike frequently when escaping) or was he on the football team in high school?

EAR was under-endowed and often not fully aroused. His penis was circumcised and was described as narrow and short. On a few occasions his organ underwent radical changes. Some heard a pumping sound which was attributed to EAR working a lubricating bottle's pumping action. On these occasions his penis was described as short but thick and not under-endowed. Possibly EAR was using a pumping device. Or...were there two suspects in the rapes?

My thoughts on this last comment are that I think it is possible that when these comments were made by victims it is possible that there were actually two different suspects. These were the occasions that Richard Shelby mentions in his book, Hunting A Psychopath. He has descriptions of someone heavier and also mentions a different penis – during the same attack. The descriptions here of the perpetrators penis change from being short and thick to narrow and short. Sounds like two different men to me. That might be the reason there is a difference in the descriptions of this man's genitals.

This composite is the one the FBI is currently
focused on in 2016-2017

This composite looks more like the man who chased me in 1971 – he had a more rounded face and heavier lidded eyes as does the composite in the Maggiore murders previously mentioned

Chapter Sixteen
AND THEN THERE'S THAT

So many stories written and so much speculation Lyman and Charlene Smith and the shift to blame them.

What the following story repeated over time tells us is that rumor, innuendo, and just plain gossip can survive over time and that gossip can change our perception of who innocent victims were. The misinformation that has been passed down over time by many close and not so close to the couple, the crime and even the investigation show how blame on those who are innocent is shifted seemingly slanting the story to the side of blaming the victims. There were many articles written over time that speculated about who the victims were or who various sources thought they were. This is sometimes unfortunate if the speculating casts an inaccurate light on the subjects. I have to ask – what was the point of articles such as the one that follows? The murders of Charlene and Lyman are certainly not an amusing subject. The things this author states and talks about are merely things he thinks he knows about Lyman. Why talk about things that were not proven or not held to be true? Where did this author find his information? If Lyman had been alive he would have called it slander.

When a person is murdered even if they are somewhat high profile in a community how is it the right thing to do to write things such as this after so many years? Obviously I find this very disrespectful.

This article is just one that speculated on who Lyman and Charlene were. Rumor is of course not fact. The fact that a business associate was prosecuted with only the word of a preacher that wanted attention was very unfortunate. Mr. Joe Alsip is and was innocent. The accusation and prosecution because someone needed to be blamed had a profound effect on Mr. Alsip and his family. Rumor and false information threatened to destroy a person and his family and in the end probably did.

Many articles were published that cast Charlene Smith in a bad light and there were also comments made about her husband Lyman Smith that are not or were not verifiable. The stories continued to be copied and distributed. In my research the following is one example of what is out there about the couple. I have reprinted parts of this article as it was written in 2012. The Smiths were murdered in 1980. The speculation and misinformation was repeated 32 years after they have been dead. I have included bits and pieces of the article in order to show how long and how widespread rumors and misinformation can last especially when a crime goes unsolved this long. The Sloan Canyon Boxer written about in the article I found was a gentleman who was an investor in a venture with Lyman Smith and others briefly in the 1970's.

I have picked out just a few pertinent paragraphs from the article to examine. My comments throughout are bolded. This is how the article begins:

"The Sloan Canyon Boxer was a suspect in one of SoCal's strangest murders. Back in 1947, a powerful and charismatic fellow named A.E. "Bud"/ "Haystack" Sloan bought the old Stevens Ranch on Torre Canyon Road in Piru. He picked up the Stevens Ranch for a bargain ($130,000 for 6,500 acres). Sloan earned the name of "Haystack" during his brief boxing career during the 1930's, in which the giant heavyweight amassed a pro record of 7-4. Interestingly five of his wins were by knockout, and in all three of his losses he was KO'ed. Thirty years later, he would briefly be a suspect in one of the Southland's most sensational murder trials."

The article continues:

"The ex-pugilist was questioned in a complicated murder mystery 45 years ago involving the fledgling Maverick International Airlines. Sloan was a major investor in the line, which specialized in shipping prize cattle to the Shah of Iran. The planes were converted to hold thousands of pounds of cattle and horses."

(The timeline is incorrect in the article. 45 years ago would have made the crimes 45 years old). If it were 45 years ago it would have had to have happened in 1967) This article was written so long after the crimes yet the timeline is still completely

inaccurate. **The Smiths were murdered in 1980 – 37 years ago from 2017.**

Because Lyman was involved in business dealings outside of his law practice and while he had some losses with his investors funds it was speculated that he had done things that were not exactly orthodox. It was speculated that the first year of operation, Maverick grossed $17 million hauling livestock and returning with things like melons from Israel and auto parts from Italy. It was reported that while Maverick took in $17 million, they spent $20 million.

"After the '70s, the Shah didn't need prize cattle, as he was deposed by the Iranians with the Ayatollah Khomeini. And, with poor management and deadheading (the practice of an aircraft returning with empty seats or cargo holds), Maverick's future wasn't looking good. It was also speculated that the business partners were hiding money offshore in the Cayman Islands.

Sloan's partners? You couldn't write a dime novel any better than the real life of the controversial Ojai couple, Lyman and Charlene Smith."

In one article I read it stated "that Charlene was noted for carrying out several very public sexual affairs." As this particular story shows authors took some pleasure in spreading gossip about Charlene as well as telling a story about Lyman that was never proven. Financial information written about in articles about business dealings was not

432

substantiated by this author, he merely passed along gossip. The article goes on to say:

"In 1980 the couple was found brutally murdered in their Ojai mansion. Both were bound by rope and bludgeoned to death with a log. Charlene had been raped. The suspects were many including Charlene's various lovers and Haystack, who wasn't too happy at losing seven figures on the couple's high lifestyle.

According to court records, Alsip was a lover of Charlene's and had visited with the couple the night before the murders." Bonus: for some oddball reason, Alsip confessed. As one police investigator commented: "This is better than 'Law and Order.'"

"The Alsip trial was spectacular. A flashy and showboating attorney ended up getting Alsip acquitted. Today, Alsip runs a fishing boat in Hawaii. For years, the case was dead. Haystack was absolved of any wrong doing."

"It wasn't until 2001 when DNA evidence linked this Original Nightstalker to the Smith couple's murders from 1980. This Original Nightstalker/East Area Rapist is viewed as one of the top serial killers in American history, credited with at the very least 50 official murders. There are no clues to his identity."
END OF QUOTES FROM ARTICLE

My comments are as follows:

There is so much misinformation here including the statement that "This Original Nightstalker/East Area Rapist is viewed as one of the top serial killers in American history, credited with at the **very least 50 official murders."** These statements as well as many others in this article are completely inaccurate.

There have fortunately **NOT been 50 murders** committed by the Original Night Stalker. There were at least 50 rapes and a possible 13 murders. The above authors' speculations about Charlene and her private life or who she may have slept with are also exaggerated. **Alsip was never Charlene's lover. The couple most certainly did not live in a mansion in Ojai.** They lived in track housing and had a view of the ocean, but the home was actually modest by today's standards. The Lyman and Charlene Smith murders had the distinction of being sensationalized the most and also the distinction of having people speculate that somehow they had brought their own murders on to themselves. Whatever business dealings they were involved in the article above makes many statements that are pure conjecture and inaccurate reporting which make me wonder who the author's sources were.

It seems that time has only made it easier for people to continue to speculate about a couple who were brutally murdered through no fault of their own. Do we really need to compartmentalize or define the victims of crimes in the ways that we do? Why do reporters or story tellers pick apart victims of violent crimes after their death? Is this truly something that needs to be done?

This couple was not the only one written about in this series of murders. Personal disclosures were made about several of the victims and their lives that may or may not be true. Things have been said about the Harrington's and Janelle Cruz in particular. The Smith's murders had more rumors, more innuendo than some of the other murders because they were what many call "High Profile." I have speculated in this book about the perpetrator. I have said that I am not an expert and I have identified when I use facts versus my own speculations and that of others in this case. There is a huge difference in speculating and conjecture versus fact. In the Smith murder case it seemed there was a lot of rumor and speculation that was later passed along as fact. Unfortunate.

Sensationalism at its finest!

Chapter Seventeen
The Backstory

Originally I had many more pages for the backstory from journaling my research and where it took me. In the interest of anonymity, I have not included many of these pages in order to keep the confidences of people who have been kind enough to share with me not only information about what they do regarding this case but also in order to keep all of us safe.

December 2014 through February 2016 is not included in this publication. I pick up in March with intermittent chosen sharing of postings.

March 13, 2016

36 years ago tonight Lyman and Charlene were bludgeoned to death in their bed. Found side by side they died with the last moments of their lives violent and painful. The fear and the brief knowledge that they would not survive this maniac must have been devastating. You have to have some sort of awareness that this is it.

There are a select few people who are volunteers as well as retired detectives in every jurisdiction who are determined and diligently working this case and all of the other murders, working from lists of possible suspects. One by one they have meticulously worked through looking at evidence. Were they in the area, did they fit the profile? Inch by inch, piece by piece year after year, trying to put the pieces of this case together so that investigators and law enforcement will have the chance to look this perpetrator in the eye and ask him questions. Hoping for answers about who he is and why he did such unspeakable things to so many people.

I know that every family of the victims and every victim mark the events that changed them forever. Those that were left alive who have memories that still include the history and the story of the man who is still out there free and able to hurt others. He is not yet too old to do that. He may be slower at movement or he may not able to jump a fence as he did in the 70's and 80's but make no mistake, he is still very dangerous as he is not afraid to use deadly force. He will take out whoever gets in his way. This is how he stayed free from the beginning.

We are genuinely lucky to have protectors out there. Men and women who care enough to hunt down criminals and work on cases even long after they have retired. The Original Night Stalker is the worst serial offender by far that the State of California has ever seen. How can we let it rest? How can we not catch him in the end?

In this case there have literally been thousands of suspects that have come in from tips and many other sources since the 1970's. In this case law enforcement has DNA which will possibly find the killer/rapist someday. Even if testing on potential suspects were to be allowed they must have probable cause, they must have circumstantial evidence that paints a very thorough picture of where the suspect was, if he has an alibi, if he truly could be tracked to all of the areas that his DNA was found. Back in the 1970's a case was built by circumstantial evidence and eye witness testimony as well as possible fingerprint or trace evidence. There was no ability to really test DNA the way they can today. In essence this case has to be built backwards from the old way.

The DNA is there linking this one person to many of the crimes listed in this book. The problem for many years when DNA first came into being is that they could only test one sample at a time every now and again, a very slow process. Now they can test 12 at a time several times a year. Each suspect has to have a case actually built prior to asking to test a man's DNA to see if he is a match. DNA could be collected without the suspect's knowledge I suppose to see if the detectives are on the right track, but it is preferred to find the suspect, build the case the "old fashioned way" and then get the DNA. The case must be very tight and it is tedious and time consuming to get all the details that are forty plus years old now. It is slow going to make this case of circumstantial evidence that then creates probable cause to test a potential suspects DNA. Once the case is built to a very certain certainty then probable cause can be established and the question can be asked of the suspect – can we have a sample of your DNA? A warrant most certainly would be issued to get DNA from a suspect if the judge thought there was probable cause. Once again, I am not an expert in this area.

About DNA

DNA testing in order to extract a profile

"Semen confirmatory tests will not help identify the perpetrator. In order to do this, investigators need a DNA profile. A DNA profile is essentially a set of numbers which will highlight the polymorphic regions on a person's DNA; these regions are unique to the individual and a complete DNA profile can help accurately discriminate between different people. No two individuals can have the same exact DNA profile (with the exception of monozygotic twins).

Once the DNA profile has been extracted it can be compared to the DNA profiles of any suspects to look for a match. In cases where no match is found, investigators and police might run a search in a DNA database. A DNA database will contain the DNA profiles of convicted criminals (the criteria for adding a person's DNA profile into a government DNA database vary from country to country; moreover, there may be a time frame after which a DNA profile will be removed from the database). The USA has CODIS (the Combined DNA Index System), compiled and run by the FBI, as well as the National DNA Index System (NDIS). If a DNA profile extracted from a sample at a rape scene is matched with a DNA profile in CODIS or NDIS, the identity of the suspected perpetrator may be known. However, a match between two DNA profiles does not necessarily confirm the person is guilty of the crime and is the true perpetrator. Other evidence will be needed to support the case."

"When a law enforcement agency is investigating a given sexual assault it is possible that they can compare their forensic samples to the database in hopes of finding a match. In other cases, once there is a suspect found or identified, testing of this person can be required in order to prove or disprove their involvement in the crime. This technology is relatively new and laws protecting citizens from agencies looking at database DNA are constantly evolving."

http://www.forensicmag.com/article/2015/01/dna-forensic-testing-and-use-dna-rape-kits-cases-rape-and-sexual-assault

It would seem if a suspect was brought forward and if he was actually guilty of these heinous crimes, he would certainly say no to the question of voluntarily giving a DNA sample. In this situation law enforcement will have to have a warrant for the DNA. Asking for DNA constitutes a search under the Fourth amendment. The perpetrator of these crimes it would seem will have an exit strategy if he becomes a major suspect. After being free all of these years and having had the opportunity to live his life as he pleased since the murder of Janelle Cruz he can either accept responsibility and give the DNA so that he can take credit for his crimes or he may have stashed a load of money to get the heck out of Dodge. Or... lastly maybe he would decide to take his own life. That way he would be in charge of what would happen to him. That seems a little farfetched to me as I would think that the intention of this man really is to take credit for what he has done so that he can be named and have books written about him and a movie made about him. This has most certainly been his claim to fame. This way if he is taken into custody he can have a page on Wikipedia that under occupation it will state: Criminal. Ted Bundy has his own Wikipedia page. Jesse James does as well. Their occupations say Criminal and then the crimes are listed. He will be famous forever, be a celebrity forever. This may have been his original intention as he began daydreaming of who and what he was to become. The only drawback in this scenario is that it will most certainly upset the family that he has as they come to understand that they have lived with a monster all of these years.

May 5, 2016 - I spoke to one of the counties today and when I asked about whether all of the DNA testing was done in one county for all jurisdictions I was told it is all done in one place. I am told this just happened and this particular individual is not aware of how this came to be. It is also believed that no matter who the suspect is that the detectives and police are 100% committed to following this case through and would do whatever it takes to solve this crime no matter who the perpetrator turns out to be.

Paul Holes is an investigator that helped link the DNA of all of the crimes to one person. Paul Holes has said that Goleta and Sacramento are key to solving these crimes. I agree from what I have read and the maps I have seen which are similar to the neighborhood that this suspect likely came from.

June 2016 – I received a call from one of the people close to the case. I was told to watch for the press releases in approximately two weeks to commemorate the 40-year anniversary that the East Area Rapist began his crimes in Sacramento June 1976. The person who contacted me says that other counties will also be doing the same thing. Orange County, Santa Barbara County and possibly others.

Here is what was sent out to victims and victim's families prior to the press release regarding the FBI becoming actively involved in the case once again.

Here is the text of that announcement:

Dear _____

The Sacramento County Sheriff's Department and our allied agencies have continuously been investigating the East Area Rapist/Original Night Stalker series since its beginning in 1976. We want to assure you this investigation has not ceased and the cases have not been closed.

In 2011, a Working Group was created consisting of all involved agencies from Northern and Southern California in an effort to better communicate and work together in identifying this still unknown offender and bring him to justice for so many victims. To that end, the anniversary date of the first known assault is approaching. The Sacramento County Sheriff's Department, along with several other agencies and with the assistance of the Federal Bureau of Investigation (FBI), is planning a large scale media release on June 15, 2016.

This media release will consist of a press release, social media dissemination, billboards, video interviews, podcasts, etc. And likely will be picked up by national media outlets as well.

We want you to be aware of these actions. And, despite our efforts to protect the identity and maintain the privacy of victims and their families, the media and general public can be aggressive and tenacious.

If you are contacted by any media outlet, you are under no obligation to speak to them unless you choose to do so. If you have any questions or concerns:

END OF ANNOUNCEMENT

June 15, 2016

I watched the Sacramento news online because I knew the press release was coming about the Original Night Stalker. It was short and to the point. I am glad they are asking for help from the public however, I worry that they will scare the guy into hiding to tell the truth. If he was unaware of the powers that be were looking for him and if he thought no one was looking maybe he was complacent. Now he is warned and I worry that gives him the edge.

As a side note: June 15, 1981 from an article:

35 years ago to the day there was an article in Sacramento that says it all. The title was When Terror Reigned. By Thom Akeman – I have taken clips from this piece as follows:

"He emerged from a drainage ditch in Rancho Cordova. And within a year, he was one of the most feared men in Sacramento County."

A slight man, some said. Athletically built, said others. Little was certain except that the man was terrifying.

On his forays, the rapist ignored floodlights, bypassed guard dogs, went through alarm systems and circumvented some sophisticated locks to get to his victims. Such intrusion skill and daring and word of the rapists' mind-controlling routine quickly caused a near hysteria throughout the East Area."

"We'll never lose interest in this guy... He's very dangerous." **END OF QUOTES**

Yet, this man still remains free.

June 20, 2016

I had been looking at the Visalia Ransacker timelines so I asked someone who has worked the case for several years their thoughts on VR. I am thinking he was practicing breaking and entering in a community that was smaller than a city with easy escapes. The person I spoke to says they go back and forth on that connection. The more I have looked at these cases the more I believe they really could be the same individual. It makes sense. This guy was studying and schooling himself on how to be the ultimate outlaw. I truly believe that he wanted to be extremely prepared for what he was about to do next. Breaking in and raping women. This guy was logical practiced and ready when he raped in Sacramento for the first time. It must have been a most exhilarating high for him to do it and get away with it. It was an adrenaline rush never before experienced. So, I do believe the Visalia Ransacker could be the same guy. The timeline fits. Many aspects of the MO certainly fit.

I think one of the guys (suspects) graduated from high school in 1973. This is the age I think at least one suspect is. I think he set about learning his trade as an outlaw soon after his graduation. I also think that it is something he tried to do as a teenager in his own neighborhood and then thought better of it. He moved out of the range of his home. By the time he started the rapes in Sacramento he was very well practiced. There were over 125 crimes in Visalia over the time span of April 6, 1974 until December 10, 1975. I think the suspect had relatives in the area of Visalia and he stayed with them during these crimes if in fact EAR and the Visalia Ransacker is the same guy. When the crimes ceased in Visalia six months would go by before the first reported rape in Sacramento June 18, 1976. If EAR is NOT, the Visalia Ransacker it is my belief that he still practiced burglary as a way of fine tuning his game probably in Sacramento or elsewhere in the state while staying with others. He was ready when he began his attacks in Sacramento.

In the 1970's there was quite a lot of crime and certainly there were many perpetrators out there committing burglaries and rapes. There was not too much fear of the relatively minor consequences to rape.

June 21, 2016

I am certain the FBI has had tons of calls about this case. The Facebook page also shows some of the silly remarks made by many. I wanted to post that this is not a joke, it is not funny. People were forever hurt and some lost their lives. The comments that are not helpful or useful or sincere are most likely not appreciated by the FBI – their job is hard enough. I could be very far off in my analysis or I could be partially correct or even completely correct in my ideas about this man's neighborhood of origin and what motivates him, and what is potentially wrong with him and so on.

We will see if he is caught, or if they are caught. I still believe it is entirely possible two brothers are responsible for these crimes and that the older one could have convinced the younger one to ride with him in several of the cases. There were reports several times from witnesses who saw and described two suspects. This may be why he or they have been so successful in evading capture. The variance on description must have been somewhat confusing to law enforcement and the public. I think that the brother may know what happened in Southern California and he had stopped going along with his brother when he realized how far his brother wanted to carry this.

My intent originally was to go further and deeper into the different aspects of the investigation as well as add more information about the different investigations in the many different counties. The scope of this story is huge. I have left it, and will leave it to others to write about each of the crimes in detail. In the end I wanted this particular effort to be less complicated and more focused on the perpetrator himself. I wanted people to know the story more from the perspective of someone who watched the story unfold up close. Maybe that way the victims will be remembered more as the good people they were with more than a page or two describing only the crimes. Upon reflection I wanted to keep it simple. In the interest of time which is running out for those of us who were there in the 1970's and 1980's I wanted to publish this as soon as possible in the hope it can help in some way. If this manuscript is of any help to law enforcement or to one of the victims or victim's family members then this has been time well spent.

This case has so many components to it and so many avenues that one could go down that in the end when writing the story, the result could be a book series of mass proportions. So, it is my hope that this book has enough information in it to jog someone's memory. To make people think back to a lifetime ago to whom they knew and what they knew about them. If my descriptions of the criminal sound like someone you know or did know those many years ago and if this manuscript causes you to call in tips to the FBI, then it has served a purpose. Often times it is something very small and seemingly insignificant that someone remembers that could lead to the identity of this man. One piece is missing to the puzzle. Perhaps someone out there who reads this will have that one piece.

There is so much information and misinformation, and speculation as well as individual theories about how this guy chose his victims and what kind of a person he is. I wanted to be more focused on the descriptions and crimes of the man who has done these terrible things. His MO is important and where he was geographically is important. To those who write stories and who write articles in the future it is my hope that the details that are mentioned are facts. We have to separate what is fact from speculation or fiction. I have tried to make sure in the writing of this book that I have said these are my thoughts, this is speculation. I have also presented and tried to report the facts that we have on these crimes as facts when they are discussed. We need to care about getting the details and the facts right. This story is serious and not fun. It should not be discussed in the same vein and in the same way as fun stories about haunted houses or ghosts.

There are things that have been posted on the internet like "What is the most scary thing about EAR and ONS stories?" Here is what my response would have been: "The most scary story or part of this story is when Law Enforcement drives up to your house to tell you someone in your family has been murdered and then they tell you that your son or daughter has been bludgeoned to death by an unknown intruder." And now, I would say that another part that is awful is when Law Enforcement for all intents and purposes said to my grandfather in 2001 "I am sorry Mr. Smith although we have tried to solve your son and daughter in laws murders on and off for 20 years we still don't know who did this awful thing." And now after 37 years, after my grandfather Lyman Jones Smith has been dead for 16 years since 2001, I would say "the most awful thing is that there is no money for cold cases and no money to actually solve the crimes of a murderer who has been free and unaccountable since 1979-1980." (When the murders began) I would say that someone somewhere needs to make this case a priority as though the crimes just happened last week. I would say to the FBI and to different counties, "Why are these crimes unsolved? Why is this case still on the back burner?" There are large gaps of time between contact and any news. Year, after year, after year.

My tribute to the victims and the families is very heartfelt. No one deserves to be a victim of violent crime and certainly no one deserves to wait a lifetime to discover who did this terrible thing.

Chapter Eighteen

Post-Traumatic Stress
The cost of trauma

Everything in this chapter was written prior to the FBI announcement of their reinvestigations of these crimes

This is a story that would not leave, would not go away. I wanted to write about a million other stories and this one did not cross my mind at all. This was a story that I tucked away and did not look at for more than 30 years. Any information I knew about the case I found out accidentally along the way. I left Sacramento in 1984. Four years after Lyman and Charlene Smith's murders in Ventura County, four years' after Patrice and Keith Harrington lost their lives in Orange County. I had no desire to live in a city, especially Sacramento where I did not feel safe. I wanted to go somewhere else. I know bad things happen everywhere but I wanted to put the place and the summer heat behind me.

Post-Traumatic Stress is a difficult thing. My own symptoms that stemmed from fear are as follows:

I learned at a very early age (14) to not call attention to myself and to try to be invisible as much as possible. It was reinforced when I watched the aftermath of the murders in 1980. I have hidden from work men in the bedroom while my husband interacted with appliance repair people, furniture delivery people, carpet cleaners; you name it I would try not to be seen in my own home in these instances. When I moved from one house into another, from a neighborhood I was familiar with for eighteen years into another that I did not know I was worried for a couple of years. I did not know who belonged in the neighborhood and who did not. When cars drove by my house and I was gardening near the road each time a car would go by I would freeze hoping I would not be seen.

I usually walk to the mailbox when there are no cars on the street. If I am in the driveway and I hear a car I will turn around and stand still until they are gone. I automatically move, hide or freeze or all three. This particular action seems illogical to me and goes against everything else that I am, yet I still repeat the behavior over and over, year after year. I know that others, family members of murder victims sleep with the lights on, install alarms, and have dogs and guns, anything to feel safe. I hide and freeze. Sometimes I am fine.

For years I also did not feel comfortable going anywhere at night alone. If forced to do so there was a period of time where I would tuck my hair inside my coat to make it harder to notice, I am female. I have made sure I was not being followed home by passing by my street and driving around until the car behind me is gone. These are things that do not occur as much now that I am older, but they were as much a part of my everyday thinking at the times they happened as combing my hair or eating dinner. These were behaviors that became a part of what I did every day to feel safe. Eventually I got better. Most of these things don't happen anymore. I fought my fear and began to relax in my new neighborhood.

In retrospect looking back at the pattern that happened in my case there were several things that occurred in rapid succession to help me feel afraid. First was being chased down my street in 1971, and then a month later my mother was gone. I came home from being with friends to discover she was in the hospital and that my parents were separating. There was much shame and depression that happened as a result. My mother was gone for more than two months. When she came back my father moved out. It had only been three months since I was chased. There was no one to talk to about anything as I then discovered my parents were divorcing. So for me it was chased, mother gone, dad gone, mother home briefly and then mother gone again. I was not yet 15. This was 1971. My brother and I were alone in our house the next three years until 1975. In 1976 EAR showed up and was present everywhere in the news the next two plus years apparently leaving Sacramento in 1978. And then by 1980 the murders happened in the family. All of this equaled for me that there was no safety. I moved away in 1984.

In 2001 I saw a report accidentally on MSNBC. As I was cleaning house one day the television was on. The victims killed in Southern California pictures flashed by me on the screen. In particular, the pictures of Lyman and Charlene were on the screen. My grandfather had died in 2001 still not knowing who had killed his son, but knowing that the perpetrator was a serial killer and was linked to several murders. I had long ago hoped and assumed that the person who had been known as the East Area Rapist had been caught and long ago put away. It was not so. He had become The Original Night Stalker. My grandfather had not shared this with me. He did not speak about it. These crimes were connected. I sat down on the couch and listened.

Amazingly the crimes had not been solved; the perpetrator was still out there. I was to learn that all of the victims of murder by the Original Night Stalker who is a serial killer are one and the same person and he is also EAR. I called my mother, I called my father. Holy crap I told them, I can't believe it. My fascination with serial killers had begun in 1980 without knowing that all of the victims in these cases were tied together and had in fact been killed by one. This case, as I slowly became aware of the particulars over time was surprising to me because like many from Sacramento we believed the East Area Rapist must have been caught. I would take it out and look at it once in a while, read about it and found that it still terrified me too much to really study the case.

Here it is 16 years later and he is still out there. In 2012 and on I began to look at this case in depth and then study it. I did not want to keep it in the dark recesses of my brain any longer. I wanted to research and search out what I now know.

These were such horrible brutal crimes and so senseless that it became something that was never discussed in some families. As if by some chance if the words about the brutal way they were lost was not said out loud then the loss could somehow be more normalized. That a member of our family had been lost, but to speak of the how or why made it harder to bear. I know there are families who do not speak about these horrible crimes anymore. It is too painful and it has gone on too long. Yet, there are a few family members who are outspoken and who fight to bring justice for the victims every day.

Another journal entry from the backstory 2016:

The different counties need to focus on this case as a priority. The anniversaries are marked and nothing changes. I know there has been a tremendous effort by law enforcement and detectives, criminalists and examiners over time, but this case has at times been on the back burner for long periods of time because new crimes and new murders also need to be solved. I am grateful for all of the work done that has been done.

September 2017

It is my belief that there is very little being done actively by LE on this case even now, even after the FBI's announcement last year. I also believe the shows being done about the cases are doing little to spur any real investigative time spent actually following leads and information. What I am saying is the shows are good to inform the public about these cases and to let them know The East Area Rapist Aka the Original Night Stalker has never been caught. But, it seems these shows do little to motivate Law

Enforcement into spending more investigative time into these crimes. Likely they truly do lack funding to really put together a cold case unit and to put forth a great effort with time and people power to solve these crimes. If anyone knows facts about what is truly being done, please tell me. There are large gaps of time that go by in every step of investigations. We are running out of time.

I and many others feel the frustration at the lack of information available 41 years later. I cannot obtain a copy of the police report or crime report. I am told I cannot receive any information from the medical examiners' office because County Police Homicide Detectives prefer that I not see them. After 30 to 37 years? I know that family members of victims in these cases feel that they should be allowed access to these records. The reason for my frustration is that after 41 years it would seem there would be a time limit on the exemption laws. That an update to this law and what can be released would change after 41 years. It would seem that the advancement of Forensics and the inclusion of DNA evidence would make it possible that this exemption list could be challenged and updated. I am certain other family members have run into the same walls from the beginning.

June 2016 and now June 2017

In less than two weeks it will be 40 years since the East Area Rapist first attacked in Sacramento. And now another year has gone by. Another year has gone by let me say that again, "41 Years." There will be stories written, possibly again press releases in Sacramento County, Orange County, and other Counties. No new information, no new leads will be announced. They will merely be marking the length of time that has passed since this criminal began in earnest. Will the public service announcement generate new leads? Let us hope so. Hope is all that remains. Time is running short.

I am certain that my grandparents would be behind me and that they would approve of my pursuit of honoring them and also of pursuing the truth. The truth is out there. Someone knows this murderer. They will be shocked to discover what a monster he really is. These crimes must be solved. But, they may not be.

Don't you know

there comes a midnight hour

when everyone has to take off his mask?

- Soren Kierkegaard

Chapter Nineteen

Tribute to victims in this case

When these crimes occurred, one by one the stories of all of the victims became frozen in time. Their once beautiful family photographs were to become the picture, the one snapshot of the people who were now forever labeled "victims". They were so much more. This is what motivates me to help in any way I can to shed light, to find the culprit and to put this story to rest. This case needs to be solved. This case needs more attention. This case and many others who are left to the archived boxes of reports and unsolved crimes need to be solved.

There is no excuse in this day and age with the DNA testing which has evolved over time to a fantastic opportunity to punish those who think they long ago got away with murder to think again and to watch their backs. In this generation of criminals, we need to send a message that if you do these terrible things, rapes, murders, that there will be no place to hide. That no one will rest, law enforcement, medical examiners, DA's and detectives who will hunt you down.

You will not have the luxury of waiting and letting sleeping dogs lie as it were. We should as people who care about justice make sure there is funding for cold cases to be worked on and solved. The cold case units are not funded as they should be. The people who work on these crimes when they become somewhat dormant are not paid most of the time.

The people who tirelessly work to solve the mystery on cold cases are frequently retired detectives and volunteers. They are people who are dedicated and who do not want crimes such as these to go unsolved. That is the real crime. Families needlessly go a lifetime without knowing who took their loved one from them. Criminals should not go without punishment. I hope that the victims of these crimes can be remembered as they were rather than only being connected to a serial killer.

The impact of losing a loved one to violent crimes is multifaceted. Family, friends and communities are forever impacted in some way. Even the resources we spend in man/woman hours through law enforcement as well as the monies spent from these same agencies to try to solve the crime and find the perpetrators of crime cost all of us. The rape victims many times suffer from post-traumatic stress issues and are never the same. The cost of mental health care as well as time lost from work, time lost in general to these victims and their families as they try to deal with the aftermath of such attacks is catastrophic. These are the practical costs. The families of the murder victims suffer in all of the same ways mentioned. The impact is emotional suffering and of course the loss of their loved one makes it so that life will never ever be the same. The lost opportunity of the sharing in the lives of the people murdered and vice versa. The cost to communities and futures of the lost as well as their loved ones takes a toll. In these murders there were many families affected. Their loved ones missed an entire lifetime of love. The communities they came from felt the loss of the legacy the murdered victims should have been able to leave.

There were children and grandchildren that were not born to these families. The families were forever altered. The cost has been very high to all of these people that remain. Of course the obvious is that the lost, murdered humans in this story can never be replaced. They did not get to live out their lives, experience joy and laughter. The contributions the murder victims would have made to so many have been felt and have been missed for all of these 37 plus years.

These lives would have and could have intersected with many, many others. They were born and were meant to be here except for the sick rages of a person who could not deal with his own self. It was more important to him that he act out on others to feel in power and control. The motivations he had were born of his inability to cope with his own low self-esteem. Because of the absolute rage ONS had towards women it led him to obliterate and destroy those that he chose to control. This is a man who could never be rehabilitated. He is a narcissist who is all powerful and it truly is and was all about him. He has no empathy, no remorse and he is arrogant about the idea that he thinks he got away with these horrendous acts against actual human beings. So far he has.

"No man really knows about other human beings
The best he can do is to suppose that they are like
Himself"

- John Steinbeck

"I believe there are monsters born in the world
To human parents"

- John Steinbeck

Bits of information learned since publishing the first edition of this story

After speaking to select Law Enforcement and reading Larry Crompton's book about the attacks I was able to put this story into perspective from a Law Enforcement person's eyes. I met with Larry in person in February 2016 traveling to meet him in his neck of the woods. I speak with him by phone and email.

I have interviewed Hal Barker, Lyman's best friend four or five times and as of the writing of this edition I look forward to meeting with him again. Mr. Barker is a very stand-up guy and has been a pleasure to talk to.

I have spoken to Paul Holes who is an investigator for Contra Costa County still working this case as much as is possible. We have talked six or seven times as of the writing of this edition. We have typically spoken for an hour or more. What we discuss remains confidential. He is of like mind with me on these cases and believes the man we all look for could very well still be in Sacramento and is from there. Mr. Holes has stated this many times in television interviews.

One of the questions I have had about the investigation so far is this: Have the latest techniques and forensics been used and is there enough DNA left to test using today's methods? The answer is yes. Also, have they figured out his eye color from this definitively?

The answer is yes. More information should be forthcoming. A possible new composite sanctioned and authorized by LE could be released soon. These things are discussed on the internet regarding this case and so should already be information that is public knowledge.

After the first edition of this book came out I finally tracked Colleen Cason down. I have emailed and also spoken on the phone with Colleen three or four times, most recently in June 2017. Each time we spent an hour and a half or more discussing this case from a past perspective as well as currently discussing our views. Colleen had interviewed and spoken to many of the involved characters in the Smith stories. In 2001 Ms. Cason wrote a detailed account as much as was known of the story at that time. She had gathered information from those involved in the 1980's as well as contacted and interviewed some involved twenty years after the fact. Most of what we discuss is also confidential but I will disclose the following information as we agree on a couple of points as well.

All of these years many have believed that EAR might have gone to the same high school Lyman Robert went to (although 20 years after he did). Some believe that EAR lived in Citrus Heights or in East Sacramento and that is where he came from. It could be. Some have believed there was a possible connection because they believed my grandfather Lyman Senior had always lived in Citrus Heights and still resided there during the attacks in 1976 – 1978. Some have believed there could be or was a connection geographically to the Smiths' murders because they came from Citrus Heights and Sacramento thinking that EAR might have run across them. In discussing this with Colleen it was made clear to me that she had believed my Grandfather had been in Citrus Heights during the attacks all of these years later. The fact is that when my grandfather Lyman Sr. married my grandmother Veonia he rented his home out to family members in Citrus Heights for a couple of years.

Lyman Senior moved to West Curtis Park in 1960 when he married my grandmother. Lyman Senior left 16 years prior to the attacks in Citrus Heights. There was no connection to the Smith's being in residence there as some have believed during the 70's. My uncle on my grandmother's side of the family rented the home in Citrus Heights and my Uncle Don Smith lived with my aunt and uncle in Citrus Heights in the 1960's briefly. He wanted to finish high school graduating in 1962 from San Juan High School. Don soon enlisted in the Navy. That was the last time a Smith resided in this area. The home was sold before 1970.

I see the details as extremely important and these details or facts could affect the outcome of investigations. The details are what are important. There have been many who have asked me "How do you know these details?" I know them because I was there and this is my family.

Colleen Cason and I agree that there could be a connection to how ONS saw Charlene and one possibility is he could have seen her in Sacramento. So here it is: My grandparents lived on West Curtis Park. Veonia's first husband purchased the house in 1928. Lyman Smith moved there in June 1960 when he married my grandmother. Lyman Robert and Charlene would visit my grandparents in Sacramento across from the park and in South Lake Tahoe from 1973 until they were murdered in 1980. Is it possible that there is a connection from Sacramento to where Lyman Robert lived in Ventura with his wife Charlene? Is that too farfetched for that to be a possibility? Colleen and I agree that it could be a possibility. Paul Holes and I agree this should be looked at. They coincidentally lived across the street from a very nice park very close to the Highway 99 freeway which was a mile from the house and the neighborhood I grew up in.

Because Sacramento is also close to Lake Tahoe is it possible that EAR/ONS saw Charlene in Tahoe? Lyman and Charlene visited my grandparents in Tahoe several times from 1973 until 1979. Every possibility should be looked at. Lyman and Charlene attended (Bob's) high school reunion in 1974 coming from a visit to Lake Tahoe and then going to the 20-year reunion for San Juan High School in Citrus Heights. These are some of the things I shared with Colleen Cason. The rest of our discussions must remain confidential at this point.

Here are a couple of brief disclosures from our emails this year.

Hi Anne,
"This is all sounds fine.
I truly believe your geography theory is valid.
The fact that he drew that "punishment" map is
very telling of his obsession with place.
Good luck in Sacramento.
Best,
Colleen"

Another one:

"I wish you every success in your promising
research and writing and hope it ultimately leads
to solving this case. For the sake of you, your
grandfather and every other person whose life has
been destroyed or forever changed by this
monster.

Best,

Colleen"

There are researchers on this case who I have
spoken to in the past. They anonymously work the
case and have done so for more than ten years. They
have much of the investigative files from Contra
Costa County. They received these files from a time
frame when no one was investigating these crimes.
They were very cold cases so these people
volunteered to work it. They have tirelessly shed
light and worked to discover this man's identity.
They have put many things together and made many
connections in their research. Unfortunately, the
crimes remain unsolved.

These researchers have some records that came from the Sacramento crimes. They were not all destroyed as some thought after the statute of limitations on the rapes ran out in 1984.

Epilogue

If we could somehow reach back into our pasts and remember that we may have come in contact with the someone described in all the descriptions included in this book we can show the perpetrator and everyone else across the country that if you commit crimes such as these you may be free today but sooner or later because the victims, the families and law enforcement will never give up in the hunt for you that you will be found. You will be found and exposed and be held accountable for the crimes you commit.

With the advances in DNA testing that are made every day we will be able to definitively know without doubt who actually committed crimes everywhere. We will know the color of your eyes and what you look like. We already have the capability to break it down knowing whether the criminal is African American or Caucasian, or other races as well. If we can solve this case which began forty-one years ago and apparently ceased 31 years ago it can send a message to would be perpetrators that they cannot get away with hurting innocent people as this man did.

I know it seems a lifetime ago that these crimes took place. It was a lifetime ago. This perpetrator went to school with some of us. Please read through the descriptions of who this person might have been when you may have known him. Does anyone from the past stand out in your mind that possibly had some of the personality traits described? He could have been the guy who always had trouble fitting in or the guy who seemed a little strange but tried not to call attention to himself. Re-read the personality disorders section included in this book and think about who you may have known that had difficulty regulating his emotions or was frustrated and angry in classes. Because every teen has these difficulties from time to time I am talking about frustration that is over and above what could be called "normal" teenage frustration or anger. Was there someone you knew who appeared to have no respect for authority or for the consequences of any actions he may have taken in the face of authority? He tried to live under the radar just trying to get out of school so he could be free to commence destruction on our communities.

Or... he could have been like Ted Bundy who at first glance and first encounter seemed like a regular guy. He was and is able to pull off a persona of his own making.

I also must discuss how I really feel about law enforcement and volunteers who have worked this case and who are still working this case.

I am aware that some comments I have made throughout this unfortunate story may be construed as somewhat critical or unflattering to certain people who have been involved with this story. It is not my intent. What you hear and what I have stated is my frustration and disturbance that this man was not caught in the early stages of his career. It seems that

469

although law enforcement worked very hard to do their best to stop him that in fact this guy caught every break along the way. It seemed that if anything was going to be missed by witnesses or others everything that could go wrong when it came to finding this guy, it was always the criminal who caught the breaks in this case. That is certainly not law enforcements fault.

To be fair, this criminal also thought nothing of using deadly force when cornered and always did use deadly force when necessary to escape. He is a very dangerous individual. Yet law enforcement puts their lives on the line every day. I do have great respect for everyone who worked so diligently on this case and who still do. I am grateful as I have said that we have protectors out there who try to stop evil and who many times do. To all law enforcement everywhere I thank you for the hard work and the lifetimes of sacrifice not only from you as individuals but also to your families who live with the fear for your own wellbeing and safety. I have to say it again, Thank You. I also am appreciative of all of the volunteers and people who give of their time to endlessly track down leads and to research possible POI's. I really do commend you for your dedication.

Tips for the whereabouts of the man now in custody from areas of the crimes can be called in to the Sacramento County Sheriff's or FBI 1-800-CALL-FBI

Photo Album: After the murders - Lyman Jones
Smith and us after the loss of Lyman Robert and
Charlene. My wedding reception May 10, 1980

Previous page top: Guests at my wedding reception May 10, 1980 grandpa and grandma on the far right lower part of the picture. Right behind Lyman Senior was Bill and Melanie Harvey. Bill was a news man for KCRA in Sacramento at the time.

Bottom left previous page: Lyman J. Smith and Veonia Smith and guests at my wedding reception in Roseville CA, May 10, 1980. Two hours before Lyman had been crying at the church in the vestibule at the wedding in Auburn, California

Above photo: November 1980 8 months after the murders. Thanksgiving in the kitchen Lyman J. Smith carving the turkey with my uncle from my grandmothers' side of the family. We had Thanksgiving together my entire life until they passed away.

Lyman Jones Smith Shriner event May 11, 1982
raising money for the Temple Building Fund

Top left: Lyman and Veonia Smith at my cousins graduation from College June 1985 Fullerton, CA

Top right: At home Curtis Park 1984 Grandma on Grandpa's lap. Married 24 years in this picture.
Bottom left: Dinner senior citizens Christmas party 1984

Myself, Grandpa and my son 1986 backyard collecting oranges from the orange tree

Curtis Park Home

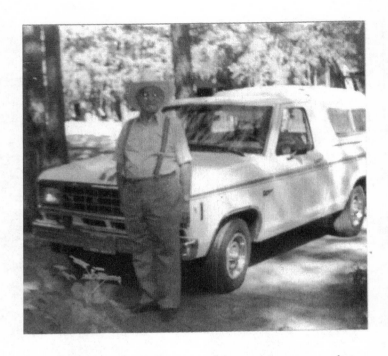

In Tahoe my grandpa was always in suspenders
(these were rainbow colors) Cowboy hat was new.
So was the truck. June 1985 at the cabin. Grandpa
was the only man I had ever known who wore
suspenders.

Lyman Jones Smith and Veonia Smith this was the last portrait they had taken in approximately 1987. They had been married 27 years at the time of the photo.

Fall 1990 Left to right: Laurie, Lyman Senior, Veonia and my aunt and uncle on my mothers side of the family and my 8 year old son. This was taken right around my grandfathers 81st birthday and in less than 2 months my grandmother would have a stroke and pass away. One of our last group photos with Veonia.

My home 1990, Grandpa Lyman Senior with my son laughing at something. This was my son's 8th birthday. My grandparents always came to my son's birthday dinner. He was the last baby they took care of in Sacramento.

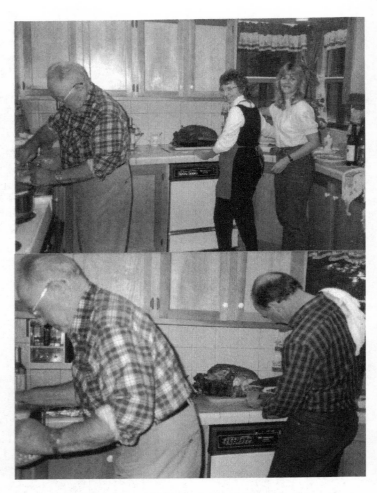

Both photographs: 1990 in the kitchen cooking for Thanksgiving dinner. Top photo is Grandpa on the left with my mother and me on the right. Bottom: Grandpa getting ready to carve the turkey with grandson in law. This was our first Thanksgiving without my grandmother who had passed away Oct 15, 1990.

Laurie and Lyman Easter 1991 on the way to church – this was grandpa's first Easter without my grandmother so we all went with him downtown to the First Baptist church.

In front of West Curtis Park Home

Easter 1991 Lyman Jones (Grandpa) with my son.
We brought Grandpa an Easter basket

He had held us on his lap and he was now grandpa
to my children and my brothers' children

Grandpa Lyman Jones Smith with my son and his
cousin Easter 1991 on the way to church

Lyman Jones Smith Senior in the kitchen Curtis Park 1992 (I took the picture). You can still see the twinkle in his eye. Lyman lived until 2001 to the great age of 92 almost 93. It is conceivable that his son Lyman Robert could have still been alive today had he and Charlene not been taken.

This journey began as unfinished business. When the murders occurred in the Smith family I buried the trauma and put a lid on it except for my Post Traumatic Stress. The fear limited what I felt comfortable doing and also affected the times I would be out and when I would travel. Fear also had an impact on my comfort level out in the world, and in trying new things. I have written about this earlier in the book. I bring it up again because the journey I have had while researching this case, and in writing a book about it, as well as expressing my thoughts and ideas or theories has brought me many surprises.

Digging up the past has had many up sides and a few downsides. The upside for me has been the happy memories I had with my grandparents. This journey has reminded me of what losing them meant. It has also reminded me of how much we shared and how lucky I was to have had them in my life. We shared so much time, memories, laughter and all of the things that families share.

When I turned 16 and got my driver's license and although I was driving a Volkswagen and they knew they would have to squeeze into the back seat they wanted to make me feel important so they called me one day. They said "can you drive us to the airport and drop us off?" They were going on a trip and did not want to leave their car at the airport. So I went over picking them up very early and on time. They trusted me and helped me to feel like I could do something for them.

My grandparents were there always and had my back on occasions I needed help in my life. Lyman and Veonia Smith took care of me and my newborn three-week old baby taking me in when my husband lost his job right before our son was born. We lived with them for five months while my husband and I got back on our feet.

When I went back to work full time the first year my grandparents took care of our new baby while I worked. I dropped him off every day at 7:30 a.m. and picked him up at 5:15. When my marriage ended once again they were there and I stayed with them for a month while I looked for a new apartment. When I moved back east for a time they were devastated at losing contact for a year with their great grandson. When I came back to start a new business they gave me a place to stay. I was told to just pay them for the utilities. They were doing the job that parents do for their children. All of these lovely pictures brought back great memories for me

Life did go on and we were fortunate to have ten more years with both Lyman Senior and Veonia. We had more time with grandpa after her loss while he was adjusting to life without her. So, feeling my feelings throughout the experience of researching and writing this book has been good for my own healing. I have done what I could to work through it, study it and work towards helping to identify the man known as EAR and ONS. There is still unfinished business because we do not yet know who changed us all in these cases. We deserve to know the name of the man who is EAR and ONS.

I have found that even now after all these years whether I am researching this case or simply reading various articles that people have written about the Smith's and their murder's, the speculation about their lives, I still feel this pain in the pit of my stomach because there are so many stories out there and so many reports about these two people. The speculation, the rumors that are in print without real basis of fact sometimes makes my stomach ache. This story is not a report or a manipulation of hearsay to have the desired effect in order to capture or keep a strangers' interest, this story is personal. I feel uneasy each and every time I read the actual facts and also the attempts at sensationalizing this story as though it can be talked about in the same way that Big Foot or stories about aliens are.

There are many who did write stories and articles about every aspect of what they know about these cases. There are those who have written stories about the murders in Ventura County and other counties as a way of calling attention to themselves through blogs and crime diaries hoping to make careers or to become famous in some way. Everyone involved has their own motivations.

There are many armchair sleuths out there who are sincere, kind and helpful who truly want nothing more than to solve this case or to help solve it. Thank you to all of you for your attention to detail in this case and for all the many hours you spend and have spent in working on finding the one detail, or the one POI. Finding the one something or anything to help end the victims and family members stress over this case. I admire the tenacity and endurance of the many of you out there.

It would have been my wish to never have had to try and integrate this experience into or out of my life. I needed to look at this as a mature adult and to try and purge the fear. Some days it has been harder than others. When one focuses on this type of subject matter for a couple of years intensely, especially a story that is laden with fear there are times when driving up to the mail box in the dark, and getting out of the car has me looking around over my shoulder a little bit more diligently. I find I hurry a little more to get inside, make sure the house is secure or even in summer before I go to bed I make sure the windows and doors are all locked.

These murders changed everyone in our family. As I have said I am not the daughter of Lyman Robert; I am the granddaughter of his father. I did spend over 41 years of my life loving and sharing life with Lyman Jones Smith the murder victims' dad. I did not know Jennifer, Lyman Jay or Gary Smith personally, and they did not know me because geography kept that from taking place. As small children we did meet and play. As we grew this never occurred again.

There was never contact or conversation between Lyman Robert's kids after the murders with our side of the family until 1989. Jenny, Lyman Jay and Gary saw my grandfather in Santa Paula, but he was getting older and travel became more difficult. The Smith children's parents were divorced in 1972, and then Lyman Robert was lost to them in 1980. I have much empathy for them in the loss of their father especially because of the way he and Charlene were taken. I did not see this experience from their perspective nor could I have. I only saw this experience through the eyes of our grandfather and through my own eyes as a witness and as a family member.

It was unfortunate for Lyman Robert's children they did not get to share in our grandfather's life on an almost daily basis like I did and our part of the family did.

It does not surprise me nor would it if Lyman Robert's grown children have no memory of any of our names since we were not raised near each other. Lyman Senior was grandfather to 7 grandchildren and several great grandchildren from our side of the family.

The last time I saw Lyman Robert's kids was in 1989 in Napa, California for our Grandfathers 80th birthday celebration. My Uncle Norm and his wife felt it important that they be invited to share in Lyman Senior's birthday. Lyman Robert's grown children looked great. They looked to be healthy people who were glad to be in Napa that day September 15, 1989.

All of our lives have always been on different paths. I was lucky to share the same grandfather. I was glad to have Lyman Senior as a role model and as a father figure to me all of my life. He served as grandfather to me and my brothers, to my children and all of the children in our family.   I am grateful.

For Homicide survivors or family members of homicide victims:

If you are a homicide survivor or experiencing grief, you may feel:

- Unable to understand or believe what happened to your loved one
- Helpless and powerless over your surroundings
- Preoccupied with your own personal safety and the safety of surviving loved ones
- As if you somehow could or should have protected your loved one from harm
- Haunted by images, nightmares, and flashbacks of the murder, even if you were not a witness
- Afraid of strangers and worried that the perpetrator, or any perpetrator, will strike again
- Intense rage toward the perpetrator(s)
- Distrustful of others and of the world around you
- A desire to avoid people and places that remind you of your loved one or of the homicide
- Physical symptoms, like head or stomach aches, difficulty sleeping, eating or focusing
- Blamed, isolated, exploited, or stigmatized by law enforcement, health care providers, news media, and your own friends and family

- Anger and blame in many different directions – toward yourself, other family members, witnesses of the homicide, law enforcement, spiritual leaders, and God

How a violent crime can affect you:

It can be extremely frightening to experience a violent crime. As well as possibly being hurt or injured physically, you can be very seriously affected emotionally.

Many people find it hard to deal with the feeling of being powerless when they are threatened. Other common feelings include:

- finding it hard to believe what has happened, and feeling numb

- feeling deeply upset

- feeling that your life is completely out of control

- physical symptoms such as 'the shakes', sleeplessness or crying all the time

- extreme anger towards your attacker

- self-blame for being in the wrong place at the wrong time.

All of these reactions, and more, are completely normal responses to experiencing violence.

Resources for Victims of Violent Crimes

Victims of Violent Crimes Resource Information

National Center for Victims of Crime

http://victimsofcrime.org/

http://victimsofcrime.org/help-for-crime-victims

Help for Crime Victims

The National Center for Victims of Crime has a number of resources available to assist victims of crime. Our National Help Line, VictimConnect, provides help for victims of any crime nationwide, and can be reached by phone at 1--855-4VICTIM (1-855-484-2846) or by online chat.

Find Law: http://criminal.findlaw.com/criminal-legal-help/crime-victim-resources.html

National Organization for Victim Assistance http://www.trynova.org/

A Note of Thanks

I must thank those who tirelessly answered my questions, listened to me, and always showed patience and concern as I began this particular journey all the way to end of this manuscript. Thank you to Tim, Jon, Kathleen and Larry for your infinite patience and for always trying to listen. Thank you to Mark Smith who after the first edition came out discussed the case with me and bounced ideas back and forth. Also thank you Mark for your patience when the frustration of this case made me crazy. Thank you as well to the many more who when the discussion turned to serial killers you would look at me as though I was nuts. Thank you for your honest reactions! I know that these individuals will continue to be as wonderful and as giving in the future whether or not these crimes are ever solved. Thank you to the select few of you that spoke to me about this story. It meant so much to me to be able to speak with you. Grace and generosity are the words that come to mind as I think of you.

Thank you to all of the rest of you who unknowingly made it easier to walk through this path and who were peripheral and necessary in my brief disclosures to you about this story. I know I must have seemed obsessed as I informed you about a story that not enough people were talking about. I needed to bounce some of my thoughts around with you out in the world. Thank you to my family for their long and appreciated patience.

It is truly my hope that this manuscript helped someone, anyone who has been touched by this story either directly or indirectly. This is an unfortunate story, but the families of the victims and the victims/survivors go on. They work and fight to make things better for others. We are all connected and we are all in this together. Finally, thank you to everyone who reads this book and contemplates any shred of information that might be helpful in solving the puzzle.

And now we know the name of the man responsible for these crimes. On April 25, 2018 the criminal who uses the name Joseph James DeAngelo, Jr. was arrested. His DNA is a 100% match. He is the evil perpetrator of ALL of the vicious crimes against the innocent. We will see justice preserved. We will see the final chapter in this story as it evolves in real time in our lifetimes. Thank God. I am glad he is still alive so that he can feel the loss of power and control over his own life. I am glad he will know how it feels to be awakened by bright shining lights in a jail or prison as his captors, police officers he underestimated, thinking he was smarter in the end proved that the was the one who was not smart at all. He is the one who now sits in a box. I take great pleasure in that fact as do the many, many survivors and family members of the deceased.

Stay tuned for the final, final chapter. Much love to the victims, the families and the survivors.

Anne/Laurie

New Chapters

After the capture of suspect Joseph James
DeAngelo age 72, of Citrus Heights, CA

It has been three weeks since the capture/arrest of
the suspect mentioned above. I will not mention his
name again except with the words Criminal, Creep,
Suspect, or other words like that. I try not to use his
name as he does not deserve one bit of recognition as
an actual person. The initials JJD will be used if
needed.

In a court of law, he is presumed innocent until
proven guilty beyond a reasonable doubt. This case
and many others like it in the age of DNA have to be
prosecuted differently because in this case the
Creep's DNA matches the profile of the East Area
Rapist, Original Night Stalker, Golden State Killer
100%.

I suppose it is possible the public defender will try
to say somehow that the match could be faulty and
she/they could offer up some scientific data and
experts who will make us doubt the match that says
this is the guy. The old fashioned police work that
has been done, and that will be done to tie JJD to the
places and the times of the crimes will all prove we
have him at long last. It seems like such a waste of
time and money to try and prove this man is guilty –
because we know HE IS.

In the three weeks since this man's arrest I will add
what I personally know right at this moment. It is

subject to change as this story evolves. JJD is now older and appeared to be pitiful in his first court appearance. I will elaborate in the chapter

In the creeps second appearance he at least was standing in a cage in the Sacramento Superior Court Room. When he had been surveilled the previous weeks he was seen riding a motorcycle, walking around his yard and acting to quote Paul Holes "more like a man 50 years of age" So the pitiful show in a wheelchair either had to do with feigned weakness or possibly the perpetrator was sedated when on suicide watch.

The next court date in slated for May 29 in Sacramento which I have read will be more of the same. Motions being filed and nothing much being done to move this along. The wheels of justice although 42 years late for some will take their time as they always do. For those of us up close this part will also be excruciating because we want this to be done. JJD sits in a box for all the world to see, yet we are eager to hear HIS final sentence before he can escape his story by dying. At 72 he could live at least another 15 years while we take up at least the next five years deciding what jurisdiction will get the pleasure of trying him for murder first. Many maneuvers and wrangling will happen as the legal system moves forward. The long haul ride into the beginning of any trial will last at least the next two years in my humble opinion.

So what we know at the moment is actually pretty extensive as we try to track where this man was and what he was doing during the attack timelines. The sleuths who have been after this man have never stopped and will not stop until the last T and the final I's are dotted, and even then there will be those who are still unsatisfied with some of the answers we may receive.

The retired detectives who worked this case have different opinions about what will happen. Richard Shelby form Sacramento has said he believes that JJD will talk at some point. I think if he does he will take his sweet time about it. Likely not until AFTER he is convicted. This man is selfish enough to make his family go through a trial and waste the community tax payer dollars in order to convict him. For me and I am sure many others, we would be just fine if he stood up like an actual man and took responsibility for his crimes. At least BTK did. He said "You got me" "I am BTK."

This man, this creep in waiting will play it out until the end in my opinion. This is what I think looking at this three weeks in. I will add just a fraction of what the media is reporting here and it will be subject to change as we move forward.

DNA Succeeds in finding him at last:

First, how we ultimately found the guy suspected of being the Golden State Killer aka Original Night Stalker aka East Area Rapist.

It must be said that the suspect Joseph James DeAngelo was not on any – repeat any POI (Person of Interest) list until six days prior to his arrest in Citrus Heights, CA on April 25, 2018. There were 8,000 names on lists, but not his. Old fashioned police work had gone down many paths over the course of forty plus years never giving resolve to these cases. Lots of discussion about using DNA and genealogy to track the killer using a footprint he never considered that he had successfully left behind at his crime scenes went on for years. Privacy issues with ancestry sites and legal discussions I am certain went on behind the scenes over time.

For me – waiting for them to JUST DO IT became more and more a question. I wanted to know what is taking so long? This guy who had about an 85% chance of still being alive when we finally found him, the longer we waited the higher the statistics went that the possibility he would die before being brought to justice.

The genealogy site that the killer's profile was fed into tracked the killer back in time to his great-great-great grandparents. Sort of reminds me of that movie with Dennis Quaid called Frequency where the characters have the ability to track a killer over decades tracing him back in time over a generation.

They had the ability to know the outcomes and the footsteps of the killer in the movie. We had the whole story, we knew what he had done and we tracked and connected the dots the best that we could over the course of forty plus years. Going back to the early 1800's this family had no way to know that this man who could be traced to current times had become a monster. JJD had left his invisible genetic markers that could be traced over the generations back to the early 1800's. Tracking the code branch by branch of JJD's family tree which created 25 trees containing thousands of relatives. Tracking and tracing. I can imagine when they got to 1900 they had to be getting energized at their progress.

The story of JJD being a disgraced cop likely came as no surprise to the current investigators which did include Paul Holes, a criminalist until March 2018 with Contra Costa County. Apparently a team of five investigator's spent four months building family trees name by name. Connecting the dots with census records, obituaries, gravesite locators as well as police databases and other commercial databases they worked to track each relative until they came to JJD.

GED Match was used to upload the killer's DNA profile to compare with roughly one million profiles. A lab in Ventura County amazingly had put duplicate samples from Charlene Smith's rape kit into a freezer in 1980 which was used by the lab to convert into a format that could be read by the site. GED Match analyzes hundreds of thousands of DNA data points to determine relatedness.

Once the tracking brought them to DeAngelo they waited and watched until a discarded item could be picked up and tested to see if JJD was a match to the killer. It was. Now charged with 12 counts of murder.

Where was he hiding?

JJD was working for Save Mart grocery store for 27 years at the Roseville Distribution Center. He retired last year. According to people he worked with "none of his actions would have led us to suspect him of any crimes that are being attributed to him." JJD started working at the distribution center in 1990.

As we know if we have followed the case DeAngelo worked for the Auburn Police Department from 1976 until 1979, being forced out after being charged with stealing a hammer and dog repellent from a Citrus Heights drug store off Greenback Lane.

Prior to arriving at the Auburn Police Department JJD worked in Exeter PD from 1973 until 1976 with fewer than 10 officers patrolling with a population of about 5,000. He was known as always serious. While in Exeter which was East of Visalia near the Sierra Nevada Foothills, an old edition of the Exeter Sun quoted JJD as commenting about law and order, he said "Without Law and Order there can be no government and without a democratic government there can be no freedom." Law Enforcement is his career, he says, and his job is serving the community."

To all of the sleuth's tracking this man for all of these years it came as no surprise that JJD was a cop and that he had been in the military, and we had determined him to have been in the Navy.

JJD went to Folsom High school, but received a GED rather than diploma. He also attended Sierra College and Sacramento State College, not far from many of his attacks. JJD obtained a degree in Criminal Justice.

What I have read about what fellow officers said about the theft of dog repellent and the hammer leads me to think that it might have been something he was using so much of in his attacks that possibly they needed to sign out what they used on the force. Maybe JJD was trying to replenish his supply without having to sign out any more of the repellent on the job. He also wanted no record of his usage or his purchase of it just in case it was ever questioned. And as we know this theft ultimately lost him his Police job. After his firing and by the end of the same year JJD began murdering in earnest.

I have to interject a thought here: I really think that after JJD's firing from the Auburn Police Department that he was already a man who thought he was above the law and smarter than the officers in every jurisdiction. I think he was a revenge type killer moving forward. He satisfied his twisted view of rape, sex and terror already very much in place for several years. Once he was fired in 1979 he played with all law enforcement taunting them in his own way setting out to make sure they never caught him. He knew if he crossed into different jurisdictions changing some of what he did that LE would have a much harder time putting the pieces together.

He also likely knew that it was not often that Law Enforcement would look at their own to find a serial burglar as in the Visalia Ransacker cases. It was not something to be looked at in Sacramento in the beginning either. The idea that a department would really look into one of its own in Exeter or in Auburn was as foreign I think as the idea that reporting prowlers was back in the 1970's. People many, many times never picked up the phone.

The same thing can be said with the inability to look inward by departments back in the day. If they had done so, if they had looked at any fired police officer, if they had tracked his movements from the beginning of the Visalia attacks, to Sacramento and then outward, if they had tracked this guy in real time all the while looking for any irregularity in any of their own departments, if they had ever considered, REALLY considered he could be one of their own we would have learned JJD's identity long ago. We would not have had to wait for DNA to solve these crimes because the answers were right in front of us all along.

Old fashioned hard core police work would have found all of the answers if they had only looked within. I had begun to look around at the small towns surrounding Sacramento for the perpetrator of these crimes. I had discussed a small town a little southeast of Sacramento this year with Larry Crompton. I mentioned it to Paul Holes because it was not far from Highway 80 which leads to 680 and 580 South. It was a place no one had yet checked. Like many sleuths I was possessed with looking everywhere, but especially around Sacramento. For a while I was convinced we would find him in South

Sacramento. He did attack there twice, knowing the layout of every place he went well.

I had not yet looked north to Auburn. But, of course in retrospect it makes sense. I kick myself at not looking there first. I had looked at another jurisdiction at other cops. And was now looking at a town South East of Sacramento. I was also looking at collecting the DNA of a POI from Citrus Heights on the Wednesday 4-25-18, the day JJD was arrested. I had my map and the address in the car for that trip to Sacramento. The address I had in mind was 2.1 miles away from Canyon Oak in Citrus Heights a mere six-minute drive from JJD.

It turns out the pencil necked guy that Shelby had seen in South Sacramento during the attacks was just a pencil necked guy. Lots of them there in the 1970's.

More to follow soon.

Sources

Materials presented in this book that are photographs of victims were taken from the internet on various image sites. They are published for educational and informational purposes only in the interest of this book and I am using them as set forth under Section 107 (the Fair Use doctrine) of the U.S. Copyright Act of 1976.

Other photographs were taken during my research and in an effort to disclose an area of Sacramento. Photographs were taken by myself, Anne Penn, and are copyrighted materials from 2016.

I have listed and credited other sites and articles by various authors listed in the bibliography. I have secured permission from as many individuals and authors that I could reach. These articles are also used under Section 107 of the Fair Use doctrine of the U.S. Copyright Act of 1976 and are used for informational and educational purposes to enlighten the public on crimes committed by this perpetrator.

Various news articles from the Sacramento Bee are also reproduced in the hopes of helping to make the public aware of this criminal's activity and his MO as the East Area Rapist and the Original Night Stalker from approximately 1975 until at least 1986. They are published for educational and informational purposes only in the interest of this book and I am using them as set forth under Section 107 (the Fair Use doctrine) of the U.S. Copyright Act of 1976.

News articles are presented in their original form and are typed into the manuscript for clarity and to inform the public of the crimes committed by this perpetrator. Once again these are used for Educational and informational purposes in the interest of telling the stories of criminal acts perpetrated in Sacramento California from 1975 or 1976 until 1981. The articles are used for informational purposes and to inform the public of the type of criminal that he is. He is a dangerous man and still walks among us. The articles are published for educational and informational purposes only in the interest of this book and I am using them as set forth under Section 107 (the Fair Use doctrine) of the U.S. Copyright Act of 1976.

The various sites listed for Victims of Violent Crimes are taken from the internet from their websites in order to provide helpful information and awareness of the help that is available to victims of violent crimes as well as their families. They are published for educational and informational purposes only in the interest of this book and I am listing them as set forth under Section 107 (the Fair Use doctrine) of the U.S. Copyright Act of 1976.

Thoughts and opinions are wholly mine and no one else's. I did not collaborate in any way in the writing of this book. The responsibility is mine. My background and education lie in the following experiences.

I have almost 40 years of experience studying serial killers from 1980 until now. I have a Psychology and

Sociology background as well as Criminal Justice. I am an Addiction Specialist and have worked in a jail with inmates teaching Health Education Addiction Recovery programs. I was a Computer Installation Analyst installing and training computer operator's. I have run small businesses training and hiring people to become successful. I have been writing throughout my life, but more consistently since 2006. Prior to that I have enjoyed writing since childhood having written poems by age 12. In the beginning I helped start a school newspaper along with others by age 13. I have written another book prior to this one that was published 3 months ago under my real name.

I grew up in South Sacramento attending schools there as well as colleges there. My father was a Parole Officer working for the California Youth Authority and in programs designed to help young men between the ages of 17 and 21 from 1968 and for many years after. He also worked at the Preston School of Industry in Ione during his time with the California Youth Authority. He also worked for the Department of Rehabilitation also for the State of California.

My stepfather was a Parole Agent also working for the State of California and the Community Treatment Programs. He worked extensively with the Youth of the community in South Sacramento and in Sacramento general trying to teach young men a better way of living and how to make better choices in life. Both of my fathers worked at this diligently throughout their careers. They were my examples. I think our society can be hard on young men and that it can be a huge challenge on the way to becoming contributing men in our societies.

Various articles were taken off various sites from the internet. Some I could not identify the origins of. I have tried to credit and acknowledge those that I could identify who the author was as well as the location and time frames of the articles written. All were found on the internet in some capacity or another. Some of the websites are dedicated to telling everyone about this perpetrator and what his crimes were. I have only highlighted just a few of the articles of the times as well as articles of opinions that were published in the hopes of getting more of the public's help in finding the man responsible. They are published for educational and informational purposes only in the interest of this book and I am using them as set forth under Section 107 (the Fair Use doctrine) of the U.S. Copyright Act of 1976.

There are many other resources and books written on the subject here are just a few:

Crompton, Larry. *Sudden Terror: The True Story of California's Most Infamous Sexual Predator, the East Area Rapist Aka the Original Night Stalker.* Bloomington IN: Author house, 2010. Print.

Shelby, Richard. *Hunting a Psychopath: The East Area Rapist: Original Night Stalker Investigation.* Bradenton, FL: BookLocker.com, 2015. Print.

Penn, Anne Murder On His Mind Serial Killer, First Edition Amazon March 2017. Print. Kindle January 2017.

There are multitudes of Podcasts available on every aspect of this case from many different sources

Anne Penn podcasts:

Dan Zupansky Blog Talk Radio July 2017

http://www.blogtalkradio.com/dan-zupansky1/2017/07/13/murder-on-his-mind-serial-killer-anne-penn

Alan Warren Seattle July 2017 KKNW Seattle

https://www.podomatic.com/podcasts/houseofmysteryradio/episodes/2017-07-08T13_00_03-07_00

Websites: there are many sites available as well as Facebook pages just type in key words. These two sites should be a very good start.

http://ear-ons.com/investigate.html

https://www.fbi.gov/news/stories/help-us-catch-the-east-area-rapist

NEWS OF HIS ARREST AND APPEARANCE IN COURT TODAY April 27, 2018

http://www.kcra.com/article/suspect-in-east-area-rapist-case-in-court-for-1st-time-1/20088759

Bibliography

BVDA - BVDA: Materials and Equipment for Crime Scene Officers and Forensic Laboratories. N.p., n.d. Web. 10 March. 2016 *Author: M.J.M. (Theo) Velders, Politie Brabant Zuid-Oost, Eindhoven, the Netherlands.* N.p., n.d. Web. 10 March. 2016 IAI Educational Conference St. Louis, Missouri; August, 2004 Presenter: J.N. (Jan) Zonjee, BVDA, Haarlem, the Netherlands website:http://www.bvda.com email:info@bvda.nl

Velders, Theo. "Visualization of Latent Fingerprints on Used ... - Bvda.com." N.p., n.d. Web. 6 Sept. 2016.

Http://independent.academia.edu/TheoVelders. "Visualization of Latent Fingerprints on Used Vinyl and Latex Gloves Using Gellifters." *Academia.edu - Share Research.* N.p., n.d. Web. 20 August 2016.

Photographs of ligatures and knots as well as footprint were retrieved from the internet and were listed under images in general

Authored by Ken LaMance, Legal Match Law Library Managing Editor and Attorney at Law. "California Statute of Limitations on Sexual Abuse." *Find a Lawyer.* N.p., n.d. Web. 09 Dec. 2015.

Dryden-Edwards, MD Roxanne. "Antisocial Personality Disorder Symptoms, Treatment, Causes - What Is the Difference between Antisocial

Personality Disorder and Psychopathy? -
MedicineNet." *MedicineNet*. N.p., n.d. Web. 08
April 2016.
http://www.medicinenet.com/antisocial_personality
_disorder/page2.htm

Erin Hallissy and Charlie Goodyear, Chronicle Staff
Writers. "DNA Links '70s 'East Area Rapist' to
Serial Killings / Evidence Suggests Suspect Moved
to Southern California." *SFGate*. N.p., n.d. Web. 06
Oct. 2015. Published 4:00 am, Wednesday, April 4,
2001

"Glove Prints." *Wikipedia*. Wikimedia Foundation,
n.d. Web. 10 May. 2016.

Lyle, D. P. *Forensic Science*. Chicago: American
Bar Association, 2012. Web. 5 April. 2016
Web. According to *Forensic Science*, there are three
types of fingerprints. D.P. Lyle, *Forensic Science
(ABA Fundamentals)*, p. 255 (2012):

McDonald, Karl M. "DNA Forensic Testing and
Use DNA Rape Kits."
Http://Www.forensicmag.com, Forensic Magazine,
1 Jan. 2015.
http://www.forensicmag.com/article/2015/01/dna-
forensic-testing-and-use-dna-rape-kits-cases-rape-
and-sexual-assault

"Mental Health: Conduct Disorder." *WebMD*.
WebMD, n.d. Web. 05 Dec. 2015.

"Mental Health: Oppositional Defiant Disorder."
WebMD. WebMD, n.d. Web. 06 Dec. 2015.

"Original Night Stalker." *Wikipedia*. Wikimedia
Foundation, n.d. Web. 06 Jan. 2016.

Rule, Ann. *The Stranger Beside Me*. First ed. New
York: Norton, 1980. Print.

Items found in Ted Bundy's car in Utah 1975 –
Ted's "Kit" By Source, Fair use,
https://en.wikipedia.org/w/index.php?curid=259674
14 02 Sept. 2016

"Sacramento County Sheriff's Department." *East
Area Rapist/Original Night Stalker*. N.p., n.d. Web.
Dec.-Jan. 2015 - 2016.

Staff, By Mayo Clinic. "Intermittent Explosive
Disorder." - *Mayo Clinic*. N.p., n.d. Web. 05 Dec.
2015.

"Ted Bundy." *Wikipedia*. Wikimedia Foundation,
n.d. Web. 06 Nov. 2015.

"Tie Hinted in Pair of Goleta Murders -
Jjmcgr.org." N.p., n.d. Web. 6 Feb. 2016.
Malnic, Eric *Los Angeles Times*, 29 July 1981, pg.
A20.

"East Area Rapist/Original Night Stalker." *East
Area Rapist/Original Night Stalker*, ear-

ons.com/crimes.html. http://www.ear-
ons.com/contact.html

"Why the Backlog Exists." *Homepage.* N.p., n.d.
Web. 06 Oct. 2016.
*http://www.endthebacklog.org/backlog/why-
backlog-exists*

"http://www.ear-ons.com/nightstalkerprofile.pdf."
Ear-ons.com. N.p., n.d. Web. 7 Feb. 2016.

Http://www.jjmcgr.org/BK/Clippings/770518.pdf.
N.p., n.d. Web. 7 Feb. 2016.

Crompton, Larry. *Sudden Terror: The True Story of
California's Most Infamous Sexual Predator, the
East Area Rapist Aka the Original Night Stalker.*
Bloomington IN: Authorhouse, 2010. Print.

Shelby, Richard. *Hunting a Psychopath: The East
Area Rapist: Original Night Stalker Investigation.*
Bradenton, FL: BookLocker.com, 2015. Print. I am
using a quote from this book as set forth under
Section 107 (the Fair Use doctrine) of the U.S.
Copyright Act of 1976.

Leslie D'Ambrosia, Special Agent. "Florida
Department Of Law Enforcement Miami Regional
Operations Center in consultation and review by
Detective Sergeant John Yarbrough, Los Angeles
County Sheriff's Department Homicide Bureau."
"http://www.ear-ons.com/nightstalkerprofile.pdf."
Ear-ons.com. N.p., n.d. Web. 5 Oct. 2013.

Meyer, Richard Judge regarding the release of public information law

Heurich, Charles Cold Cases: Resources for Agencies, Resolution for Families www.namus.gov Web. 20 June 2017.

Rule, Ann – paragraph of letter from Ann to old friend Jim appear and are published as set forth under Section 107 (the Fair Use doctrine) of the U.S. Copyright Act of 1976.

https://www.forensicmag.com/article/2016/08/dna-phenotyping-recreates-face-alleged-serial-killer Web 28 July 2017 Augenstein, Seth

https://www.forensicmag.com/article/2015/01/dna-forensic-testing-and-use-dna-rape-kits-cases-rape-and-sexual-assault Web. 25 July 2017 McDonald, Karl M. 1-26-2015

https://en.wikipedia.org/wiki/California_Proposition _69_(2004) Web 20, June 2017

Baumgardner, Randy W. Sheriff Hal Barker information was taken from the FBI National Academy book Web 25 June 2017

Smith, M.J. lives in Visalia

http://www.visaliatimesdelta.com/story/opinion/201 5/03/25/visalia-training-ground/70406130/

Kelly, Peggy: Lyman & Charlene Smith murder revealed to be work of serial killer Web 20 June 2017, article October 13, 2000 Santa Paula News

Made in the USA
Lexington, KY
24 August 2018